Table of Contents

Disclaimer (Exclusive clause)

The author and all employees disclaim any incorrect interpretation, wrong answers to questions or text, harm including emotional, psychological, and physical or any form of the liability to the reader/listener or being given information by third parties. Furthermore, this disclaimer protects all contributory people, directors, employees, 3rd parties, authors and will not be liable for any injury caused.

Dedication

I dedicate this book to my niece in Ghana, Dora Okine, who has a nursing degree. And all my readers be on a journey to a psychology degree.

Acknowledgement.

As with all the previous seventy-two books I have written and published, I acknowledge the Guardians' help, knowledge, wisdom, and the direction Almighty God has given me to write this book. It would have been impossible to finish writing these books because when I started writing,

i. never knew how and when I was going to end or where to conduct my research, but once I began to, I got more and more guidance from Almighty God. Without him, this book would have never been written. He directed and gave me the resources; therefore,

the real author of this publication is God. For example, initially, I aimed for one book of 400 pages, but God gave me so many resources that this book is about 800 pages. Therefore, I have more information to write three volumes.

Forgive and love every then, trust, believe and have faith in God. This FORMULA IS THE KEY TO HEAVEN.

PREFACE

Definition; Psychology is the scientific study of the mind and behaviour in humans and non-humans. Psychology includes the analysis of the conscious and unconscious. That encompasses the study of phenomena, including feelings and thoughts about human behaviour, development, personality, emotion, motivation, and more.   It is an academic discipline of immense scope, crossing the boundaries between the natural and social sciences. Psychologists seek an understanding of the emergent properties of brains, linking the discipline to neuroscience. The first letter of the Greek word psyche from which the term *psyche* from which the term psychology is derived, is commonly associated with the science

Abnormal psychology It is the study of abnormal behaviour and psychopathology. This speciality area is focused on research and treatment of various mental disorders and is linked to psychotherapy and clinical psychology. Biological psychology (biopsychology) studies how biological processes influence the mind and behaviour. This area is closely linked to neuroscience and uses MRI and PET scans to examine brain injury or abnormalities. Clinical psychology focuses on assessing, diagnosing, and treating mental disorders.

Cognitive psychology studies human thought processes, including attention, memory, perception, decision-making, problem-solving, and language acquisition. Comparative psychology

is the branch of psychology concerned with studying animal behaviour. Developmental psychology is an area that looks at human growth and development over the lifespan, including cognitive abilities, morality, social functioning, identity, and other life areas. Forensic psychology is an applied field that uses psychological research and principles in the legal and criminal justice systems. Industrial-organizational psychology is a field that uses psychological research to enhance work performance and select employees. Personality psychology focuses on understanding how personality develops and the patterns of thoughts, behaviours, and characteristics that make each unique.

Social psychology focuses on group behaviour, social influences on individual behaviour, attitudes, prejudice, conformity, aggression, and related topics. As social scientists, psychologists aim to understand the behaviour of individuals and groups.

About the Author

What motivates me to write this book is my experience in life, from being an abandoned child eating from bins/gutters in Ghana to being one of the most successful businessmen in Europe.
I have visited most European countries and wish to share with my readers through poems.
Through miscarriage of justice, all my wealth, dignity and family were taken away. Having attempted suicide five times and the conspirators unable
to kill me, I realise that God had a mission for me, which has resulted in me having much more than before, given to me by God. I regard myself as the living memory of God's prophets who suffered, but God saved their life. The suffering at the hands of people in authority positions, including my siblings, who appeared to love me when I provided for their needs for over 30 years from their childhood and even brought them to the United Kingdom. My voluntary work helping people in natural disaster areas, poor and needy, made me feel sorry for humans on Earth.
I have proven that "going down is an accident or God's calling, but staying down is a choice.

Chapter 1

The Contribution of Survey Methodology to Our Understanding of Learning

Content

Introduction

Discussion

Conclusion

Introduction

Various methodological approaches exist for individuals or students interested in conducting research in psychology, such as the experimental method, survey method, and text-based or literature review method. Selecting a research approach is dictated by several factors, the availability of resources, the type of research question, and the purpose of the research. The current paper aims to describe the survey research method as one approach to conducting research and critically evaluate its contribution to our understanding of learning. Survey research is "collecting information from a sample of individuals through their responses to questions" (Bohle & Immergut, 2018, p. 34). It can also be described as "questioning individuals on a topic or topics and then describing their responses" (Sivertsen, 2019, p. 62). This research methodology allows a researcher to utilise various methods to recruit participants, collect data, and employ multiple instrumentation methods. With the survey research method, a researcher can employ quantitative research strategies like closed-ended questionnaires, qualitative research strategies like open-ended questionnaires, or both strategies as mixed methods. Since surveys are regularly used to explain and examine human behaviour, they are often used in psychological and social research. Also, due to its flexibility and efficiency, survey research contributes greatly to the und understanding g in psychology.

Discussion

Sivertsen (2019) posited that developmental psychology strives to explain why and how cognition and behaviour change with time or over the lifespan. The broad field of psychology enhances diverse de-analysis degreases, including adult life phases, teaching and learning, language and cognitive development, identity development, attachment relationships, and genetic-environment relationships. Therefore, the research methods used by developmental psychologists are equally varied. As social expectations, activities, and environments change, developmental psychologists develop strategies and paradigms to research the impacts of these recent occurrences on human development. For instance, how social media affects young children's growth and thinking or their literacy development is influenced by texting.

Nevertheless, the primary issue throughout psychology research is the researchers' position regarding epistemology. In the context of psychology, "epistemology is the development of knowledge and how it is acquired" (Slaney, 2020, p. 67). Most research in psychology has utilised the survey research method, mainly because it is qualitative and qualitative, with two significant traits which have outstanding contributions to the field of psychology research. First, the researchers can measure variables using self-reports. For example, researchers asked respondents to report their behaviours, feelings, and thoughts directly. Secondly, researchers can pay special attention to sampling procedures. Notably, using the survey method, researchers prefer large random samples since they give the most exact approximates of the whole population. Therefore, survey research results or outcomes can be generalised based on the sample population.

The results can be generalised widely whenever the sample is more prominent or significant. According to Scudder & Colson (2019), survey research is the only methodology in psychology that routinely uses random sampling. Surveys can be short or long. Historically, survey studies have entailed data collected from a large population. The survey's main objective is to speedily acquire information describing the traits of a large sample of people. Examples include comprehensive census surveys that provide data that reflect personal and demographic characteristics and consumer feedback. Surveys can be conducted through the mail, by phone, over the internet, or in person. Surveys can be about anything or any topic that is achievable to ask people about and receive meaningful feedback. While survey data are usually analysed with statistical methods, various questions can be processed using qualitative methods. The survey is often non-experiment describes single variables and explores or evaluates evaluate statistical relations between variables (Scudder & Colson, 2019, p. 270). However, they can also be experimental. Most researchers in psychology have used self-report measures with large national samples in their research. Furthermore, their use of independent variables to assess their impacts or influence on a dependent variable make their works experimental.

The contribution of survey research in psychology originates in American and English "social surveys" dating back to the early 20th century by reformers and researchers who sought to record the degree of social issues like poverty. By the early 1900s, the U.S. administration carried out surveys to record social and economic issues among the American people. The necessity to conclude the whole population accelerated improvements in sampling practices. Most surveys conducted around this time were predominantly election-related and market studies. However, surveys quickly made their way into multiple fields of academia like public health, sociology, psychology, and political science, where it continues to be a practical approach or method of collecting data. Starting in the 1930s, psychology researchers made significant improvements in designing a questionnaire, including techniques like the Likert scale (Xu, 2019, p. 481). Also, surveys closely relate to studying prejudice, stereotypes, and attitudes. Also, pioneer attitude researchers were among the early psychologists to employ large and more varied samples than the expediency samples routinely used by university students in psychology. Until the present, university students still use small samples in their research.

Survey research keeps on being an effective method in psychology today. For instance, survey data have been helpful or valuable in estimating the pervasiveness of various mental illnesses and identifying statistical relations between these illnesses and other multiple factors. One of the reasons why survey research is essential in psychology today is because most researches in psychology have individuals as the unit of study. According to Sivertsen (2019), survey research "is best suited for studies with individual people as the unit of analysis." While researchers can also use a survey to explore other units of analysis like dyads or groups, these studies usually use a specific individual from each group as a "key informant" or a "proxy" for that unit. Also, such surveys "may be subject to respondent bias if the informant chosen does not have adequate knowledge or has a biased opinion about the phenomenon of interest" (Xu, 2019, p. 841).

The contribution of survey methodology to the understanding of learning lies in the strengths of this research method. The survey method has several intrinsic or natural strengths compared to other research methodologies. To begin with, the survey is an excellent approach for assessing a broad array of unobservable data like people's factual information, behaviours, beliefs, attitudes, traits, and preferences. The survey method is also best suited for gathering data remotely about a sample that is too large to observe directly. For instance, a large area like a whole country or region can be covered using telephone, email, or mail-in survey using "careful sampling to ensure that the population is sufficiently represented in a small sample." Thirdly, because of its unnoticeable nature and the option for participants to respond at their convenience, the survey is the most preferred research methodology by researchers and respondents (Nardi, 2018, p. 80). Here, the survey is often achieved by the use of a questionnaire. Also, there is no available sampling framework for specific population groups like illegal immigrants and the homeless; therefore, an interview survey is the only appropriate way of reaching these groups. Another strength of the survey method is that a sample survey may allow researchers to detect minor effects even when analysing numerous variables. Researchers can also compare subgroups of the research population or sample based on the survey design.

As argued by Bohle and Immergut (2018), survey research methodology is cost-effective in terms of cost, effort, and time compared to other methods like case research and experimental research. However, having mentioned all these strengths or advantages, it is also important to note that the survey method has some limitations. For instance, this type of research is subject to multiple biases like recall bias, social desirability bias, sampling bias, and non-response bias. However, survey research has recently evolved into a meticulous approach to research, with systematically tested approaches detailing representative samples and survey methods and reducing non-response errors to guarantee quality research processes and findings. The phrase "survey" reflects an array of survey administration methods, data collection tools, recruitment and sampling strategies, and research aims (Slaney, 2020, p. 71). Considering this array of alternatives in the conduct of survey research, survey research consumers or readers need to understand the likelihood of bias in survey research and the tested methods of reducing bias to draw proper conclusions. Also, various strategies for reducing errors in survey research have been developed.

Researchers in psychology use survey software to conduct research, an influential tool psychology researchers use to collect data. Sophisticated survey software developers provide survey solutions for all survey research designs, including phone surveys, paper surveys, and online surveys, to the recently introduced mobile surveys. This availability of survey options has resulted in the extensive use of quantitative designs throughout all survey designs to collect, process, and utilise data to conclude (Leman & Bremner, 2019, p. 86). When psychology researchers execute survey research correctly, it can benefit them with reliable and usable data and improve learning in psychology.

As discussed earlier, surveys are comparatively cost-efficient. Mobile and online surveys particularly have very minimal costs per respondent. Even if researchers give incentives to respondents, the cost remains far less compared to the cost of administering a phone or paper survey, and the possible number of responses can be thousands. Also, survey research is valuable in describing the traits of a large sample or population (Nardi, 2018, p. 89). No other research design can offer this extensive capability, ensuring a more accurate sample to collect targeted outcomes to make conclusions and reach significant decisions.

Furthermore, researchers can administer surveys in various models. For instance, they can employ a mixed survey research design for hard-to-reach or remote respondents. Here, they can administer both paper and online surveys to collect feedback and compile the responses into one data set that can be analysed statistically. Most importantly, anonymous surveys enable respondents to respond with more frank and valid answers. Accurate data can be obtained only when respondents are as honest and open as possible with their solutions (Xu, 2019, p. 841). Researchers conducting research anonymously offer an opening for more genuine and transparent responses than other research methodologies, especially if they clearly state that those survey responses will remain confidential.

Conclusion

The survey research method is one approach to conducting research that significantly contributes to our understanding of learning. Survey research " collects information from a sample of individuals through their responses to questions." With the survey research method, a researcher can employ quantitative research strategies like closed-ended questionnaires, qualitative research strategies like open-ended questionnaires, or both strategies as mixed methods. The contribution of survey research in psychology dates back to the early 20th century, and survey research remains an effective method in psychology today. The contribution of survey methodology to understanding learning generally lies in this research method's strengths.

Reference List

Bohle, D. and Immergut, E.M., 2018. Introduction to Research Methods.

Dawson, C., 2019. *Introduction to research methods 5th edition: A practical guide for anyone undertaking a research project*. Robinson.

Leman, P. and Bremner, A., 2019. *EBOOK: Developmental Psychology, 2e*. McGraw Hill.

Nardi, P.M., 2018. *Doing survey research: A guide to quantitative methods*. Routledge.

Scudder, T. and Colson, E., 2019. From welfare to development: A conceptual framework for analysing dislocated people. In *Involuntary migration and resettlement* (pp. 267-287). Routledge.

Sivertsen, G., 2019. Understanding and evaluating research and scholarly publishing in the Social Sciences and Humanities (SSH). *Data and Information Management, 3*(2), pp.61-71.

Slaney, K.L., 2020. Is there a waning appetite for critical methodology in psychology? In *Problematic Research Practices and Inertia in Scientific Psychology* (pp. 86-101). Routledge.

Xu, F., 2019. Towards a rational constructivist theory of cognitive development. *Psychological Review, 126*(6), p.841.

Chapter 2

The Contribution of Experimental Methodology to our Understanding of Memory in Real-World Settings

Content

Introduction

Discussion

Conclusion

Reference List

Introduction

Memory has a broad history within the context of psychology, and we can find a lot of new and old research examining its complex nature. The way humans process, store, and use information has been a contentious topic in psychology's history, as eventually, it dramatically influences who people are and how they behave. In psychology, most researchers have experimented with and investigated multiple aspects of human memory, leading to a better understanding of what affects our memory and how it works (Sternberg & Pickren, 2019, p. 82). For instance, researchers can reduce neural memory mechanisms through lesion studies, and findings from delicately designed psychological tests can assist them in reaching conclusions about how memory works (Sheehy, 2017, p. 61). An invaluable research methodology in the study of memory is the experimental method. This method allows us to understand memory in real-world settings. Therefore, the current paper explores experimental methodology's contribution to our understanding of memory in real-world settings.

28

Discussion

Experimental psychology presently has a broad application from the primary scientific quest to increase vital knowledge about how the "world works" concerning brain functioning, human thinking, and behaviour to applying simple manipulation to the environment to transform behaviour (Sheehy, 2017, p. 62). Furthermore, experimental psychology is becoming more and increasingly in designing and developing "artificial bits of intelligence" and other computer algorithms that could interact with or imitate human users. Greer (2005) described empirical or experimental research as a study that rigorously follows a scientific research design. The research encompasses a hypothesis, a variable that the researcher can manipulate, and variables that the researcher can measure, calculate, and compare. Most significantly, the researcher or researchers conduct experimental research in a controlled environment. The data collected by researchers and subsequent results either support or rejects the hypothesis (Schacter, 2022, p. 68). For this reason, this research method is also referred to as deductive research or hypothesis testing.

Experimental research aims to determine a relationship or correlation between two variables, namely the "dependent variable" and "independent variable." Here, after carrying out an experiment-based study, researchers can either reject or support a relationship between a particular aspect of a subject and the variable under investigation (Long et al., 2010, p. 59). Considering this aspect, data used in this type of research must be quantifiable or measurable. For instance, data gathered could be growth, time, weight or volume, density, etc. Nevertheless, the being should be observed qualitatively or described using photos or words.

According to Greer (2005), an experiment is a "set-up for measurement that allows the testing of a hypothesis" (p. 51). Here, an experiment hypothesis is deemed to be more than just a question. In a way, it predicts the correlation between two or more variables. We can describe a variable as some measurable factor or element considered to be at play in a situation. Therefore, for researchers to initiate experimental research, they should think about what diverse factors are at play in their case that might be interesting. They can then convert these into measurable or quantifiable variables. This process of turning elements at play into measurable variables is termed operationalisation. The researchers can then design an experimental framework to study these variables' correlations. For example, one might need to query how a variable like the volume of a sound relates to a variable like how an observer perceives the loudness of this sound.

Fechner's book "Elements of Psychophysics" (1966) marked the beginning of "psychophysics" as an area of inquiry and, more significantly, of psychology as a "natural science," just like biology, chemistry, and physics. The move presented a challenge for psychologists since the psychology topic is the "observer"; therefore, the objectivity fundamental to natural science is debatably unavailable. Fechner solved this hitch by employing experimentation to explore how events "in the physical, real-world setting correlate with observers' experiences. He envisioned that psychophysics should be understood here as an exact theory of the functionally dependent relations of body and soul, or more generally, of the material and the mental, of the physical and the psychological worlds" (Fechner, 1966, p. 112). From these words, Fechner meant that how people perceive, and experience things internally cannot be measured objectively; however, the correlation between these internal and external spheres allows the researchers to measure indirectly and study the external stimuli' mental representations. Fechner justified the employment of the assumptions intrinsic to other natural sciences in mental constructs and representations, providing the basis for such study to be carried out with similar tools universal to the other natural sciences. These tools are the experimental control and treatment of variables to find out their influence on another measurable variable, implying that the majority of studies in psychophysics are comparatively straightforward. These studies treat value A and measure response B while holding everything else constant (Fechner, 1966, p. 117). However, this uncomplicated design allows alarming rigidity, and the stimuli presented to the subject can become incredibly intricate.

From the 1960s, experimental research methods quickly expanded past psychophysics, widening the psychology research areas. Nonetheless, psychophysics better unpacks experimental methodology's methodological principles and focuses on two thresholds. These thresholds are categorised into two classes. The first class is the simple 'absence or presence of a stimulus representation', and the second class is the 'magnitude of change' in a stimulus needed to produce a change in a stimulus representation. The first class can also be referred to as the "detection thresholds" and is an example of the practicality of the other natural sciences at play in the science of psychology. These thresholds link a change or transformation in the real-world setting with behaviour based on a mental representation. Also, these constructs strive to explicate the outcomes using theories of legitimate processes and structures on the two sides of the mental-physical divide (Scholtz et al., 2020, p. 8). Therefore, they demonstrate the necessity of comprehending causal correlations and the postulation of a deterministic system native to physical sciences.

After conceptualising and operationalising a mental process into a task that gives rise to performance measures, experimental methodology deal with "quantitative" data-variables like score or data, categorised as "measures." Quantitative data encompass natural measurements, like height or weight, but also contain calculated values from participants' responses, such as the number of items recalled correctly in a memory experimental study (Scholtz et al., 2020, p. 18). Despite the particulars of the measure, this type of data will share some essential traits relating to the conceptual ideology of what makes data "quantitative." Experimental studies generate quantitative data; therefore, researchers can employ statistical tests to reach conclusions about their findings. Although there are multiple ways researchers can use to analyse experimental studies' data, analysis often results in null hypothesis significance testing, which enables researchers to understand how confident they can be that any discrepancies in the data are because of the impact of the experimental manipulation, but not just because of chance fluctuations in the data (Pike et al., 2021, p. 21). In other words, researchers can know whether they can confidently accept or reject the null hypothesis. This aspect is as vital in experimental research in psychology as it is in all other areas of research utilising quantitative data.

Psychology researchers can use experimental research studies to examine memory in the actual world. For instance, scholars have developed diverse experimental paradigms to examine or explore false memories. The "misinformation paradigm" is the most common, set in the 1970s. Most of these researchers have discovered or established that the original event's accuracy is notably lower whenever subjects provide misleading information compared to a control group, leading to what is referred to as "the misinformation effect." Researchers have found the said effect using leading questions, misleading narratives, and interactions with co-witnesses (Pike et al., 2021, p. 23). Research has also established that circumstances could mislead subjects into falsely or wrongly recalling past childhood occurrences and that misleading information further influence or affect short-term food preferences (Pike et al., 2021, p. 26). Studies on tricky questions triggered a substantial theoretical and methodological debate on why the effect comes about and what transpires with the original memory. For example,

Scholtz et al. (2020) first argued that the initial memory could not be accessed because it was overwritten.

Nevertheless, other researchers argued that "the effect resulted from response bias and that the original memory was retained" (Schacter, 2022, p. 72). The researchers designed an experimental framework that eliminated social factors and response bias to address some of these issues (Schacter, 2022, p. 81). They hypothesised that if similar post-event info permanently changes a memory, they should still find the effect after a delay.

Conclusion

The Understanding of memory has been a hot topic in psychology's history because it dramatically influences people and their behaviour. Researchers have experimented with and investigated multiple aspects of human memory, which has led to a better understanding of what affects our memory and how it works. Invaluable research methodology in the study of memory is the experimental method since it allows us to understand memory in real-world settings. This methodology presently has a broad application in psychology and is primarily aimed at determining a relationship or correlation between two variables, namely the "dependent variable" and "independent variable." Experimental research is a "set-up for measurement that allows the testing of a hypothesis." The experimental methodology deal with "quantitative" data; therefore, researchers employ experimental research studies to examine memory in the real world.

Reference List

Fechner, G., 1966. Elements of psychophysics. Vol. I.

Greer, C., 2005. Crime and media. *Criminology*, pp.157-82.

Long, M., Wood, C., Littleton, K., Passenger, T. and Sheehy, K., 2010. *The psychology of education*. Routledge.

Pike, G., Havard, C., Harrison, G. and Ness, H., 2021. Eyewitness identification procedures: Do researchers and practitioners share the same goals? *International Journal of Police Science & Management*, 23(1), pp.17-28.

Schacter, D.L., 2022. Memory: from the laboratory to everyday life. *Dialogues in clinical neuroscience*.

Scholtz, S.E., de Klerk, W. and de Beer, L.T., 2020. The use of research methods in psychological research: A systematised review. *Frontiers in research metrics and analytics*, 5, p.1.

Sheehy, K., 2017. Ethics, epistemologies, and inclusive pedagogy. In *Ethics, equity, and inclusive education*. Emerald Publishing Limited.

Sternberg, R.J. and Pickren, W.E., 2019. The Cambridge Handbook of the intellectual history of Psychology.

Chapter   3

Contribution of Discursive Methods To our
Understanding of Social Aspects of Language

Content

Introduction

Discursive methods are instrumental in the study
of the following social aspects of language:
 How language is used to construct social identity
 How language is used to build social
relationships
How language is used to construct social reality
An Overview of the Main Approaches to
Discourse Analysis
The Advantages and Disadvantages of Using
Discursive Methods to Study Social Aspects of
Language
Evaluation of the Role of Discourse in Shaping
Our Understanding of Social Aspects of
Language
How Discourse Can Be Used To Investigate
Social Aspects of Language
Assess the Usefulness of Discourse in Studying
Social Aspects of Language
Reference

Introduction

Discourse has been defined as a stretch of language perceived to be meaningful within a culture. It is how language is used to create meaning within a social context. Discourse is not just about the words spoken or written but also about how these words are used. It includes language structure, grammar rules, and combining words to create meaning. It also has how language is used in different social contexts, how it is used to create relationships, and how it is used to communicate identity.

Discourse is a social phenomenon. It is shaped by the culture in which it is used and by the social relationships between the people who use it. The power relations between different groups of people also shape it. Notably, discourse can be used to create social change. It can be used to challenge dominant ways of thinking and to promote alternative ways of thinking. It can raise awareness of social issues and promote social justice.

Discursive methods are beneficial in studying social aspects of language because they allow researchers to analyse how language is used in a particular context. So, it is because discursive methods focus on analysing the content of spoken or written language rather than on the form of the language.

Discursive methods are instrumental in the study of the following social aspects of language:
 How language is used to construct social identity
 How language is used to build social relationships

How language is used to construct social reality

How language is used to construct social identity

Discursive methods are instrumental in studying how language constructs social identity. These discursive methods allow researchers to analyze how language is used to construct identity in a particular context. For example, discursive methods have been used to study how language is used to construct gender identity. Studies have found that language is used to construct gender identity highly variable across cultures and contexts. For example, in some cultures, women are more likely to use language that emphasises their femininity, while in other cultures, women are more likely to use language that emphasises their masculinity (Davies & Horton-Salway, n.d.).

How language is used to construct social relationships

Discursive methods have also been found to be particularly useful in the study of how language is used to construct social relationships. Discursive methods allow researchers to analyze how language is used to construct relationships in a particular context. For example, discursive methods have been used to study how language is used to construct family relationships. Studies have found that how language is used to construct family relationships is highly variable across cultures and contexts (Davies & Horton-Salway, n.d.). For example, in some cultures, family members are more likely to use language that emphasizes closeness, while in other cultures, they are more likely to use language that emphasizes distance.

How language is used to construct social reality

Discursive methods have also been found to be particularly useful in the study of how language is used to construct social reality. Additionally, discursive methods allow researchers to analyze how language is used to construct reality in a particular context. For example, discursive methods have been used to study how language is used to construct political reality. Studies have found that language is used to construct political reality highly variable across cultures and contexts (Davies & Horton-Salway, n.d.). For example, in some cultures, politicians are more likely to use language that emphasizes their power, while in other cultures, politicians are more likely to use language that emphasizes democracy.

An Overview of the Main Approaches to Discourse Analysis

Discourse analysis is the study of how language is used in texts. It can be used to analyze both spoken and written texts. There are three main approaches to discourse analysis:
1. The linguistic approach focuses on studying language at the level of words, sentences, and

grammar. It is concerned with the way that language is used to create meaning.

2. The sociolinguistic approach: This approach looks at how language is used in social contexts. It concerns how language use is affected by factors such as social class, gender, and ethnicity.

3. The psycholinguistic approach: This approach focuses on the way the brain processes that language. It is concerned with how people understand and produce language.

Each of these approaches has its advantages and disadvantages. The linguistic approach is suitable for analyzing the structure of language. However, it does not consider the social context in which language is used. The sociolinguistic approach is suitable for understanding how language is used in social contexts. However, it does not always provide a detailed analysis of the language itself. Finally, the psycholinguistic approach is suitable for understanding how the brain processes language. However, observing how people understand and produce language is not always possible.

The Advantages and Disadvantages of Using Discursive Methods to Study Social Aspects of Language

Discursive methods have several advantages when studying social aspects of language. Firstly, they allow researchers to access various data types, including spoken and written texts. They can provide a complete picture of how language is used in different social contexts. Secondly, discursive methods can help to uncover the hidden meanings and ideologies that underpin language use. It is because they involve close analysis of how people use language to construct and communicate their ideas and beliefs. Finally, discursive methods are generally highly adaptable, meaning they can be used to study a wide range of social phenomena.

There are also some disadvantages associated with using discursive methods to study social aspects of language. One of the main problems is that these methods can be time-consuming and resource intensive. It is because they often require researchers to collect and analyze large amounts of data. Another disadvantage is that discursive methods can be complex and challenging to interpret, particularly for those without prior experience using them. It means that there is a risk of producing inaccurate or misleading results. Finally, discursive methods often rely heavily on written texts, limiting their applicability to spoken language studies.

Evaluation of the Role of Discourse in Shaping Our Understanding of Social Aspects of Language

Discourse is an essential tool for shaping our understanding of social aspects of language. It allows us to analyze how language is used in different contexts and explore the relationships between language, power, and social structures. Discourse analysis can help us to understand how language is used to construct and maintain social relationships. It can also help us to identify how power is exercised through language. Discourse analysis is a valuable tool for students of language and linguistics, as it allows us to critically examine how language is used in different contexts. It can also help us to understand the relationships between language, power, and social structures.

How Discourse Can Be Used To Investigate Social Aspects of Language

Discourse can be used to investigate social aspects of language in several ways. One way is to examine how language is used in different social contexts. For example, you could look at how people use language in different settings, such as at home, work, or social settings. Another way to investigate social aspects of language is to look at how different groups use language. For example, you could look at how men and women use language or how other age groups use language. Finally, you could look at how language is used in different cultures. For example, you could look at how English is used in different parts of the world or how diverse languages are used in different cultures.

Assess the Usefulness of Discourse in Studying Social Aspects of Language

For several reasons, discourse is a valuable tool for studying language's social aspects. Firstly, discourse can examine how language is used to construct social reality. In particular, it can analyze how power and identity are negotiated through language. Secondly, discourse can be used to study the interactional effects of language, for example, how specific linguistic strategies can create or reinforce social inequalities (Davies & Horton-Salway, n.d.). Finally, discourse can be used to investigate the role of language in social change. For example, it can be used to study how language can be used to challenge dominant social norms and values. Remarkably, discursive methods are concerned with how language is used in social contexts and how this can reveal important insights into the nature of social interactions and relationships. In recent years, there has been an increasing interest in using these methods to investigate a wide range of social phenomena, including power relations, identity construction, and social change. Despite the disadvantages, discursive methods have significantly contributed to our understanding of social aspects of language. This significance is because they have provided detailed and nuanced insights into various social phenomena. They have also been used to study how language is used to construct and maintain social relationships. In the future, discursive methods will likely continue to play an essential role in understanding social aspects of language.

Reference

Davies, A., & Horton-Salway, M. (n.d.). Chapter 9: Why focus on discourse? Discursive Psychology and Identity.

Chapter 4
Planning for survey

It is essential to plan before starting a survey.

You may begin with a checklist. Survey design

Obtaining a practical design for a survey is essential, not just to be able to get valid data. Efficient survey design is also vital for ethics since asking participants to fill in a study and not using the data they provide breaks the 'terms and conditions they have consented to. So, if researchers tell participants they will be using the data and then don't, they would effectively have lied to them. Deception is covered under ethics advice.

Use the following checklist to help design and finesse your survey so that it complies with ethics protocol and can be signed off by your tutor.

Participant information is paramount.

Consent of the party must be obtained since participants cannot answer questions without consenting first.

This is an option for setting up a question in Qualtrics, an online survey.

When using Qualtrics, Participants are not asked to provide withdrawal codes which could identify them after data collection.

The debrief must be set as the 'end of survey message'.

Since survey options show that responses are anonymous, No personal information is requested,

categories must not overlap, for example, Age: 20 to 40, 41– 60… should be 20 to 60,)

Questions are only asked for multiple responses if indicated by the measure used.

Ensure the participant questions help you answer your research question and hypotheses.

Check that the data you are collecting can produce continuous data for multiple regression (MR) or principal components (PC) analysis.

checklist before launching a survey

Surveys need thorough checking before launching. Mistakes in the questions, or ethics protocol, can undermine the data collected and create ethical challenges that are difficult to fix after the survey launches. A successful launch of a survey means careful attention to final checks. This specification is designed to help the researcher's survey succeed.

To ensure you are launching your survey correctly, please carry out the following prelaunch checks, for which you are responsible.

You have checked that the t spelling and grammar on questions are correct

You have checked that questions are not invalid for example, by being vague or unclear)

You have checked that the data each question produces is suitable for the type of analysis (e.g., consider that multiple regression and factor analysis need continuous data. Avoid collecting numerical data, for example, age, via textboxes)

You have had confirmation of ethics approval for my survey

You have checked that my survey is fully anonymised and does not collect IP addresses, and I have switched off the collect IP address switch for my study in Qualtrics.

You have checked that no identifying information is collected or used to contact participants.

You have shown my final version of the survey to my tutor by sharing the link that will allow them to edit the study (NOT the link sent to participants). Please check Appendix 2 below for how to do this.

Your tutor has reviewed and tested the survey and given the green light.

The tutor will sign and date it to confirm that you have carried all the above.

Guidance in writing up Survey results - Multiple Linear Regression

When one receives the result of the survey from the participant, insert them into the SPSS analysis
you then produce a result section in your document

Start with an Introduction sentence. Example: "Multiple linear regression (MLR) was used to examine the relationship between two potential predictors: revision intensity and subject enjoyment".

Characteristics of the sample

What was the total number of participants who answered back, and what were their types?

Once you have noted any exciting patterns, such as bias in your sample, you may also wish to arrange a table to present your sociodemographic variables (even if these are also part of your multiple regression).
Inform the reader what is there and what to observe before you present the summary.
Look at advertised papers to see how the professionals write up this information.

Sociodemographic characteristics of the sample

Characteristic;

Gender – male or female. Their age, variable ect
Do Sample size, which includes; Number or mean expressed in percentage or SD standard deviation.
You may use keys such as n to denote the total sample size.

Chapter 5

Consider using numbers and percentages for categorical variables and mean/standard deviation or median/IQR for your continuous variables. Again, you may need advice from your tutor if you need help deciding which to use.

Some people may use cross-tabulation. This means splitting the data by another variable, such as gender. Tabulation. Please see the FAQs thread in the Software Forum for Surveys.

1. Descriptive statistics

For some projects, it may be applicable to show a table that shows the mean and standard deviation for each domain or construct determined.

In some cases, you may have figures in the scale validation paper about the descriptive statistics for the samples used in the validation, and you can describe whether the sample is similar or different.
Suppose you have changed your scale or been advised to do this analysis by your supervisor. In that case, you should report "Cronbach Alpha" for each domain to argue whether your sample responded internally consistently.

Instance similar characteristics of people replying identical to the scale items.
If you have used a validated scale without change, you will have given the Cronbach Alpha from the validation paper in the methods section, and you may not need to calculate your alpha.

Decimal

It is advisable to use two decimal points after the decimal (e.g., 10.73; 1.25; .56 –

P-Value

For p-values, you can use the symbol $<$ if the value is smaller than .01 (e.g., $p < .01$ or even as small as .001). Where you show frequency data or several participants, use whole numbers because you cannot use a fraction for a human being.

Regression analysis

First, show the assumptions checked to ensure the data was appropriate for the chosen analysis. Start with a sentence to remind the reader that you are doing a multiple regression and then introduce the assumptions:

Name the type of regression used, i.e. enter method, hierarchical etc.] Multiple regression was performed to investigate relationships between [DV] and [IVs/predictor variables]. The data were

considered to be suitable for the analysis because.'

Finally, we get to the MLR itself. Give a model equation, an advantage of a predictive model. Make sure that the write-up has the following elements:

The proportion of variance is explained by the model as indicated by the R2.

The model brief Includes the F statistic and statistical significance.

The contribution of your different variables to the model. Most papers reporting a multi-variate test like MLR will give a table to

Show the variables in the model. Something like this:

Table: Multiple regression model to predict a variable in [DV].

Model	Unstandardised coef	Standard error	Standardised coefficients Beta	Statistical significance (p)

	ficie nts B			
Constant				
IV1				
IV2				
IV3 [amend the number of rows as needed]				

The statistic is part of calculating the p-value, so it sits next to the p-values in the table.

Unstandardised coefficients

Unstandardised coefficients are the ones that go into the predictive equation.
They are 'unstandardised' coefficients since they are each determined in the units they were collected. These units could be the scales used or the values assigned to categories.

standardised coefficients

Standardised coefficients are used to compare and contrast variables directly because the standardisation process turns each coefficient into the same measure for all variables, so you are comparing like with like.

You only need to recognise that you are looking for the most considerable number (regardless of whether it is positive or negative).

The most significant variable number is the variable that makes the biggest contribution to the model.

One cannot establish cause and effect with survey data. Still, the variables contributing the most in the model may be a valuable full focus for future research, which could provide more substantial-ger evidence about causality.

Greek β

The standardised beta coefficients (shown by a Greek β) are the ones that are reported in the results when you are making the argument about which variables are statistically significant in the model.

Writing up Survey results in PCA ("Principal component analysis)

You could start with an Introductory sentence: "Principal component analysis (PCA) was using varimax rotation was used to analyse fifteen questions related to teaching style."

Characteristics of the sample

What was the total number of participants who responded, and what were their characteristics? Once you have noted any exciting patterns, such as bias in your sample, you may also wish to provide a table (see example) to present your sociodemographic variables (even if these are also part of your PCA). Remember to tell the reader what is there and what to notice before you present the table. Look at published papers to see how the professionals write up this information.

Sociodemographic

Characteristic; Gender – male and female, age plus any other variable in the study

Number of mean (% or SD)

n = (give the total sample size)

Consider using numbers and percentages for categorical variables and mean/standard deviation or median/IQR for your continuous variables.

One may use number or mean (% or SD)

n = (give the total sample size)

Some people may want to break down the data by another variable, such as gender Awn as cross-tabulation.

Descriptive statistics

This describes the variables, which can be supported by a table showing all the main variables. This includes all your demographics, e.g., age, and the items used in your PC.A Provide a general description noting any unusual issues (including skew, sample bias to sex or similar topics); you can finish with "See below summarises the means and standard deviations."

The table below will have the following appearance or similar
Descriptive

[insert here any other categorical demographics or variables

Variable	Factor 1	Factor 2	Factor 3
VAR1	.76		
VAR9	.65		
VAR6	.66	.42	
VAR4	.41		
VAR8		.68	
VAR3		.64	.44
VAR7		.50	
VAR5			.56
VAR2			.54

Decimal point

Use two decimal points after the decimal (e.g., 10.73; 1.25; .56 –For p-values, you can use the symbol < if the value is less significant than .01 (e.g., $p < .01$ or even an s small as .001). Where you show frequency data or several participants, use whole numbers.

Principal components Analysis

Providing rationale for the principal components analysis you did

Begin with something like: "The principal components analysis used varimax rotation (direct oblimin)" – give a reason why, e.g., "…because the aim was to establish components that were assumed to be independent. " (or if oblimin was used …" that were assumed to be correlated."

Advice:

Only use oblivion if you have reason to believe that factors are correlated.

KMO sampling adequacy & Bartlett's sphericity is equivalent to checking the assumptions for doing a PCA.

Start with a statement such as "Inspection of the KMO suggested the data would factor/not factor well (see Appendix for table)."

If your assumptions are violated, do not panic! You may be unable to fix problems at this level, which is not a disaster. Discuss with your supervisor.

Describe the factor space.

Under factor headings, you must state how many factors are extracted based on scree plots and eigenvalues and describe the factor space, factor size, or even how much of the variance they report for.

You can use a scree plot in your results section OR refer to it in the appendix. However, if you use a scree plot, you still need some narrative in the results section.

An example from the module materials is: "Using both the scree plot and eigenvalues > 1 to determine the underlying components, the analysis yielded four factors, explaining a total of 60.66 per cent of the variance in the data."

Here maintained based on the rotated components matrix or pattern matrix (for direct noblemen). You may use a table for summarising

the factors and their loadings. This will be based on the rotated components matrix (or pattern matrix if direct oblimin rotation was used).
" below table provides a summary of the loadings across the item space. (Factor loadings smaller than .40 have been suppressed, and the table is sorted by size of loadings."

Describe each factor:

"Factor 1 accounts for 45% of the variance and contains items that express…. This factor was labelled <factor name> and included k items to interpret the findings quickly.

Factor 2 accounts for 12% of the variance and comprises items that refer to…. This factor was labelled <factor name> and contains k items" ….
If you ran a varimax PCA, you do NOT need to deal with the Component transformation matrix. If (and only if) you used direct noblemen do you need to comment on the correlation between components using the data from the Component correlation matrix?

"Inspection of the factor correlation matrix shows significant positive correlations between factors a, b. (r=.67, p<.001) factor c and d were uncorrelated (see Appendix for SPSS output)."

Chapter   6

Content of Participant Information Leaflet

Content

Project details include study Title

Participant Information Leaflet Voluntary

participation & confidentiality

How will the data collected in the interview be

used?

How do I give consent to take part in the study?

Questions, comments or complaints

Data Protection Privacy Notice

What personal information will be collected from

me?

Why is this personal information being collected?

How long will the data be retained?

Will my taking part in this study be kept

confidential?

How will the data collected from me be used?

Will my data be shared with others?

Informed Consent Form

Project details

Name of researcher

Name of Institution researchers represent…..

Reason of conducting research……..

Brief summary of the proposed project, written in a language that a lay person would understand. It should be no longer than a few sentences and should describe the topic].

What is the hypothesis, or the findings hope to achieve

To the participant

You have been invited to take part in the research because [briefly explain inclusion criteria and exclusion criteria]

If you agree to participate, you will be invited to participate in an interview conducted via [Skype/Zoom/Microsoft/telephone teams; give the participant the choice if you can, as they might be more familiar with one of these apps].

Please note that you do not need to have used these apps before to take part. Detailed instructions will be sent to you before the interview, and I would be happy to discuss any concerns you may have about the technology involved.

If you do not have access to a stable internet connection, it may be possible to conduct the interview using standard mobile or landline network. Please contact me to discuss this option.

The interview will likely last up to ..... and will be recorded for research purposes. You will be asked questions about ....

Voluntary participation & confidentiality

Participation in the study is entirely voluntary. After you have read this information, please feel free to contact me if you have any questions or concerns. If you are happy to participate, please complete the Informed Consent Form provided

Note that if you wish to withdraw from the study at any time before, during or after the interview, you can do so simply by letting me know. You can withdraw at any time, for any reason, and you will not be asked to explain your reasons for withdrawing. Note, however, that once the interview has been transcribed, anonymised and analysed (expected to be by(insert date), it may not be possible to withdraw your individual data from the research.

There is no direct benefit to you as a participant from participating in the study. However, you will contribute to research on ..., and you may enjoy sharing your views and experiences. In terms of risks, there is a possibility that you may become uncomfortable when answering some questions. Note, however, that you have the right not to answer any question, and you can stop the interview and withdraw from the study at any point.

How will the data collected in the interview be used?

Data collected will be stored confidentially and transcripts will be anonymised. Before agreeing to take part, please read the Data Protection Privacy Notice below which explains in detail how the data will be managed after collection.

How do I give consent to take part in the study?

If you are happy to participate in the study the easiest way to give consent is by return e-mail. All you need to do is reply to the email, and, within the body of the message, indicate 'yes' to each statement listed below, and then enter your name and the date. A copy of the email (including the header information with email address and date) will be retained with the project files as proof of consent. I will e-mail you back to acknowledge receipt, and this e-mail will serve as proof that I have taken your consent (if given) and that I agree to the terms set out in the consent form. We strongly recommend that you keep a copy of this e-mail for your records.

Please note that the consent form will be kept separately from the transcription of the interview. Also, your name will be removed from the transcript, and information that could directly or indirectly identify you will be removed. Only anonymised quotations will be used in the final written report and any publications derived from it.

Once I have received the consent form, I will contact you to schedule a suitable interview and discuss technical arrangements.

Questions, comments or complaints

If at any point you need more information about the study or you have any concerns, please get in touch with me by emailing (insert your student email). You can also contact the project supervisor (insert your supervisor's or organisation)

Thank you for your time, and I look forward to hearing from you, ideally before [enter date],

Researcher name

Date (Leaflet given to a participant)

Chapter   7

Data Protection Privacy Notice

The research study complies with UK General Data Protection Regulations (GDPR) and the UK Data Protection Act 2018. The data collected in this study is anonymous. That means when taking part in this study it is not possible to identify you individually.

What personal information will be collected from me?

As part of the study, the researcher will record your [name, gender, age, city/town of residence, education, and occupation; remember only to collect the information you think is relevant to the study]. The nature of the research is such that you will not be asked to disclose sensitive personal information. The project does not require you to disclose special category data (ethnic origin, political views, religious affiliation, trade union membership, health issues, or sexual orientation [edit/delete as appropriate]. However, if you choose to share such information about yourself, it will be kept confidential as described in this document.

Why is this personal information being collected?

We are collecting this personal data to understand the characteristics of the participants who took part in the study. Please also note that [Microsoft for Skype and MS Teams, or Zoom], the company that owns the software that will be used to conduct the interview, collects a limited amount of electronic data from users (e.g. their location, IP address, e-mail if you have an account with them, and so on), in line with its privacy policy.

How long will the data be retained?

Interview recordings and consent forms will be kept for a maximum of a year. In contrast, anonymised interview transcripts may be kept longer (subject to participants not withdrawing consent before the insert date). All data and consent forms will be stored on the researcher's password-protected hard drive, with a backup copy on an encrypted or password-protected external drive. Except for a copy of the consent forms, e-mail correspondence with participants will be destroyed immediately after collecting the data.

Will my taking part in this study be kept confidential?

Measures will be taken to ensure the confidentiality of participants. Your name will be removed from interview transcripts, with all information that could directly or indirectly help identify interviewees removed to ensure that any risks are minimised.

How will the data collected from me be used?

What the result of the study be used for

The study's author reserves the right to publish the findings as an academic publication or in another form. The report and any subsequent study's authors are either presented in aggregated form or using quotations with pseudonyms.

Will my data be shared with others?

 Your data will only be available to the researcher, their supervisor and, in exceptional circumstances,

What if I am not happy with how my data has been managed?

Suppose you have concerns about data protection and how your information was handled. In that case, If you feel that your problems with data handling have not been resolved, you have a right to complain to the Information Commissioner's Office (ICO), the relevant regulator for data privacy and protection matters. The ICO can be contacted at Wycliffe House, Water Lane, Wilmslow, SK9 5AF, and you will find more information at https://ico.org.uk.

Chapter   8

Informed Consent Form

This must be given to the participant to sign before he or she commences the survey.

I, the undersigned participant, hereby confirm the following:

Please indicate 'yes' or 'no' next to each item by deleting the option that does not apply.

I have read and understood the information in the Participation Information Leaflet and the Data Protection Privacy Notice and have had the opportunity to ask questions about the research, interview process and my participation. [YES/NO]

I voluntarily agree to participate in this study and understand that I am free to withdraw without explaining and that I will not be penalised for doing so. [YES/NO]

I understand that I cannot withdraw my data from the study after [insert date]. [YES/NO]

I am aged 18 or over. [YES/NO]

I understand that my participation will contribute to psychological research, but I will receive no reward, payment, or other direct benefit. [YES/NO]

I was advised of any risks or disadvantages of participating in this research. [YES/NO]

The use, storage and destruction of my contributed data (including the measures taken to secure confidentiality) has been thoroughly explained to me [YES/NO]

I consent to my interview being audio recorded. [YES/NO]
I consent to anonymised quotes from my interview used in the research report and any publications derived from it. [YES/NO]
I understand that by returning the consent form by e-mail, I am giving my informed consent. [YES/NO]
Participant

name:_______________________________

     Date:_____________________

Chapter   9

Ethics and Data management for survey methodology

Content

Definition

options for survey design

Research Proposal and Ethics

Data Management Plan

Ethics is a vital component of the research project.

Think positive, choose a topic suitable for the methodology

Internet Facilitated Research

Avoid the following

What constitutes personal data?

Which are considered 'special categories?

Informed consent should include the following;

Helpful questions to Develop One's Data Management Plan

Keep in regular contact with One's tutor/professor.

Important Documents

Definition

• A survey quantifies people's experiences or beliefs

• It is a questionnaire that measures and compares people's hidden attitudes, opinions, knowledge or beliefs

• Rating scale items are tested for face validity, construct validity, concurrent validity, test-retest reliability, split-half reliability

• Data are analysed using statistical tests related to seeing relationships between variables – correlations, regression (different kinds), factor analysis

options for survey design

• Two options:

• Option 1: Combining existing scales to develop a predictive model = Multiple regression.

• Option 2: Development of a new scale based on an existing scale = Principal components analysis.(PCA)

• Open-text surveys are not an option as they are not part of the survey methodology.

Research proposal and Ethics

• A correct participant and ethic form must be used. Plus

• Project proposal:

• A project summary (Section 1)

• project details (Section 2)

• A One's survey questionnaire items

• Ethical approval form signed by the ethics team or the professor.

• Answers to sections 1 and 2

• A name and today's date (these can be inserted electronically)

• A participant information leaflet and participant consent form using the appropriate template for a method specialism.

Data Management Plan.

In ethics, Consider the following; Dilemma, compliance, wrong, choice, Benefit, Morals, Right, and Values.

Ethics is a vital component of the research project.

Without ethical approval, a researcher cannot begin collecting the data needed for One's research. Therefore, it is essential to read the ethics guidelines carefully and ensure. One's research proposal takes complete account of the guidelines. In addition, to avoid later ethical issues, one needs to develop a research proposal that does not include vulnerable participants; those who are under 18 years of age, have experienced acute emotional or physical trauma, or may be easily manipulated, such as elderly participants or those with mental health problems.

Choosing topics that both researcher and participants will enjoy engaging with is better. An excellent point to keep in mind here is that One's study will not generate more marks if it is more complex, uses more participants, or if it covers sensitive topics. It is good to choose an exciting topic, and you should pick One's topic based on how easily you can carry out the research and write the results. Remember, you gain marks for how well you write up the project rather than for how you do it.

• Be mindful of ethics throughout the research process
• At the outset, principal concerns are with the topic and potential participants' stress levels!
• Discuss the topic ideas early with a tutor to be agreed
• Stay away from any topic which surrounds negative emotions or experience

• Ethics proposal form must be signed before you recruit participants.
• Ethical wrongdoings can reduce the overall project grade

As a researcher, one will need to adhere to the code of research, including;
• Respect - for the dignity and welfare of the participants
• Competence – acknowledge limitations
• Responsibility – be trustworthy, avoid harm, manage power
• Integrity – be honest, truthful, accurate

Think positive, and choose a topic suitable for the methodology.

Refer to The (British psychological society) BPS Code of Ethics updated Apr 2021 https://www.bps.org.uk/news-and-policy/bps-code-human-research-ethics and APA (America Psychology Association) ethical guide advice: avoid any topic which surrounds negative emotions or experience.'
• Creative thinking makes it possible to turn a negative or problematic proposal into a positively orientated one.
Some topics are 'riskier' than others.

Crucial Issues to consider in ethnic/methodology

• Informed consent

• Participant safety

• Researcher safety

• Confidentiality and anonymity

• Debriefing participants

• How can participants obtain further information/discuss the research & additional support/disclosure issues?

• Possible need for additional support/disclosure issues

• Right to withdraw from the study

• Safe storage of participant information and data

• Disposal of participant information and data

• Act within the professional competence

• Sound research design

• Maximise benefits – at all stages, inc. dissemination – minimise risks.

Internet Facilitated Research

• The right to withdraw should be stressed, and autonomy can be validated by minimising the number of forced answer questions.

• If participants quit by closing their browsers, they will not be debriefed.

• Design the project with opportunities for the participant to quit (or ask them to confirm if they wish to continue at regular intervals); if they choose to stop, ensure they access the debrief page.

• If participants do not click the consent option, they could be re-directed to the debrief page.

• Consent and age questions are paramount.

Avoid the following in research.

• Participants under 18

- Vulnerable people
- Inequality in power
- Sensitive topics (e.g. sexual behaviour; illegal activities, political behaviour; abuse)
- Unnecessary deception
- Accessing confidential information
- Psychological stress, anxiety or humiliation
- Research involving invasive intervene
- Research that may harm employment or social standing
- research that may lead to 'labelling' (e.g. 'I am stupid /not normal')
- Research that involves the collection of human tissue, blood or other biological samples
- Payment

Participant concern

Participant has a concern about some of the survey questions
The participant wants to take a look at the entire survey before agreeing to data collection
The participant wants to know how well they did
The participant wants psychological advice

What constitutes personal data?

• Name

• Identification number

• Location data

• Online identifier

• Online identifiers include IP addresses and cookie identifiers which may be personal data.

• Which are considered 'special categories?

• Racial/ ethnic origin

• Political opinions

• Religious beliefs

• Union membership

• Biometric data

• Gender orientation

• Mental health data

Informed consent should include the following; Purpose of the research

• A statement that participation is voluntary and the right to withdraw at any time without any consequences or loss of benefits that the person is otherwise entitled to receive.

• Procedures involved in the research.

• Length of time the participant is expected to participate.

• All foreseeable risks and discomforts to the participant (if any).

• Benefits of the research to society and possibly the individual human participant.

• What data will be gathered

• How data will be stored and any plans for preservation and sharing

• Who will have access to it

• How will data be anonymised/pseudo anonymised

• Contact details of the researcher [you] and institution

• Does the template in the One's Resources tab meet all these?

Helpful Questions to develop One's Data Management Plan

• How will the data be collected?

• Will the data collected be anonymous?

• Are you collecting categories of sensitive personal data?

• How will the data be stored?

• Who will have access to the data?

• Will the anonymous data be shared with a third party?
• When will the data be destroyed?
• How will the data be destroyed?

Data may be collected using Qualtrics.

2. (All data should be anonymous at the point of collection. This will include not automatically identifying participants' IP (computer) addresses when designing a study in Qualtrics.)

3. (For example, data concerning racial or ethnic origin, political opinions, religious or philosophical beliefs, trade union membership, health, a person's sexual orientation, etc.)

4. (For example, downloaded from the Qualtrics site and stored in a password-protected file on a password-protected PC.)

5. (For example, researcher, project supervisor.)

6. (For example, if planning to publish, some journals have data-sharing policies.)

7. (Usually, this will be at the end of the study when you have received One's DE300 module results. However, if you plan to publish One's project report, you may need to retain the data for extended periods, such as ten years.)

8. This should explain how the data will be permanently deleted and no longer retrievable.)

Keep in regular contact with One's tutor/professor.

• Remember one's tutor is supervising and has overall responsibility
• Your tutor needs to know how things are progressing
• Vital if you have ethical or design questions
• Your tutor will help with ethics questions

Essential Documents to include with survey methodology

Ethics Status Document

Participant Information and Consent Template

Survey Project Proposal Form

Survey Project Data Management Plan

Survey Design Checklist

Chapter   10
Ethical approval form

Ethical approval form

Important: please note the following. Your tutor must approve your project before you begin participant recruitment and data collection. Your tutor should electronically sign and date the final version of the Project proposal and Ethical approval form; final copies must be included with your Project report forms are evidence that you have gained ethical approval for your project and that your tutor has approved your design.

Inform the forms with your report to avoid trials in the. In particular, you should read pages 1–26 of the BPS's Code of Human Research Ethics.

Topics you should consider include:

informed consent – you should include a copy of your draft consent form with the Assignment participant instructions – again, a draft of your instruction sheet should be submitted with

materials (including draft questions, video/audio material descriptions, draft word lists, etc.)

participant safety

researcher safety

researcher distress – investigating a sensitive topic can be upsetting to the investigator

confidentiality and anonymity

debriefing participants

how participants can obtain further information or discuss the research

possible need for additional support/disclosure issues

right to withdraw from the study

storage of participant information and data

disposal of participant information and data.

Now complete the following two questions:

1. What are the ethical considerations that may have an impact on your study?

The necessity for informed consent, in which survey respondents participate and are conscious of the nature and prerequisites of the research, is one of the ethical considerations that may impact the study. There would also be a requirement to explain any uncomfortable feelings or harm, dignity hazard, privacy invasion, and how their safety would be guaranteed. As the research community has become increasingly concerned with human subject safeguards, one area of worry is the potential damage in asking persons to report on emotionally painful issues, mainly when there is no reward for respondents. Depression, changed self-concept, anxiety symptoms, diminished confidence in others, guilt, humiliation, fear, humiliation, boredom, irritation, getting unfavourable facts about oneself, and inconvenience may occur but on a small scale.

Furthermore, participants must be informed of any anticipated results to research facilities or the subjects themselves from gaining new knowledge. There is also a need to notify people of the methods employed to protect their privacy and a disclaimer stating that involvement is entirely voluntary and that nobody will be penalised for refusing to participate.

Respondents can narrate their tales as they interact with the survey questions. Following completion, they will need access to the study to clarify and recognise their involvement in the survey.

2. How does your study demonstrate respect for people (participants)

The study will guarantee the respect of both prospective and enlisted participants. Consideration involves, but is not constrained to, preserving their personal information closely guarded and retaining their privacy, honouring their ability to choose if the research does not align with their interests, changing their minds, and resigning without penalty. It will be accomplished by guaranteeing that all respondents are shielded from unauthorised publicity. The study considers and fosters participant safety by protecting their data, notifying them about the research and relevant issues, and protecting their human rights.

The survey is designed to meet the seven fundamental principles of an ethical survey to demonstrate respect for the participants. They include Social and therapeutic significance, Scientific credibility, Appropriate subject selection, the Risk-benefit ratio favourable, Independent evaluation, Informed consent, and Consideration for potential and enrolled topics. The study intends to respond to a specific issue, an attitude towards mental health. The solution would improve Knowledge in this area and help to enhance accessibility and provision of health care services to people with mental health. In essence, there is value in doing this study because it lessens the risk in the community regarding persons with mental illness.

Besides, responses to the question would add to a scientific understanding of mental health and enhance the methods of preventing, diagnosing or caring for individuals with this condition.

I have read the BPS guidance and confirm that, to the best of my knowledge, my study and project adhere to these principles.

Researcher name … …………………………….

Chapter   11

Project proposal

Below is an example of a survey methodology

1. State the proposed title of your project:

> A_Survey that explores the relationship between Age and Attitude towards mental health/ wellbeing

2. State your research question or hypothesis (as suitable for your chosen analysis)

> RQ/ AIM Does age influence emotional, psychological, and social attitudes towards mental health wellbeing?
>
> Hypothesis/Testable statement; Age influences emotional, psychological, and social responses towards mental health/wellbeing.
>
> Using Survey Methodology/MR

3. Provide a **brief outline of your project**; indicate the type of survey you are planning;

describe the kind of data you will collect and display the type of analysis you will undertake

This paper aims to assess age's influence on attitudes toward mental health/disabilities, using primary sources to determine the trend and impact of these attitudes and why opinions have changed.

I will conduct a survey and collect qualitative data. The study will collect information from 18 years and above respondents to determine their socio-demographic backgrounds and views on mental health/disability. DV will be Attitude, and the IV will be 1)age 2) scale of answering questionnaires 1-5) which will be grouped under the headings scale: 1) Inclusion, 2) Gains, 3) Discrimination, 4) Prospects.

The scale of 1-5 will represent: 1: Agree strongly 2: Agree slightly 3: Neither agree nor disagree 4: Disagree slightly 5: Disagree strongly.

For reliability/validity, I will keep the existing questionnaires relatively the same.

I will then use SPSS and multiple regression to determine any correlations in the data.

Before doing the analysis, I will run some dummy data through SPSS and see what it looks like with the IVs/DV I propose.

The sample will be generated using an opportunity-to-sampling process to guarantee that it represents the general population.

Mental health covers anxiety disorders, mood disorders, psychotic disorders, eating disorders, personality disorders, dementia, and autism.

The stigma associated with mental health disabilities in the population substantially impedes treatment and recovery. Fortunately, the majority of these mental disabilities are treatable.

4. Explain which psychological theories/ models your project relates to.

This study is rooted in the cognitive school of thought. In this theory, the emphasis is on thinking rather than doing. As a result, a feedback loop exists between the individual's preconceptions, dispositions, consequent perceptions and inferences.

Emotional and psychological differences in personality influence individual acceptance of mental health. Personality traits are the main component of several psychological structures used to explain people's attitudes and behaviour in this context.

The personality assessment postulates innate psychological factors that impact the things and methods people learn as they grow up. As a result, two of The Five-Factor Model of Personality's qualities are openness to experience and extroversion.

 Individuals' receptivity to experience reflects their aesthetic and intellectual capacities.

5. Which degree are you currently studying for:

☐ BSc Psychology BSc Social Psychology

☐ BSc Forensic Psychology ☐ Other, please name:

6

Briefly explain how if you are doing Psychology with Counselling, Forensic or Social Psychology. Your project relates to your degree

The researcher can give brief description about him or herself.

Section 2: Project details – Survey project

Please explain how you will conduct your project (using the questions below for guidance).

Questions	Your answers	Tutor use only
Outline how you will operationalise the measurement of your data to facilitate your analysis, i.e., use existing scales, develop a scale or other.	The measurement of the data will be operationalised through an existing questionnaire. It covers a wide range of aspects, but the key among them is capturing the thoughts of personality and mental health/disability based on the answers given by the respondents. These answers would be marked on a scale of 1 to 5 where 1 represents strong agreement with the question and 5	

	represents strong disagreement. In some cases, a scale of 1 to 7 would be used to indicate how comfortable the participants are able to share information about a given situation. The questionnaires have been selected in a way to help determine whether a person responding can associate with psychological problems and physical health issues and its impact on society.	
Why do you feel your chosen method (survey) is the most	Stratified random sampling is more appropriate because it is more precise than random sampling. Simple random samples	

appropriate for your project?	and stratified random samples are both typical data collection strategies. A basic random sample is utilised to depict the whole data population and randomly pick people from the group. In contrast, a stratified random sample splits the sample into different segments, or strata, depending on shared traits. As a result, stratified sampling ensures that members of each category are involved in the data analysis. Moreover, it focuses on a smaller sample, saving time and money to complete the project. Furthermore, because this method provides	

	information representative of the entire population, the results will be more representative.	
What design issues may be pertinent to your potential study (e.g. measurement scale, question wording)?	Stratified random samples, as opposed to simple random samples, are employed with populations that may be readily divided into multiple subgroups or subsets. These groups are created based on different parameters, and components from each are drawn randomly in proportion to the size of the group compared to the population. Leading questions may cause respondents to be directed to a specific response. Assumptions	

	of prior understanding may also lead to incorrect and ambiguous answers. Compound questions may cause respondents to believe they are being asked for more information within one request. These issues may be pertinent to my potential study.	
Outline your participant recruitment plan. Describe your potential participants (number, demographic information). Describe how you plan to recruit them (e.g. work	It is hypothesised that attitudes about privacy concerning digitally obtained data are influenced by two key variables: environmental conditions and individual traits. Contextual circumstances may have the most impact on people's privacy thinking in matters of mental health. To this extent, I will choose respondents	

colleagues, friends, neighbours, from the Experimental Participation Website (EPW)). If you are planning to recruit a group of participants with a particular demographic or characteristic, how will you do this? Are there any participants whom you would exclude, and why? If you	from my neighbours, friends, and co-workers over 18 and from various regions of the country. Social media Facebook from my friends. A personal email or from the open university experimental participation website. I will use DE 300-participant pool and open the university DE 300 students. To avoid the problem of gender bias, a sample size of 100 will be chosen, with 50 males and 50 females. A score of 1 indicates rejection, a score of 2 indicates a low level of acceptance, a score of 3 indicates a medium level of acceptance, and a score of 4-5 shows the highest	

are planning to recruit participants by using social media or websites, please explain how.	level of acceptance. I will exclude people with mental disabilities as it is unethical.	
Outline your proposed procedure. You are expected to use Qualtrics to design your questionnaire; please discuss with your tutor if you foresee any difficulties with this. Please include a copy of your draft survey	I will use Qualtrics to design my questionnaire. The tutorials I have gone through in class would make it easy to understand how to use this tool, and I foresee a seamless process. The procedure to create the questionnaire entails numbering the questions in the order in which they are made. Then, I will click the button to add a new question, select the question type and edit the query by	

with this assignment.	clicking on a text box.	
How will you administer the questionnaire (e.g. online, face-to-face, hard copy)?	I will use the Sona to upload a copy of my survey, download the results, and type them into SPSS or Excel. Or both online and hard copy survey form administration will be utilised with participants who need to be met receiving questionnaires via email.	
What type of data will your study produce, and how will these data relate to your research question? Discuss your data analysis	I will use (SPSS) numerical data that necessitate a multiple regression analysis of the link between the (2 or 4) independent and dependent variables.	

plan.		
Outline your proposed research timetable indicating approximate dates and durations of the stages of your project.	1) Survey development – 3 months (December 2022 to 20/January/2023) 2)Identifying and updating Title, RQ, Hypothesis, DV, IVs, and participants. February 2023, 3) Running some dummy data through SPSS and see what it looks like with the IVs/DV you propose (then seek my tutor's advice) 4)working on the background study. 12th-18th March 2023 5)Literature Review and	

	identification of gap. 19th-31st March 2023 6)Working on draft methodology. February 2023 (whilst waiting for the project proposal and ethic approval by my tutor) 7)Project proposer and Ethics approval Feb/March 2023 8) Data collection – after tutor approval of the proposal and ethical. March 2023 9) March/April 2023- Data analysis and interpretation (1 week) 10) Report writing – 1 week (08/April 2023)	

	11) finalising conclusions and recommendations. April 2023 12)Editing 10/April/2023 13)Proofreading and formatting – 1 day (15/ April 2023 14) submitting the research on 20/April/2023,	

Feedback from tutor

The following procedural/ design issues must be addressed before you begin to collect data:

The following materials must be submitted for approval before you begin to collect data:

Chapter 12

Ethical and Procedural approval by your tutor.

Notes to student:

If your tutor approves and signs this Ethical approval form and approves your design and materials ,then you can start running your project.

If your tutor has requested changes to your study, make those changes and post the amended Ethical approval form in your project forum to allow your tutor to scrutinise it; you must not start the project until your tutor has approved it and signed it off.

If your tutor has serious concerns about your study, you must not begin it until you have contacted your tutor, changed your form, post posted amended Ethical approval form in your project forum for further scrutiny, and gained your tutor's approval. This is very important, and you will risk failing your project if you do not comply with this instruction.

Your tutor completes the following section.
Notes to tutor: In the box below, please provide feedback on the student's Ethical approval form, advising how to further address any ethical issues.

Please tick the relevant boxes below, then sign and date the form. Then return the Project proposal and Ethical approval form to the student.

This project is approved.		
This project is not currently approved. Your project can only proceed once changes have been made and your tutor has signed off on these. Complete the changes outlined above or		

contact your tutor if you need clarification on what is required. Once changes have been made, post a revised version of this form on your project forum and await approval.		

The design of this survey is approved.	
The materials to be used in this survey are approved.	
The Qualtrics version has been reviewed (Responses anonymised in survey options, and consent and debrief work correctly)	

You can only pilot and launch your questionnaire when the tutor's signature has been given below.

Tutor signature: .... Date:

Chapter   13

Example of Management Plan survey project
Management Plan sur survey project

TITLE:

_Altitude towards Mental Health/wellbeing

Research Question/AIM:

Does age influence attitudes towards mental health/well-being?

Hypothesis/Testable Statement:

 Age influences attitudes towards mental health/wellbeing.

 1 How will the data be collected?

Researchers obtain quantitative data by asking closed-ended or multiple-choice questions via surveys, censuses, quizzes, and other approaches. For this survey, the data will be collected from a survey completed by the mentors and mentees using Qualtrics. Closed-ended surveys encourage participants to respond with yes or no, while open-ended surveys allow them to offer as much detail as they like. The survey approach used in this study would aid in collecting demographic information such as age, gender, income, and employment. Participants would also be asked to score some of the questions on a scale by providing a proposition such as I strongly agree, agree, disagree, or strongly disagree.

Will the data collected be anonymous?

If the data is traceable or can be linked to the person (directly or indirectly), the method of gathering information cannot pretend to be anonymous. The responses in this survey would be recorded in a way that protects participants' data to maintain anonymity. This process involves removing the names and any information that could identify participants indirectly within the transcription. The participants' IP (computer) addresses would not be automatically collected within the Qualtrics survey design settings. Confidential information is frequently coded so that the subject can be identified. The identity of the individual is kept distinct from the code and data.

3 Are you collecting categories of sensitive personal data?

NOT for survey

Most of the data collected are not of sensitive personal nature, but there are aspects of religious or philosophical beliefs and health matters, though on a general level, to be able to address the research objectives. When working with sensitive data, remember that great care should be taken to collect, process, handle, and store data throughout the research process. Sensitive data is information that must be safeguarded against unauthorised disclosure. Access to sensitive information must be restricted. Sensitive data security may be necessary for legal or ethical grounds, concerns about personal privacy, or commercial interests.

How will the data be stored?

A storage system would be implemented to meet the project's needs. USB drives, hard drives, and disks provide cheap and easy solutions, but their security can be compromised, lost, or destroyed. For this case, local storage solutions such as lab servers and cloud services like drive and Google drive would be deployed to the Qualtrics site server as backup options. The access to data would also be password protected to eliminate illegal access, be it on a PC or server file.

Who will have access to the data?

Access is a person's capacity to access or retrieve data in a database or other repository. The research data will be accessible to the project researcher, project supervisor, and, in exceptional circumstances, to the Module Team members. These users could save, retrieve, move, or change data stored on various hard disks and other media.

Will the anonymous data be shared with a third party?

The survey would be sent via email, which would help keep the responses anonymous. The report is scheduled for publication as an academic article. Some of the anonymous data will be shared with a UK data repository in SPSS and Excel format. In addition, the institution may communicate personally identifiable information under its control with a third party for that third party to perform the tasks on that data on behalf of the institution. Still, it has to comply with the existing regulations. The sharing might be one-time, long-term, or continuous, especially when the College outsources or offers a function requiring personal data within its storage or the available data repository.

When will the data be destroyed?

Once the DE300 module results are received, the data will be destroyed on September 30th, 2023. Per the journal's requirements, some anonymous data will be stored in a UK data repository for at least ten years. Once the data is shared in the UK data repository, all project data on the researcher's computer will be permanently deleted.

How will the data be destroyed?

Shredding, drilling, and melting procedures would render the physical storage medium worthless and unreadable can to physical data once the survey has been done. The SPSS and Excel project data files would be deleted, including removal from the desktop recycles bin, to ensure the information is no longer recoverable. All data files related to the survey in the project account will be deleted, making them inaccessible.

Chapter 14

Example of a participant information leaflet

For survey research.

Title;

Attitude towards mental health/ wellbeing/disability

Research question/ RQ/AIM;

Does Age influence attitude towards mental health/wellbeing/Disability

Participant Information Leaflet

Project details.

My name is (Researcher's name,),and I am a psychology student at the Name of university As part of my studies, I am conducting research project to contribute to my degree.

My project explores the relationship between age and attitude towards mental health/well-being. I hope the findings will shed light on how age influences the individual's attitude towards mental health. Because of their direct effect on various behaviours, attitudes have long been a hot issue for scholars. More particularly, stigmatising views toward persons with mental disabilities have been closely studied in recent years due to their potential to have serious detrimental consequences for those with mental health issues.

You have been invited because your answers might help us understand the reasons behind people's different attitudes towards mental health/wellbeing.

You will be asked questions about mental health, experience with patients, attitudes towards mental health, and options available for addressing the problem. *You must* be over 18 for this survey but are advised not to participate if you have mental health issues.

The survey should take about 15 minutes to complete.

Voluntary participation & anonymity

Participation in the study is entirely voluntary. After you have read this leaflet, please contact me if you have any questions or concerns. My University personal email address is (insert the email)

To carry out this survey, the University uses the tools provided by Qualtrics, with whom the School of Psychology agrees. All information collected within Qualtrics will be anonymous – you will not be identifiable to the researcher or in any report resulting from this survey.

If you decide to participate, you can withdraw without giving a reason or negative consequences. As the data collected is anonymous, it will not be possible to withdraw from the study once you have completed the survey, as the researcher will not be able to identify you.

How will the data collected in the survey be used?

Data collected will be aggregated and analysed statistically, and summaries of the results will be included in research report. Before agreeing to participate, please read the attached Data Protection Privacy Notice below, which explains how the data will be managed after collection. If you would like a summary of the findings from the study, please email the researcher at the researcher's university email. The researcher must not insert his or her personal email.

How do I give consent to participate?

If you are happy to participate, please complete the Informed Consent Form below when prompted.

Questions, comments or complaints

If you need more information about the study or have any concerns, please get in touch with the researcher by emailing (insert researcher university email). You can also contact the project supervisor; insert the researcher's supervisor's name and email address. If you wish to make a formal complaint,

Thank you for your time reading this information. Please complete the survey by Insert deadline date for the study to be done. Then sign it.

Chapter   15

Below is the "Data protection privacy notice" used by the researcher in the survey.

You may notice some of the wording changes.

The research study complies with UK General Data Protection Regulations (GDPR) and the UK Data Protection Act 2018. The data collected in this study is anonymous. That means when participating in this study, it is impossible to identify you individually.

You will be asked to indicate your gender, age, education, religion, and occupation, but this cannot be linked back to you as an individual.

The nature of the research is such that you will not be asked to disclose sensitive personal information. The survey does not require you to disclose special category data (ethnic origin, political views, health issues, trade union membership, or sexual orientation).

How long will the data be used and retained?

All anonymous project data and consent forms will be stored on the researcher's password-protected hard drive, with a backup copy on an encrypted or password-protected external drive until the project is completed. Any e-mail correspondence with participants will be destroyed immediately after collecting the data.

The study results will be a basis for a research project report in the university model. The study's author reserves the right to publish the findings as an academic publication or in another form. The anonymous data will be presented in aggregated form in the report and any subsequent publication.

Will my data be shared with others?

The anonymous project data collected in this study will be available to the researcher, their supervisor and, occasionally, academic staff on the DE300 module team. The project data may also be stored indefinitely in a secure UK research data archive, subject to appropriate legal and ethical practices.

What if I am not happy with how my data has been managed?

If you have concerns about data protection and how your information was handled, don't hesitate to contact the course chair at (insert email for the supervisor). You can also contact the university Data Protection Team at data-protection@open.ac.uk. Suppose you feel that your concerns about data handling still need to be resolved. In that case, you have a right to complain to the Information Commissioner's Office (ICO), the relevant regulator for data privacy and protection matters. The ICO can be contacted at Wycliffe House, Water Lane, Wilmslow, SK9 5AF, and you will find more information at https://ico.org.uk.

Chapter   16

Example of Participants Questionnaire in Survey
Project

Participants Survey Questionnaire

Introduction

My name is (insert First name). I'm a psychology
with a counselling student at the open university.
I am surveying " Age attitudes towards mental
health/wellbeing."

The questionnaire may take about fifteen minutes
to complete this survey on the overall status of
your experiences and perspectives on people
with mental health issues. We value your
feedback, and your responses will be kept
confidential.
Thank you for your input.

Q 1. <u>Gender:</u>

- Male
- Female
- Others

- I prefer not to say.

Q2 <u>Age (18+)</u>

Please state your age________

 Below are some opinions other people hold about mental health/wellbeing/mental disability, and I would like you to tell me how much you agree or disagree with each one.

You will notice that I did not give the full details of the IV (I=inclusion, D=discrimination and p=prospect) to avoid bias in the participants answering the questions.

A scale of I

01: Agree strongly 02: Agree slightly 03: Neutral
04: Disagree slightly 05: Disagree strongly

		Agree Strongly	Agree slightly.	Neutral	Disagree slightly	Disagree Strongly

		1	2	3	ly. 4	5
1	Some people with mental health problems find making new friends more challenging.					
2	People with mental health issues sometimes have problems socialising.					
3	Anyone can develop mental health conditions.					
4	People with a history of mental health issues should be offered the same					

	opportunities as anyone else.					
5	Anyone can develop mental health problems.					
6	People with mental health issues have the same need for social inclusion as anyone else.					
7	Everyone should have the opportunity for social inclusion in their community.					
8	People with mental illness should be supported to manage their					

	responsibilities in a way that is helpful to them.					
9	Increased spending on mental health services is an investment in supporting people to reach their potential in life.					
10	When someone shows signs of mental health issues, they should be offered support to help them manage the situation.					
11	Residents have nothing to fear from					

people coming into their neighbourhood to obtain mental health services.					

A <u>scale of D</u>

01: Agree strongly 02: Agree slightly 03: Neutral

04: Disagree slightly 05: Disagree strongly

		Agree Strongly	Agree slightly.	Neutral	Disagree slightly.	Disagree Strongly
		1	2	3	4	5
1 2	People tend to become impatient with those with mental health					

	issues.					
13	People tend to treat those with mental health problems as if they have no feelings.					
14	People with mental disabilities should not be given too much responsibility.					
1	People					

5	with mental disabiliti es have for too long been the subject of ridicule.					
1 6	People with mental health issues have been heavily stigmati sed.					

A scale of P

01: Agree strongly 02: Agree slightly 03: Neutral

04: Disagree slightly 05: Disagree strongly

		Agree Strongly 1	Agree slightly. 2	Neutral 3	Disagree slightly. 4	Disagree Strongly 5
17	We need to be more supportive of people who experience mental health issues.					
18	Locating mental health facilities in a residential area does not					

	downgrade the neighbourhood.					
19	People with mental health problems should have the same rights to a job as anyone else					
20	We should invest time and money in supporting people with mental health					

	issues to have the opportunity to be active in society.					
21	We are responsible for providing the best care for people with mental disabilities.					
22	We need to adopt a far more tolerant attitude toward people with					

	mental disabilitie s in our society.					
2 3	Mental illness is a like any other. Physical illness.					
2 4	Less emphasi s should be placed on protectin g the public from people with mental illness.					
2	Virtually					

5	anyone can become mentally ill.					
2 6	There are good services for people with mental illness.					
2 7	No one has the right to exclude people with mental health issues from their community.					

28	People with mental health issues are far less of a danger than most people suppose					
29	The best therapy for many people with mental health issues is to be part of their community.					
3	People					

0	with mental health problems should have the same rights to a job as anyone else	145			
31	People recovering from mental health issues can lead 'normal' lives.				
32	We should show empathy and understa				

	nding towards people with mental health issues.		146			

Chapter   17

How to Write a Literature Review

1.   provide a working title for your project

2.   provide a literature review outlining the rationale for your study

three to five primary sources

3.   state your research question (RQ) or hypothesis. (what do you aim to discover)

2.   The working title should be short and mention the method and topic you wish to investigate

3.   hypothesises. This should be phrased as a statement predicting a difference or an effect

4.   Must conduct academic research. (Rationale or supported reason)

1.   background research to help to 'set the scene' (detailing current findings, methods and debates in an area of study)

5.   NB can use the literature as a rationale for the work you want to do for assignment

6.   , the aim is to include literature that gives an overview of the work that has already been

done on your topic of interest, so relevance is vital. The rationale for the study, methods, results and limitations

7.   Did the articles agree or disagree

Structure

8.   Similar to an essay, a literature review is essentially made up of three different sections: an introduction, the main body and a conclusion

8.1.   The introduction

8.1.2. Explain the broad context of your research area, the main topic(s) you are interested in, and why (defining any key terms, if necessary).

8.13. It should also include a brief overview of the format your review will take

8.2.   Main Body; (the bulk of the review)

8.2.1. details and critical analysis of the literature that is relevant to your research;

8.2.2. This should include three to five studies in academic journals or book chapters (not textbooks).

8.2.3. The review provides a critical assessment of the chosen studies comparing and critically evaluating the different contributions to the literature.

8.2.4. Go beyond simply providing a list or description of the published papers or chapters you identified in the literature search.

8.2.5. It should identify any patterns and shortcomings in the literature, which can then be used to justify or explain the need for your research.

8.2.6. Discussion (very important)

8.2.7. Discuss significant patterns, relationships or themes within the literature

8.2.8. Discuss areas where there are unresolved questions or conflicting evidence.

8.2.9. The consideration of methodological or theoretical weaknesses within different studies that need to be addressed

8.2.10.   Shap of review

8.2.11.   In the review, you should start with a general, more comprehensive view of the literature, gradually narrowing it down to address the specific focus of your research.

8.2.12.   NB; It should allow the reader to understand what you are doing and why you are doing it.

8.3.   CONCLUSION

8.3.1. summarise and evaluate the essential aspects of your review.

8.3.2. Summarise any significant problems or gaps within the existing research, supported with citations,

8.3.3. Explain how your proposed study will address these gaps or build on the current literature to produce something new.

8.3.4. It would be best to end this section with your proposed research question and hypotheses, linking your research to existing knowledge.

8.3.5. Your research question and hypothesis should be read as a logical conclusion to the literature discussion.

9.   Reference

9.1.   Complete the reference list for your literature reviews. The institution will provide their prevalence.

Example.

9.2.   Cite Them Right

9.3.   Harvard referencing style the references or bibliographies are presented in a breakdown fashion in the Harvard referencing style. ...

9.3.   MLA referencing style The MLA referencing style is extensively used and approved in most academic settings. However, it is predominantly employed in the humanities, especially in liberal arts subjects like language and literature.

9.4.   APA referencing style.

9.5.   MHRA referencing style.

Chapter 18

Example of Literature Review for a survey.

Topic;

Attitude towards Mental Health/wellbeing

Research Question:

Has the attitude towards mental health issues

changed in the various age groups using Multiple

regression of the survey method?

Hypothesis:

 There has been an improvement in stigma

towards mental health among all ages.

Introduction

It has been shown that stigma associated with mental disorders among healthcare workers, the public, and within the healthcare system is a substantial impediment to treatment and recovery and a key contributor to reducing the quality of physical care provided to people with mental disorders. These stigmatised views could lead to failure to attend to patients' medical requirements, provision of improper, and even social marginalisation of the patients.

The definition of the mental disorder depends on the types; Mental illness (Psychosis and necrosis), learning difficulties, and psychopathy. Psychosis includes schizophrenia (paranoid, hebephrenic, Catatonic, and Bipolar). Neurosis (reactive depression, anxiety phobia, ADHD, ASD, OCD/PTSD). Hallucinations, delusion, and endogenous depression are characteristic of psychotic, with no insight and cannot be cured. However, Neurosis has understanding and, therefore, can be treated.

This paper aims to conduct a judicial review to assess attitudes toward mental illness, using primary sources to determine the trend and impact and why opinions have changed.

How Attitudes of People Affect individuals with Mental Disorders.

The stigma associated with mental disorders is a significant public health issue confined to the public and healthcare professionals (Robinson et al., 2019). However, evidence suggests that many persons with mental illness claim that healthcare practitioners, who provide physical and mental health treatments, play a significant role in stigmatisation and prejudice in many nations worldwide (Kalb et al., 2019). Mental disorders are a condition causing substantial disturbance to an individual's situation, emotional behaviour, and regulation (Smith et al., 2021).

Healthcare prejudice connected to mental disorders is a topic that draws more attention and concern. Healthcare systems have not yet effectively reacted to the demands of people with mental illnesses and are severely underfunded. Besides, people with mental illnesses require social support to establish and sustain personal, family, and social ties. The workforce shortages in psychiatry are a severe problem associated with the stigma of mental disorders among healthcare personnel. According to a study by Cadge et al. (2019) in the United Kingdom, medical students' ingrained stigma against mental disorders has been identified as contributing to their unfavourable perceptions of a future in psychiatry. A scarcity of psychiatrists might exacerbate the increasing crisis in the mental health care system. According to a study by Smith et al. (2019), the availability of care for those with mental disorders is likely to be impacted by the declining psychiatric workforce. Given the situation, the stigma associated with mental disorders is widely recognised as a primary contributor to population health disparities and a significant public health concern. Much work has been done globally to lessen the stigma associated with mental disorders among healthcare practitioners (Lien et al., 2019). Given the situation, it is necessary to ascertain how people's opinions and attitudes regarding mental disorders have changed over time (Sugar et al., 2020).

According to Sugar et al. (2020), people's thoughts and perceptions about mental disorders influence how they interact with, aid an individual suffering from them, and support them. How individuals perceive and communicate their emotional difficulties and psychological discomfort, as well as whether they reveal these symptoms and seek treatment, are all influenced by their attitudes and beliefs about mental disorders. According to research by Edwards and Kotera (2021), mental diseases, such as psychiatric conditions, anxiety disorders, disorders of impulse control, and drug addiction dysfunction, are widespread and can affect anybody, with around 17.4% of individuals above 16 years in the United Kingdom suffering from mental illnesses. According to a study by Ibrahim et al. (2019) on factors affecting the attitudes of people with mental disorders, attitudes and perceptions about psychiatric conditions are influenced by their own experiences with the illness, their interactions with those who are dealing with it, cultural stigmas associated with it, media reports, and their familiarity with organisational procedures. When these attitudes and beliefs are positively articulated, they can lead to helpful and inclusive behaviours, such as the willingness to employ an individual with a history of mental disorder (Smith et al., 2019).

Trends in People's Attitude towards Mental Disorder

Robinson et al. (2019) conducted a study to monitor national views on psychiatric conditions. These researchers examined how the public perceived the efficacy of mental health treatments and how compassionate individuals were toward those with mental disorders. The aim of the study was to find estimates of attitudes regarding mental disorders at the state level broken down by specific socio-demographic characteristics, psychiatric conditions manifestations, and mental health care. At least 80% of respondents indicated that mental disorder treatment was successful. However, 35% of respondents felt that people are empathetic and compassionate toward those with a mental disorder (Robinson et al., 2019). Black, non-Hispanic, adult Hispanics, and those with less than a high school degree, for example, were more likely than other population categories to disagree that therapy is enormously beneficial, especially among women, persons with chronic diseases, and adults who are jobless or unable to work. These study findings concur with Sugar et al. (2020), whose investigations revealed that 75% of individuals with mental disorders perceive that people have positive attitudes toward individuals with mental illnesses, which is why discrimination levels are high.

In another study, Lien et al. (2019) also did a meta-analysis to determine changes in attitudes toward mental disorders. Their study involved healthcare professionals and students whose opinions and attitudes toward psychiatric disorders were measured using Social Distance Scale and Opinions about Mental Disorder. Their study, run from 1966 to 2016, was used in the current research to help shed light on this issue. Their findings showed that, over time, healthcare professionals' views on mental diseases have improved, with social distances showing an upward trend. These results offer empirical proof that anti-stigma programs benefit HCPs and can guide future initiatives to enhance clinicians' attitudes about mental disorders, which will improve treatment standards (Lien et al., 2019).

Pescosolido et al. (2021) also studied public stigma trends toward mental disorders in a study aimed at evaluating an individual's nature, magnitude, and direction based on changes in stigma associated with mental disorders over the past 22 years. The researchers did a multistage sampling of individuals above 18 years to determine their perception, and the results showed a significant decrease in stigma toward mental disorders. Although age was a conservatising variable, it was revealed that being born before World War II or the 21st century was progressive. There was evidence of stalling stigma levels for other diseases and rising public views of possible violence among individuals with schizophrenia (Pescosolido et al., 2021). These findings necessitate rethinking stigma and retooling reduction efforts to promote service utilisation, enhance treatment options, and advance population health. Generally, there has been a significant reduction in people's attitudes toward mental disorders in the past two decades.

Conclusion

Reviewing the literature above, it is evident that society and people's stigma towards mental health have wide-ranging and widespread consequences for individuals and society. Individuals who experience stigma are less likely to seek treatment, there are fewer mental health professionals available, and culture is less inclined to support the mental health industry. Therefore, studying trends in attitudes toward mental health is essential to determining strategies to mitigate challenges. This literature review demonstrates improvement in stigma against people with mental illnesses. While other studies insist that stigma is still high, the fact that there is a slight improvement shows that, in the coming years, this stigma will be eliminated. Given that the depth of stigma is declining, it is imperative to develop strategies to pinpoint causes of stigma reduction for mental health and resolve stagnation in other illnesses. Therefore, the literature review findings concur with the study's hypothesis that an attitude towards mental health has improved.

References

Cadge, C., Connor, C., & Greenfield, S. (2019). University students' understanding and perceptions of schizophrenia in the U.K.: a qualitative study. *BMJ open*, *9*(4), e025813.http://dx.doi.org/10.1136/bmjopen-2018-025813

Edwards, A. M., & Kotera, Y. (2021). Mental health in the U.K. police force: a qualitative investigation into the stigma with mental illness. *International Journal of Mental Health and Addiction*, *19*(4), 1116-1134.https://doi.org/10.1007/s11469-019-00214-x

Ibrahim, N., Amit, N., Shahar, S., Wee, L. H., Ismail, R., Khairuddin, R., & Safien, A. M. (2019). Do depression literacy, mental disorder beliefs, and stigma influence mental health help-seeking attitudes? A cross-sectional study of secondary school and university students from B40 households in Malaysia. *BMC public health*, *19*(4), 1-8.https://doi.org/10.1186/s12889-019-6862-6

Kalb, L. G., Stapp, E. K., Ballard, E. D., Hogue, C., Keefer, A., & Riley, A. (2019). Trends in psychiatric emergency department visit among youth and young adults in the U.S.

Pediatrics, 143(4).https://publications.aap.org/ped
iatrics/article/143/4/e20182192/76774/Trends-in-
Psychiatric-Emergency-Department-Visits

Lien, Y. Y., Lin, H. S., Tsai, C. H., Lien, Y.
J., & Wu, T. T. (2019). Changes in attitudes
toward mental illness in healthcare professionals
and students. *International Journal of
Environmental Research And Public
Health, 16*(23),
4655.https://doi.org/10.3390%2Fijerph16234655

Pescosolido, B. A., Halpern-Manners, A.,
Luo, L., & Perry, B. (2021). Trends in public
stigma of mental disorder in the US, 1996-
2018. *JAMA Network Open, 4*(12), e2140202-
e2140202.
https://doi.org/10.1001/jamanetworkopen.2021.40
202

Robinson, P., Turk, D., Jilka, S., &Cella,
M. (2019). Measuring attitudes towards mental
health using social media: Investigating stigma
and trivialisation. *Social Psychiatry and
Psychiatric Epidemiology, 54*(1), 51–
58.https://doi.org/10.1007/s00127-018-1571-5

Sagar, R., Dandona, R., Gururaj, G.,
Dhaliwal, R. S., Singh, A., Ferrari, A., &Dandona,
L. (2020). The burden of mental disorders across

the states of India: The Global Burden of Disease
Study 1990–2017. *The Lancet Psychiatry*, 7(2),
148-161.https://doi.org/10.1016/S2215-
0366(19)30475-4

Smith, M. S., Lawrence, V., Sadler, E., &
Easter, A. (2019). Barriers to accessing mental
health services for women with perinatal mental
illness: systematic review and meta-synthesis of
qualitative studies in the U.K. *BMJ open*, 9(1),
e024803.http://dx.doi.org/10.1136/bmjopen-2018-
024803

Chapter 19

Dissertation

ATTITUDES TOWARDS MENTAL HEALTH

Abstract

Attitudes have long been a popular research topic in mental health due to their direct impact on various behaviours. More particularly, because they tend to have highly detrimental effects on people with mental health disorders, stigmatising views toward persons with mental illnesses have been the subject of intense research in recent years. Therefore, this research aims to determine attitudes towards mental health. In particular, the study seeks to determine whether age influences attitudes towards mental health. This research is significant as poor attitudes towards mental health can lead to harmful discrimination of the patients, hindering individuals from seeking care and impacting the social integration of those with the condition. This research will help fill the gap in reducing discrimination against individuals with mental illnesses. The best way of capturing the essence of individuals' attitudes towards mental health phenomenological research design will be used. This aspect will apply a semi-structured interviewing process to gather data. Data analysis will involve the use of IBM SPSS, which is a robust statistical analysis that requires the authors to find, determine, describe and depict the participants' experience and then reveal the emergent themes. This method will thus provide highly valid and reliable results. Numerous misconceptions and myths about this condition have been addressed throughout the study. Actually, this study reveal that the perceptions towards people with mental health issues evolve with age with the shift differing for various mental illnesses. The most remarkable attitude and psychological impact of age on people's attitude towards mental health has been addressed via the inclusion, discrimination, prospect, and attitude sub-themes.

Attitudes towards Mental Health

Introduction

Mental health is regarded as a condition of well-being whereby every person fulfils their capabilities, bears typical life challenges, works creatively and meaningfully, and contributes to society's well-being. Most of what is known about the way humans think and act has come from psychological theories. Some of these theories have drifted out of popularity, while others are still widely held, but all have significantly contributed to our knowledge of human cognition and behavior. Over-generalization or inadequate attention to the impact of age on a broad spectrum of emotional functioning and conduct is among the primary issues in mental health research (Haigh et al., 2020). Indeed, few studies have examined age variations in psychological and mental health perspectives. Research utilizing actual utilization as an output parameter has often revealed that older persons are less prone to hold a favourable attitude toward mental health than their younger counterparts. However, data on attitudinal outcomes are inconsistent, with some research showing that older populations hold more unfavourable opinions and others reporting no apparent age differences (Pérez-Flores and Cabassa, 2021). Because younger and older persons have diverse experiences in life and vulnerabilities to mental health concerns, their perspectives of and perspectives toward mental health and service uptake may differ. Age difference data will prove helpful in implementing an evidence-based practice that effectively meets the distinct requirements of various age groups of minorities. The current study sought to determine whether age influences views toward mental health treatment.

Mental health is a crucial topic of discussion. In fact, Lomas and Vander Weele (2022) suggest that discussing health without dealing with mental health is comparable to tuning a guitar and omitting a few dissonant notes. One in every four persons has a mental condition at some point. Depression is considered the "common cold" among mental diseases, the fourth most significant source of disability-adjusted childhood and adolescence (Hendrickx et al., 2020 p2). There is a large body of work in psychology regarding the prevalence of stigma associated with mental health. Reportedly, the majority of persons with severe depression are underneath 20 years of age, and the National Stigma-Study data reveal that "adults prefer to stigmatize teenagers who display mental health difficulties" (Bardram and Matic, 2020). Yet not only grownups but even teenagers stigmatize. Adolescents have little information, attitudes, and prejudices about persons with mental illnesses, and they build their own opinions based on their observations and community ties (Bardram and Matic, 2020). Individuals suffering from depression indicate that the stigma and prejudice they face can be more severe than their mental illness (s). The reason for this scenario is that discrimination occurs not only via thoughts and perceptions but also when society acts accordingly based on those views, such as when seeking a job or participating in social events. There have been at least three essential explanations of the causes of mental illness across history. They are supernatural, somatogenic, and psychogenic. According to supernatural interpretations, mental illness is caused by the invasion of evil or demonic entities, the dis-favour of gods, catastrophes, planetary gravitation, spells, and sin. Somatogenic theories describe physical functioning problems caused by sickness, inherited characteristics, brain injury, or disequilibrium (Farreras, 2019). Psychogenic theories focus on stressful or traumatic encounters, inappropriate learning relationships, and perceptions, or skewed views. Etiological concepts of mental illness determine the treatment and medical care that mentally ill people get. The mental disease was believed to be triggered by evil spirits or a humour imbalance in the body, which led to highly stigmatizing beliefs. Developing stigmatic thoughts is recognizing a person with a mental disorder using clues, establishing stereotypes based on such cues, and then responding prejudiced (Farreras, 2019). Outgroup bias happens when a person from one group (ingroup) recognizes a person from another group (outgroup) as being distinct from themselves. As a result, a person with mental illness may be perceived as 'different' and belonging to an 'outgroup,' fostering prejudice. Furthermore, prejudice against an outgroup member can boost the observer's consciousness since they see the stigmatized outgroup individual with mental health challenges as being worse in social standing than themselves. Mental illness is impacted by various perspectives, including personal knowledge regarding psychiatric illness, recognizing and engaging with someone who suffers from it, cultural assumptions about mental condition, media tales, and acquaintance with organizational practices and prior constraints. In essence, they impact in terms of health insurance constraints and employment and adoption restrictions. Since such views and opinions are adequately articulated, they can lead to helpful and inclusive acts. However, when such mindsets and opinions are conveyed adversely, they can result in evasion, isolation from everyday tasks, abuse, and discrimination (Stangl et al., 2019). Aging also influences changes in attitudes regarding mental illness. Despite the widespread presence of mental issues among young people due to the development of these illnesses after puberty, discrimination is most significant among the youth, which may impede seeking medical help owing to embarrassment. Stigmatic attitudes have been proven to decline with age (Ross, 2019). Such notions include the assumption that mental diseases are weaknesses rather than illnesses. Yet, stigma is worsening with age; particularly older men have the most considerable risk of not receiving treatment because they are particularly hostile to asking for help.

Method

Introduction

This chapter describes the structure, design, and process used to conduct this research. It begins with the research question and briefly describes the study's purpose. It then discusses the research method/tool before moving on to the sampling size and technique requirements. The next aspect is the outline of the data collection method and the data analysis approach. Ethical concerns, as well as validity and dependability difficulties, will be addressed.

Research Question

The study's research topic is "Does age influence attitudes regarding mental health?" Mental health is a serious public health issue in many nations, with a high incidence in Western countries

(Colizzi et al., 2020). According to Ross (2019), most of those with mental difficulties do not recognize the symptoms and repercussions of their condition. Depending on this context, the research will look into age's impact on attitudes about mental health and assess the key issues and beliefs surrounding this topic. This question stems from the previously described literature analysis, which concluded that describing the attitudes and behaviours related to mental health disorders could serve as a platform for improving the understanding of mental health and advocacy.

The Research Method

A qualitative study technique of data collecting was used to portray the subjective experience of the respondents' lives and examine the distinct apprehension of their circumstances based on the themes of inclusion, discrimination, and prospect. Thematic analysis is the primary approach for qualitative analysis, and it entails going over a collection of data and searching for patterns in the information's context to find themes (Guest et al., 2020). It is an interactive reflexive process whereby the researcher's subjectivity is essential to making meaning of the facts. Yet, it frequently goes beyond this, interpreting numerous facets of the study issue to extract meaning from data. The primary goal of this research is to determine the impact of age on various attitudes regarding mental health. Such psychological characteristics are impacted by a person's stigmatized attitudes about mental health disorders.

While it reports on the experiences and interpretations assigned to the individuals, thematic analysis can be realist/essentialist. It is constructionist because certain factors, like incidents and experiences, depending on how society works. Additionally, context is another Thematic Analysis option that considers the fundamental components of reality and the meaning formation of the participants' experiences. What is widespread, however, is not always relevant or significant in and of itself. The structures of interpretation that TA enables the researcher to detect must be relevant to the specific topic and research issue under consideration (Vaismoradi and Snelgrove, 2019). The response to an inquiry is produced by analysis, even if, as in specific qualitative research, the precise question being addressed is only revealed via the analysis. Countless patterns can be detected in each dataset; the analysis aims to find those pertinent to answering a specific research question.

The thematic analysis enables researchers to see and understand communal or collective interpretations and perspectives. It concentrates not on having specific and unique ideas and experiences within a particular data item. This strategy is a manner of recognizing and making sense of what is similar to how a subject is discussed or written about. Thematic analysis, in essence, is the quest for themes that evolve as part of the essential criteria for defining and reporting the occurrence (Kiger and Varpio, 2020). The theme must be present to be elicited. Even though all of these "rules" must be followed and kept sequentially, theme analysis remains a somewhat flexible analytical method offering rich, detailed data.

Research Method Rationale

The thematic analysis differs from other pattern-description methodologies, such as Interpretive Phenomenological Analysis (IPA) and Grounded Theory. These two analytic methodologies seek patterns while staying bound by theories. Phenomenological epistemology is connected with IPA. IPA emphasizes understanding and decoding one's perceptions; it uncovers specific events by investigating the occurrence from a participant's experience and viewpoint (McGaha and D'Urso, 2019). Consequently, excluding one's subjectivity is not needed in this study because I will collect many attitudes that any specific incident could potentially impact. A Grounded Theory Analysis aims to construct a reasonable – and usable – theory of the phenomenon based on the facts. Grounded theory is factual; it aims to prove and analyze evidence based on an established hypothesis, much like science. As a result, unlike thematic analysis, it does not characterize any data "freely" but is constrained by a theory (Cuthbertson et al., 2020). In this research, the hypothesis is that "Age influences attitudes toward mental health."

Apparently, neither IPA nor grounded theory is as versatile as theme analysis since grounded theory, for instance, is not as detailed as thematic analysis. As a result, these two analytical procedures were instantly discarded because they were insufficient for this type of research. Ethnography is another analytical technique that could be used. It refers to the scientific study of people and their cultures, encompassing customs, norms, and practices. The members' way of life is portrayed through their eyes. Hence, ethnography encompasses characterizing a cultural group and examining symbols, rules, and behavior. Yet, data collection typically entails the study's 'immersion' into the target cultural group. The gathering and analyzing of data, in addition to the technique's goal, are entirely different from thematic analysis and certainly not following the study's goal.

A further qualitative analytical tool is narrative inquiry. The process of comprehending and enquiring into experience through "partnership between the researcher and the subject, across time, in a location or series of places, and social contact with milieus" is called narrative inquiry. As a result, narrative inquiry tries to characterize and collect information from the individual's acquired chronological perspectives. The analysis is then performed according to the memories collected concerning the context, which includes the setting and the subject's psychological and physical involvement (Emery and Anderman, 2020). These experiences are fused into a verbal synthesis offering comprehensive data analysis. This strategy is inappropriate for my mini-study and deviates significantly from thematic analysis approaches and procedures. The case study is the final analytical approach that shall contrast with theme analysis. A case study is a detailed, in-depth examination of a person, group, or phenomenon. To ultimately interpret and describe the data gathered, longitudinal research and monitoring of the target are required. I am severely constrained by time, which instantly excludes this analytical method.

Methods of Recruitment:

The attendees. The participants were selected based on the following criteria:
Participants must be over the age of eighteen and not minors.

For recruiting, gender types, regardless of kind, are considered when making decisions.

Significantly, they must be free of mental health difficulties on an individual/personal level, have no family histories of mental health problems, and have had no exposure to psychiatric illnesses/disorders displayed by their contemporaries.

The Research Tool

A structured interview is the best way of collecting data for this project. The survey questionnaire establishes a clear goal and direction for the interviewer to aim for (Roberts, 2020). The interview will be conducted using Qualtrics to promote the participant's active participation in the study. The questionnaire design included six major questions cantered on the study question. Each topic was segmented into further follow-up questions for discussion and in-depth views. All questions require the respondent to reveal as much as they deem necessary. The style of the questions began with general inquiries regarding mental health and progressed to more detailed ones concentrating on various facets of the mental disease. Previous questions helped the interviewee construct replies by introducing specific queries. Because the pilot research provided a chance for indirect input on the interview format, several questions in the preliminary study were rewritten because they were too ambiguous and inconsistent.

Data Collection Procedure

The Qualtrics survey tool was used to collect data. Participants were pushed and requested to comment on perplexing and fascinating elements and topics throughout the interview. Question recording increased the legitimacy of the replies by allowing them to be captured in writing. This approach guarantees that the interviewee receives maximum attention while avoiding letting the participants feel at ease (Pierce et al., 2022). Transcription occurred on the same day as the interview to maximize memory of the application process, and any critical verbal or nonverbal engagement was underlined.

Results

This chapter summarizes the findings of a study conducted on attitudes about mental health. In general, the verdicts suggest that the use of age affects people's attitudes toward this condition. The most apparent trend from these data is societal views and beliefs concerning mental health concerning age. Several ideas and hasty judgments regarding mental health include the various mental health categories. Numerous misconceptions and myths about this condition will be outlined throughout the chapter. The most remarkable attitude and psychological impact were "does age influence people's attitude towards mental health?" and "how does one recognize relate to mental health illness?" Both will be addressed under the inclusion, discrimination, prospect, and attitude sub-themes. The chapter focuses on socio-demographic analysis, descriptive statistics, and regression analysis.

Characteristics of the Sample

Gender

One of the queries in the survey questionnaire was about gender. The findings of this inquiry is summarised in Figure 4.1 below. Apparently, 1 represents the male gender, two is for females, three is for others, and 4 depicts those who prefer not to say instead. Actually, most of the participants in the study were of the female gender (43%), with the male respondents being 40% of the total. Interestingly, 13% of the participants preferred not to say, while the rest indicated being in the other category. Regarding gender, figure 4.1 shows an almost equal distribution between male and female respondents to this survey.

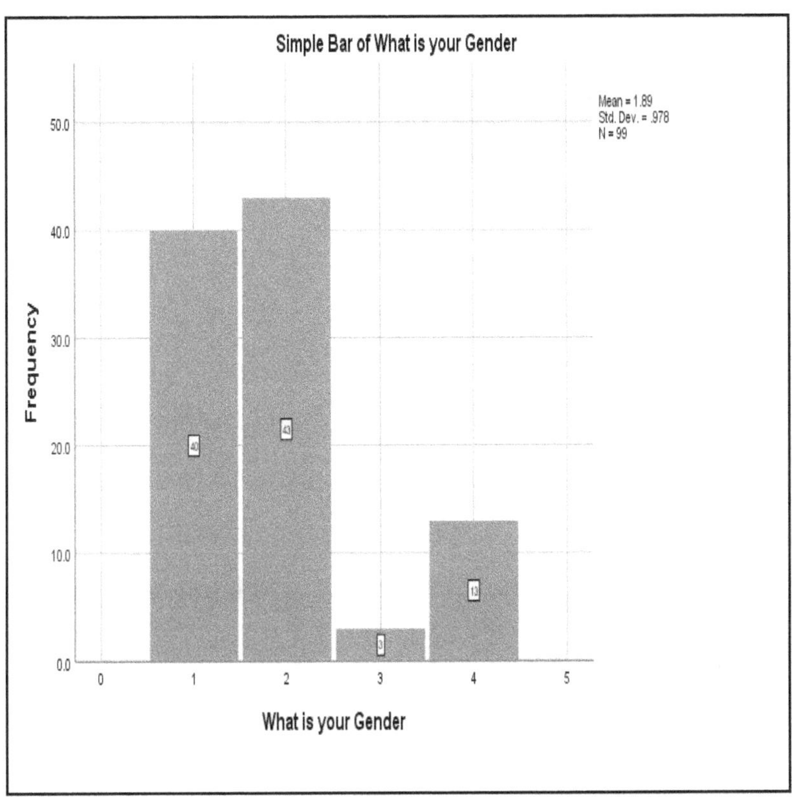

Figure 4. 1: The gender of the respondents

Age

The other question captured in the survey is the respondents' age. Figure 4.2 demonstrates the distribution of the respondents' age using the various categories in the questionnaire. Approximately 42% of the respondents are aged between 21 and 30. The next category in the rank is between 31 and 40 years which amounts to 24%. The age bracket below 20 years covers about 14% of the respondents, while that of between 41 and 50 years is about 7%. Notably, 4% of the respondents captured were above 60 years. The importance of understanding demographic characteristics such as age helps to address the research question effectively. The findings of this study are vital in determining if age influences attitudes toward mental health. Apparently, the respondents are skewed towards the left, with more than 80% being below 40 years of age, as shown in table 1 and figure 4.2.

Table 1: The frequency distribution of age

Bins	Frequency	Percentage
Below 20 years	14	15%
21 to 30 years	38	42%
31 to 40 years	24	26%
41 to 50 years	7	8%
51 to 60 years	4	4%
Above 60	4	4%

years		

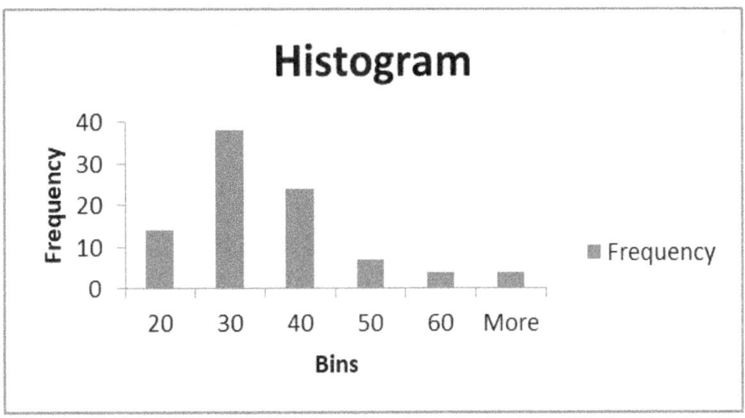

Figure 4. 2: Frequency distribution of age

Descriptive Statistics

Descriptive statistics characterize the fundamental characteristics of data in research. Descriptive statistics may responses from vast groups of people into a few basic statistics. After establishing the sample, descriptive statistics are used to determine the characteristics of the population of interest. Descriptive analysis is the data translation so that fundamental properties such as central tendency, distribution, and dispersion are described. In most cases, we would mention all three attributes for each variable in our study. A distribution's central tendency approximates the "center" of value distribution. The mean, median, and modes are the three primary forms of estimations of central tendency.

The inclusion scale has been evaluated in terms of measurement scale, the measure of central tendency, and evaluation. It is determined that the minimum and maximum of the inclusion scale are 1 and 4, based on the measurement scale as shown in Table 2. For the measure of central tendency, the analysis indicates that the mean, median, mode, and standard deviation of the inclusion scale are 1.8, 1.8, 1.0, and 0.7, respectively. For the evaluation, the descriptive statistics show that the Kurtosis and skewness of the inclusion scale are 0.6 and 0.8. The assumptions for parametric statistical testing have been met and can be used in performing an MR content analysis.

Table 2: Descriptive statistics for the scale of inclusion

ID	Inclusion
Mean	1.8
Standard	0.1

Error	
Median	1.8
Mode	1.0
Standard Deviation	0.7
Sample Variance	0.4
Kurtosis	0.6
Skewness	0.8
Range	3.0
Minimum	1.0
Maximum	4.0
Sum	181.8
Count	99.0

The scale of discrimination has also been evaluated within the context of measurement scale, the measure of central tendency, and evaluation. In terms of the measurement scale, the minimum and maximum scale of discrimination is 1 and 3.8, as shown in Table 3. For the measure of central tendency, the analysis indicates that the mean, median, mode, and standard deviation of the scale of discrimination are 2.2, 2.2, 1.8, and 0.7, respectively. For the evaluation, the descriptive statistics show that the

Kurtosis and skewness of the scale of discrimination are 0.0 and -0.4. Based on these statistics, the assumptions for parametric statistical testing have been met and can be used in performing multiple regression.

Table 3: Descriptive statistics for the scale of discrimination

ID	Discrimination
Mean	2.2
Standard Error	0.1
Median	2.2
Mode	1.8
Standard Deviation	0.7
Sample Variance	0.4
Kurtosis	-0.4
Skewness	0.0
Range	2.8
Minimum	1.0
Maximum	3.8
Sum	219.0
Count	99.0

The prospects scale has also been evaluated in terms of measurement scale, the measure of central tendency, and evaluation. In terms of the measurement scale, the minimum and maximum of the scale of the prospective scale are 1 and 3.6, as shown in Table 4. For the measure of central tendency, the analysis indicates that the mean, median, mode, and standard deviation of the scale of prospective are 2.1, 2.2, 2.0, and 0.6, respectively. For the evaluation, the descriptive statistics show that the Kurtosis and skewness of the scale of prospective are 0.0 and -0.7. In this context, the assumptions for parametric statistical testing have been met and can be used in performing an MR content analysis.

Table 4: Descriptive statistics for the scale of prospects

ID	Prospect
Mean	2.1
Standard Error	0.1
Median	2.2
Mode	2.0
Standard Deviation	0.6
Sample	0.4

Variance	
Kurtosis	-0.7
Skewness	0.0
Range	2.6
Minimum	1.0
Maximum	3.6
Sum	211.0
Count	99.0

The attitude scale has been evaluated in terms of measurement scale, the measure of central tendency, and evaluation. In terms of the measurement scale, the minimum and maximum of the attitude scale are 1 and 3.3, as shown in Table 5. For the measure of central tendency, the analysis indicates that the mean, median, mode, and standard deviation of the scale of attitude are 2.1, 2.1, 2.0, and 0.6, respectively. For the evaluation, the descriptive statistics show that the Kurtosis and skewness of the scale of attitude are -0.6 and -0.1. Consequently, the assumptions for parametric statistical testing have been met and can be used in performing multiple regression.

Table 5: Descriptive statistics for the scale of attitude

ID	Attitude
Mean	2.1
Standard Error	0.1
Median	2.1
Mode	2.0
Standard Deviation	0.6
Sample Variance	0.3
Kurtosis	-0.6
Skewness	-0.1
Range	2.3
Minimum	1.0
Maximum	3.3
Sum	208.7
Count	99.0

Multiple Regression

Multiple regression is a simple linear regression variant that helps in forecasting the value of a particular variable based on the importance of two or more other variables. The variable that is being indicated is referred to as the dependent variable (DV). In contrast, the variables used to predict the values of the dependent variable are referred to as the independent variables (IVs). In the current analysis, DV is people's attitude toward mental health, while the IVs are Age, inclusion, discrimination, and prospect. The influence of age on attitudes regarding mental health was evaluated using a multiple-regression approach. The findings revealed no significant connection between age and attitude toward mental health: $(F(1,99) = .25, p = >0.5, np2 = .007$ So, the null hypothesis cannot be rejected now. Furthermore, there was a considerable main impact between age and participants' perceptions of mental health: $(F(1,99) = 15.10, p = <0.5, np2 = >0.14.$ Multiple regression models are divided into three categories: standard or simultaneous, hierarchical or sequential, and step-wise multiple regression. The standard model test is utilized in this investigation. The value of the independent variable is predicted here using the results of more than one independent variable. In this study, one dependent variable and four independent variables are employed. The primary purpose of this investigation is to assess how much of the variance in the dependent variable can be explained by the independent factors. The model summary is shown in table 6 below.

Table 6: The regression model summary

Regression Statistics	
Multiple R	0.778338
R Square	0.605809
Adjusted R Square	0.589035
Standard Error	0.371126
Observations	99

The model summary table provides the R, R2, adjusted R2, and the standard error of the estimate, which can be used to determine how well a regression model fits the data. The R2 value of 0.995 shows that the independent variables explain 99.5% of the variability of our dependent variable.

Table 7: Anova statistics

ANOVA					
	df	SS	MS	F	Significance F
Regression	4	19.8975578	4.97438945	36.11582776	2.93508E-18

	df	SS	MS		
Residual	94	12.94702731	0.137734333		
Total	98	32.84458511			

Table 8: The coefficients for the dependent variable attitude

	Coefficients	Standard Error	t Stat	P-value	Lower 95%	Upper 95%
Intercept	0.455049	0.165304	2.752792	0.007092	0.126833	0.783264

			- 0.9760 2	0.3 315 59	- 0.00 747	0.00 2546
Age	- 0.00 246	0.002 522				
Inclus ion	0.15 343	0.065 653	2.3 369 81	0.0 215 63	0.02 3074	0.28 3785
Discri minati on	0.10 8788	0.082 269	1.3 223 54	0.1 892 59	- 0.05 456	0.27 2134
Prosp ect	0.56 4297	0.082 728	6.8 211 48	8.6 6E- 10	0.40 0039	0.72 8554

The aassumptions for the MR content analysis model are:

Dependent variable – the variable attitude is a ratio measured on a continuous scale, as shown in figure 4.3 of the normal probability plot.

Independent Variable age – is a numerical variable composed that has a direct influence on the dependent variable attitude, as shown in figure 4.4

Linear Relationship – a linear relationship exists between (a) the dependent variable and each independent variable and (b) the dependent variable and the independent variables collectively, as shown in figure 4.3.

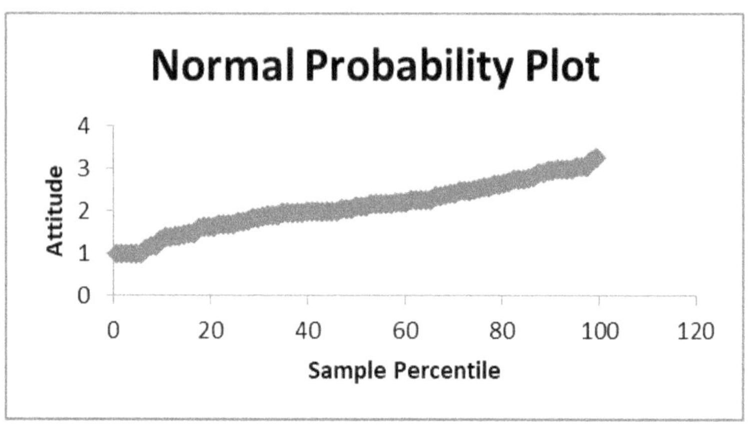

Figure 4. 3: Normal probability plot for MR model

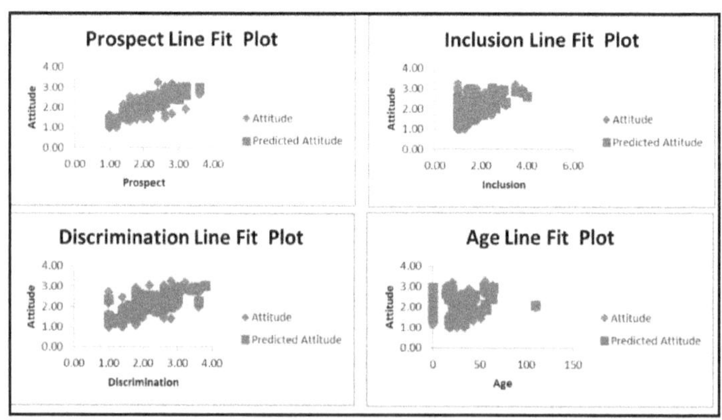

Figure 4. 4: Line of fit plots

Table 9: An excerpt of the residual output

RESIDUAL OUTPUT		
Observation	Predicted Attitude	Residuals
1	1.859854	-0.17564
2	1.5623	0.382144
3	1.26967	-0.11178
4	2.357056	-0.3015
5	1.563914	0.383454
6	2.09463	-0.09463
7	2.575966	0.213507
8	1.755191	-0.07098
9	2.450009	-0.76251
10	2.979869	-0.3132
11	2.068771	-0.64772
12	1.930022	-0.29844
13	1.643155	-0.32737

Table 10: an excerpt of the probability output

PROBABILITY OUTPUT	
Percentile	Attitude
0.505051	1
1.515152	1
2.525253	1
3.535354	1
4.545455	1

5.555556	1
6.565657	1.105263
7.575758	1.157895
8.585859	1.157895
9.59596	1.315789
10.60606	1.368421

Discussion

Because of their significant influence on various behaviours, attitudes have always been an intriguing issue for scholars. More particularly, stigmatising views toward individuals with mental disorders have been closely studied in recent years since they can potentially have serious detrimental consequences for those with mental health issues. Studies reveal that these perceptions evolve, as the literature review emphasizes, although the shift varies for various mental illnesses (Shalaby and Agyapong, 2020). For instance, most people with mental illnesses argue that health practitioners who give both physical and psychological therapies are instrumental in fostering prejudice and stigma across many countries (Kalb et al., 2019). It is essential to consider the premise that the sentiments of older people are becoming increasingly significant, considering the worldwide phenomenon of the more aging population throughout all cultures. As the number of elderly individuals increases, so will the degree of stigmatizing attitudes toward people with mental illnesses. Furthermore, this research discovered that elevated levels of stereotyping are associated with middle-aged people, implying that weak help-seeking behaviours could raise the need for psychosocial therapies in people of all ages.

Discussion of the Results

This study aimed to see if age affects attitudes about mental illnesses and how this outcome compares to earlier suggestions. The findings reveal that views concerning mental illness varied between age groups. These discrepancies, however, do not accord with our hypothesis or past research. Based on prior research, the assumption is that older people have a more favorable attitude about mental illness than younger people because of disparities in perceptual level and knowledge (Follmer et al.,

2020). The results demonstrate the inverse. The youthful participants exhibited a more optimistic and tolerant attitude in the attitude subcategories of Inclusion, Discrimination, and Prospect. This outcome means the young generation has a greater sense of inclusion and prospect toward people with mental illness.

Prior research and ideas show that the external surroundings and context influence a person's perception of mental health, which is very relevant to the findings of this study. Young individuals, it appears, are more exposed to the outside world and thus more prone to adjust their opinions toward those with mental illnesses. Young intellectuals may not have strong religious beliefs or operate following a collective culture, and they certainly show less intolerance toward mental health disorders. With the internet shrinking the world, civilizations are mixing, knowledge is more approachable than at any point in history, and society is no longer as divided as it previously was (Jin, 2022). As a result, the youthful people may have been influenced by different but complementary ideologies, resulting in differing perspectives. The properties of the multiple regression analysis could strengthen the conclusions. Because the world is evolving, developing, and shrinking in some ways, it may have lost part of its ability to discern between other cultures' attitudes regarding mental illness properly. The discovery that the significant disparity among the different age categories was in the discriminatory attitude section may necessitate reconsidering the idea that advanced age would produce unfavorable attitudes about mental disease. According to the findings, people of this age group are more likely to be compassionate towards those around them, which leads to a greater inclination to demonstrate goodwill regarding persons with mental illnesses and a greater eagerness to be nice and assist out. The results of the most and least different questions should be evaluated with caution.

Since many studies on this phenomenon are cross-sectional, it is unclear whether the patterns they provide regarding age and negative views towards individuals with mental illnesses imply a meaningful age effect. Most participants think mental disease management is beneficial, aligning with more recent findings (Cadge et al., 2019). Still, significantly fewer individuals believe others care about and sympathize with those suffering from mental illnesses. Adults experiencing mental disease symptoms report a less welcoming social environment for persons with mental illness. Adults have a more positive view toward the success of mental disease treatment because more resources are devoted to services related to mental health. They were more inclined to seek therapy and believed others cared about and sympathized with those suffering from mental illnesses. Young people are more likely to support individuals with mental disorders and to perceive that others are compassionate and empathetic to those who suffer from mental issues, implying that age positively impacts one's mindset toward mental disease.

The findings concerning positive perceptions toward mental health could be attributed to previous mental health campaigns to educate the public and the broad marketing of medications for prevalent mental diseases. Although a lower proportion of individuals disagreed that therapy is successful, even small minorities at the societal level can constitute numerous individuals who may not seek treatment. The data also demonstrate that specific individuals strongly disagree with assertions about the success of treatment for this illness. People who suffer from mental health issues may be more likely to have a variety of negative individual and social conditions if they do not seek medical treatment because they do not consider therapy helpful (Ibrahim et al., 2019). As a result, the study findings can be used to identify high-risk demographic groups and assist them in improving their knowledge about mental health and decreasing unfavorable attitudes toward the mental disease. Certain groups may benefit from public education regarding the effectiveness of various therapy methods, such as alternatives to psychiatric medicines and the chronic condition of mental disorders that go untreated for some people. Some people may not receive the emotional assistance they need for their ailments. When presented with a colleague or relative's mental illness, some react badly, adding to avoidance and isolation and perhaps compromising with recuperation. Because of the behavioral and psychological elements associated with mental health, family and close companions who are supportive are even more vital to a person's healing (Ibrahim et al., 2019). A friend, family member, or coworker can assist a person struggling with mental illness in their recovery and rehabilitation journey by providing reassurance, compassion, moral fortitude, and understanding.

Reliability of the Findings

The outcome of a study like this may end up systematically biased toward the participants' judgments of what is acceptable and socially desirable response possibilities. This tendency is known as social desirability, and it happens in most self-reports, dramatically increasing the likelihood of misleading results (Imano et al., 2022). This occurrence could have influenced the results. Responses, for example, could have been affected by how the participant understood the question. The line plots demonstrate a few outliers in the findings, indicating that these individuals answered in extreme ways to all or most of the questions. Thankfully, these data points, are quite a few, did not affect the overall results, and were thus not eliminated from the analysis.

The efficacy of the assertions regarding attitude adds to the dependability of the content validity by utilizing a tool that includes the scale of inclusion, discrimination, prospect, and age. To achieve high levels of reality, the arguments and information available to the respondents should be the same for everybody (Bhagavathi and Viton, 2022). The validity is good because the questionnaire was distributed via Qualtrics to individuals. Still, the accuracy would have been even better if the survey had been conducted directly with the participants. On the other hand, because a well-developed questionnaire focusing on attitudes regarding mental illness was utilized, the study successfully gauged people's perspectives. The research concept was validated by using a questionnaire created by competent researchers and testing the questionnaire in various previous investigations. That degree of reliability could have been impossible without a custom-designed survey. In essence, the study's concept validity is strong, and its outcomes could be used to inform future policy initiatives.

Conclusion

This study aimed to look into people's perceptions toward mental health to determine the influence of age on such attitudes. A qualitative approach was the best research method since it used thematic analysis to elicit topics based on the respondents' replies. This approach provided a concise overview of the impact of age on attitudes regarding mental health. It highlighted that stigmatization is present across all ages, and young acceptance of individuals with mental disorders is substantially higher. Nonetheless, there are still negative ideas about comprehending and handling them. As a result, in addition to highlighting the persisting mental health stigma, this research should offer an impetus to act decisively in eradicating this stigma. The findings demonstrate that views toward mental illness varied by age group in the attitude categories of inclusion, discrimination, and prospect. Participants in these groups show a better sense of kindness, social tolerance, and community cohesion toward those with mental illnesses.

The sample size was the survey's significant disadvantage concerning other investigations on attitudes toward mental health. Because large samples utilized in earlier studies were not practical at this stage, the population was confined to about n=100 by adopting a qualitative approach to research. In essence, the results could not be generalized because the sample was not typical of the intended population. Even though the queries were open-ended and non-directive, sampling bias and cognitive biases were not entirely unavoidable. These biases emerged due to judgment throughout the examination of participants' statements throughout data analysis, emphasizing relevant and current research and the exclusion of discrepant and illogical responses. As a result, both validity and reflexivity were compromised. The study concluded that participants were conscious of an absence of psychological awareness and various solutions to minimize stigma and negative feelings, which would considerably improve the well-being of people with mental health concerns.

Future research should confirm the survey's validity by considering multiple sampling populations with varied attitudes evaluated using alternative techniques. It would be equally interesting to look into views regarding mental disease in various age groups. Perhaps there is a gender or age factor, which could imply that people's views toward mental illness are influenced by their circumstances and background. Qualitative research may be beneficial in assessing attitudes toward mental health, particularly among persons with mental health problems. Additionally, questions about attitudes should center on the causes of the cognitive processes. A quantitative method should be employed to research demographic attitudes by utilizing conventional scales of inclusion, discrimination, prejudice, and attitude. The ideal research would include qualitative and quantitative methodologies to achieve accurate and comprehensive data while considering statistics and knowledge.

References

Bardram, J.E. and Matic, A., 2020. A decade of ubiquitous computing research in mental health. *IEEE Pervasive Computing, 19*(1), pp.62-72.

Bhagavathi, P. and Vitone, T., 2022. Analysis of Adolescent Barriers in Seeking Help for Mental Health Issues. *Journal of Student Research, 11*(3).

Cadge, C., Connor, C. and Greenfield, S., 2019. University students' understanding and perceptions of schizophrenia in the UK: a qualitative study. *BMJ open, 9*(4), p.e025813.

Colizzi, M., Ruggeri, M. and Lasalvia, A., 2020. Should we be concerned about stigma and discrimination in people at risk for psychosis? A systematic review. *Psychological Medicine, 50*(5), pp.705-726.

Cuthbertson, L.M., Robb, Y.A. and Blair, S., 2020. Theory and application of research principles and philosophical underpinning for a study utilising interpretative phenomenological analysis. *Radiography, 26*(2), pp.e94-e102.

Emery, A. and Anderman, L.H., 2020. Using interpretive phenomenological analysis to advance theory and research in educational psychology. *Educational Psychologist*, *55*(4), pp.220-231.

Farreras, I.G., 2019. History of mental illness. *General psychology: required reading.*

Follmer, K.B., Sabat, I.E. and Siuta, R.L., 2020. Disclosure of stigmatized identities at work: An interdisciplinary review and agenda for future research. *Journal of Organizational Behavior*, *41*(2), pp.169-184.

Guest, G., Namey, E. and Chen, M., 2020. A simple method to assess and report thematic saturation in qualitative research. *PloS one*, *15*(5), p.e0232076.

Haigh, C.B., Kringen, A.L. and Kringen, J.A., 2020. Mental illness stigma: Limitations of crisis intervention team training. *Criminal justice policy review*, *31*(1), pp.42-57.

Hendrickx, M., Woodward, A., Fuhr, D.C., Sondorp, E. and Roberts, B., 2020. The burden of mental disorders and access to mental health and psychosocial support services in Syria and among Syrian refugees in neighboring countries: a systematic review. *Journal of Public Health, 42*(3), pp.e299-e310.

Ibrahim, N., Amit, N., Shahar, S., Wee, L.H., Ismail, R., Khairuddin, R., Siau, C.S. and Safien, A.M., 2019. Do depression literacy, mental illness beliefs and stigma influence mental health help-seeking attitude? A cross-sectional study of secondary school and university students from B40 households in Malaysia. *BMC public health, 19*, pp.1-8.

Imano, T., Yokoyama, K., Itoh, H., Shoji, E. and Asano, K., 2022. Development of the Japanese version of the Depression Literacy Scale. *International Journal of Social Psychiatry, 68*(8), pp.1708-1715.

Jin, Z., 2022. *The Future of Humanity: From Global Civilization to Great Civilization*. Intellect Books.

Kalb, L. G., Stapp, E. K., Ballard, E. D., Hogue, C., Keefer, A., & Riley, A., 2019. Trends in psychiatric emergency department visit among

youth and young adults in the U.S.
Pediatrics, 143(4).

Kiger, M.E. and Varpio, L., 2020. Thematic analysis of qualitative data: AMEE Guide No. 131. *Medical teacher, 42*(8), pp.846-854.

Lomas, T. and VanderWeele, T.J., 2022. The Garden and the Orchestra: Generative Metaphors for Conceptualizing the Complexities of Well-Being. *International Journal of Environmental Research and Public Health, 19*(21), p.14544.

McGaha, K.K. and D'Urso, P.A., 2019. A non-traditional validation tool: using cultural domain analysis for interpretive phenomenology. *International Journal of Social Research Methodology, 22*(6), pp.585-598.

Pérez-Flores, N.J. and Cabassa, L.J., 2021. Effectiveness of mental health literacy and stigma interventions for Latino/a adults in the United States: A systematic review. *Stigma and health, 6*(4), p.430.

Pierce, C.D., Epstein, M.H. and Wood, M.D., 2022. Content Validation of the Behavioral and

Emotional Rating Scale–3rd Edition: Strength-Based Interview. *Journal of Emotional and Behavioral Disorders*, p.10634266221099246.

Roberts, R.E., 2020. Qualitative Interview Questions: Guidance for Novice Researchers. *Qualitative Report*, 25(9).

Ross, A.M., Morgan, A.J., Jorm, A.F. and Reavley, N.J., 2019. A systematic review of the impact of media reports of severe mental illness on stigma and discrimination, and interventions that aim to mitigate any adverse impact. *Social Psychiatry and Psychiatric Epidemiology*, 54, pp.11-31.

Shalaby, R.A.H. and Agyapong, V.I., 2020. Peer support in mental health: literature review. *JMIR mental health*, 7(6), p.e15572.

Stangl, A.L., Earnshaw, V.A., Logie, C.H., Van Brakel, W., C. Simbayi, L., Barré, I. and Dovidio, J.F., 2019. The Health Stigma and Discrimination Framework: a global, crosscutting framework to inform research, intervention development, and policy on health-related stigmas. *BMC medicine*, 17, pp.1-13.

Vaismoradi, M. and Snelgrove, S., 2019. Theme in qualitative content analysis and thematic analysis. In *Forum Qualitative Sozialforschung/Forum: Qualitative Social Research* (Vol. 20, No. 3). DEU.

Appendix

Gender	Age	Inclusion	Discrimin.	Prospect	Attitude
1	33	1.36	2.40	1.80	1.68
1	30	1.27	1.80	1.40	1.94
2	25	1.18	1.20	1.00	1.16
1	35	1.64	3.00	2.50	2.06
2	23	1.45	1.40	1.40	1.95
1	30	1.09	2.80	2.20	2.00
2	40	2.18	2.80	2.80	2.79
2	49	1.36	1.80	1.80	1.68
2	37	1.45	2.60	2.80	1.69
2	55	1.55	3.60	3.60	2.67
2	26	1.00	2.60	2.20	1.42
1	27	1.27	2.00	2.00	1.63
2	43	1.27	1.80	1.60	1.32
1	0	1.64	2.80	2.60	2.06
1	29	1.82	2.80	1.80	1.42
2	40	1.82	1.80	1.60	1.83
1	34	1.55	2.20	2.20	2.00
2	37	2.09	1.80	2.00	1.84
2	57	1.55	2.00	2.00	1.88
2	42	1.00	2.00	2.00	1.74
2	28	1.82	2.20	2.40	2.05
4	0	1.45	1.40	1.40	1.47
2	39	1.82	1.80	2.00	1.58
1	19	2.50	3.80	3.20	3.06
2	21	3.50	3.20	2.80	3.21
1	19	2.27	2.80	3.00	2.68
4	34	1.82	2.60	2.60	2.11
2	30	1.64	1.60	2.20	1.89
1	35	1.36	1.80	1.80	1.95
2	38	1.64	1.40	1.40	1.63
2	27	1.55	1.80	2.00	2.00
2	52	1.09	2.00	2.00	1.44
2	32	1.36	1.60	1.50	1.37
1	0	1.64	2.00	2.20	1.74
2	26	2.18	3.60	2.00	2.00
2	0	1.90	2.75	1.80	2.26
2	24	2.36	2.80	1.80	2.26
2	25	2.40	2.60	1.60	2.37
1	24	2.18	2.20	1.60	2.21
1	20	2.45	2.00	2.60	1.68
2	42	1.00	2.60	2.60	1.47
1	30	2.36	2.40	2.40	2.26
1	26	2.27	2.40	1.60	2.58
2	30	2.09	2.60	2.20	2.16
3	24	1.45	1.40	1.80	2.47
2	21	2.55	2.40	2.00	1.89
1	22	3.09	2.80	2.00	2.16
1	33	2.64	2.40	1.80	2.21
1	0	1.91	1.80	2.00	2.47

Gender	Age	Inclusion	Discrimin.	Prospect	Attitude
1	110	2.09	2.20	2.40	2.00
1	40	1.82	1.80	3.20	1.95
2	38	1.27	2.20	2.20	2.17
1	28	1.36	1.80	1.00	1.11
2	23	2.45	2.40	2.00	1.89
2	23	2.09	2.00	2.20	1.79
2	22	2.27	2.20	1.60	2.11
2	33	2.36	2.60	2.40	2.26
2	34	2.36	2.60	2.00	2.00
1	32	2.55	2.40	2.20	2.11
1	28	2.18	2.20	2.80	2.42
1	32	1.91	2.00	2.40	2.42
1	30	2.36	2.20	1.80	1.95
1	24	2.09	2.40	1.40	2.16
1	65	1.45	3.60	3.60	2.81
4	0	3.00	3.00	3.00	2.74
2	0	2.09	1.40	1.40	2.00
1	26	1.00	1.00	1.00	1.00
2	19	1.45	1.00	1.40	2.16
4	34	1.09	1.40	1.00	1.00
4	17	1.00	1.00	1.20	1.00
4	26	1.55	1.20	1.20	1.37
1	26	1.09	1.00	1.00	1.00
4	0	1.18	1.40	1.20	1.16
1	18	1.00	1.00	1.00	1.63
3	19	2.73	1.80	3.00	2.95
1	14	1.82	2.60	3.00	3.00
4	35	2.55	1.00	2.60	2.74
2	45	2.00	2.00	3.00	2.63
2	61	1.00	2.60	3.00	2.95
1	26	1.00	1.00	1.00	1.00
4	21	3.82	3.40	2.60	3.00
2	17	1.36	2.80	2.60	2.89
1	17	1.00	2.60	3.00	3.00
1	22	1.00	1.80	2.40	2.74
4	39	1.00	2.60	3.00	2.89
4	56	1.00	2.80	2.40	3.26
2	19	1.27	1.00	1.20	1.00
1	15	2.82	3.00	2.80	2.50
4	18	2.91	3.00	3.00	3.00
3	21	1.00	2.20	2.60	3.05
4	64	1.00	2.60	3.00	3.05
1	16	4.00	3.00	2.20	2.63
1	24	2.27	2.80	2.00	2.58
1	28	2.45	2.00	2.40	2.26
2	30	2.09	2.80	2.60	2.39
2	41	1.82	1.80	1.60	2.21
1	44	2.73	2.00	2.60	2.37
2	33	2.27	3.00	2.80	2.47
2	31	2.00	2.80	2.40	2.53

Chapter 20

1

Qualitative Research (Scenario(same-sex
adoptions in England. Appendix 1)

Question 1

Describe some key aspects of a
phenomenological researcher's methodology. 2)
State-researched question.

Question 2

**Briefly discuss a critical discursive research
methodology. 2)** State the research question 3)
Strengths and limitations to applying discursive
psychology analysis.

Reference

Appendix

Qualitative Research

Question1

      Same-sex adoption is a relatively new social issue that has recently attracting experts' attention in the pertinent psychology and education departments (New Family Social, 2021). There is still a sizable research gap when examining the experiences of adopted youngsters and their similar-sex parents, even though the necessities of adopted children who have gone through significant trauma are beginning to become defined in the literature and throughout the psychological profession. The best methodology for filling this gap is by applying phenomenological investigation. Phenomenology offers a different perspective on the things people often look at. The philosophical movement known as phenomenology directly opposed beliefs about the universe's purpose and the significance of human experiences grounded in scientific evidence (Williams et al., 2020). Phenomenology strongly emphasises distinguishing truth as people perceive it and explaining events through emergent core themes rather than exploring objectively agreed-upon conceptions. These concepts—lived experiences and critical themes—are philosophical conceptions based on qualitative research techniques. A phenomenological investigation does not involve a hypothesis that absolves the philosopher or researcher of bias. Any dogmatisms, research traditions, and methodologies that are imposed are rejected by phenomenology.

The best research question to apply in this phenomenological inquiry is: What are the experiences of children adopted by same-sex parents? The data source for this study will include all the children adopted by parents of the same sex. This will help get their perspectives, proving that same-sex adoption suits these children. The best method of capturing these data is by applying semi-structured interviews—the best way to get information on participants' experiences. According to Walker (2020), phenomenological investigators must select a suitable data collection method that permits the collection of rich and detailed descriptions of subjects' accounts of a phenomenon. This is typically done in phenomenological designs using in-depth interviews or journals.

Additionally, the interview's semi-structured format permits greater freedom in examining each person's experience while minimising the restrictions imposed by the analysts' questions and allowing follow-up questions to be influenced by the participants' descriptions. Furthermore, semi-structured interviews involve the use of open-ended questions. This aspect enables the researchers and the research participants to discuss the topic under investigation in detail.

The best method of analysis of phenomenological research is applying Collazo's method. This method of data analysis consists of seven steps. The first step is reading and rereading the subjects' descriptions of the experience to understand what they were going through and try to make sense of it all. The second step is snatching meaningful quotes relevant to the studied topic (Sundler et al., 2019). The third step is constructing interpretations for these profound assertions to reveal underlying implications. The fourth step is grouping the meanings into thematic clusters and ensuring that the participants' tales and the newly discovered information are consistent while resisting the urge to discard the data that do not fit. The fifth step is integrating the research results into a comprehensive description of the phenomenon being studied; this includes coding segments for topics, contrasting topics for recurring themes, and connecting themes for their conceptual meanings, which results in creating a theoretical model prototype about the phenomenon being studied. The sixth step is reporting the primary form of the research findings, and the seventh by validating the study findings.

Question 2

Discursive psychology is a qualitative method that examines what individuals achieve through social interaction (Riley et al., 2019). One of the various discourse analysis methodologies, discursive psychology, is a well-established methodology that is rising in popularity in family studies. Several different methodologies used in discourse analysis concentrate on language and social interaction. These methods all begin with the notion that language is performative, meaning that individuals use words to accomplish tasks (Sundler et al., 2019). Participating in practice-based research, in particular, enables practitioners to take a more active role in research intended to impact work. It allows the generation of research questions, participation in the research process, and dissemination of research results into practice. This study method is thus critical in research about same-sex adoption of children as it helps investigators view the situation in a broader sense.

It can take time to formulate a research question in discursive psychology. Many discourse investigations were reported to have poorly stated questions in a recent assessment of discourse studies (Walker, 2020). Its dedication to Prioritising a data-driven, non-researcher-directed inquiry employing inductive investigation is the focus of discourse psychology while formulating research questions. It should be noted that discursive psychology needs a clear area of study, and as a result, the research questions change as the analysis progresses. As a result, every query that directs data gathering must be open and inclusive rather than limiting that investigation. Discursive psychologists seek to comprehend what transpires in particular encounters in this manner. It permits the data to show unique and insightful concerns not planned from the start by keeping the investigation broad and open (Walker, 2020). Therefore, the best research question in this form of discursive psychology is: what are the attitudes towards same-sex adoptions?

There are various strengths and limitations to applying discursive psychology analysis. One of them is that it offers a lens through which people can look at the social world, making visible the social processes that hold people and their behaviour factually accountable. Riley et al. (2019) also adds that the ability to respecify the theoretical foundations of psychology is another strength of the discursive psychology method, in addition to its analytical rigour and technical detail. No matter their field of study or point of view, interaction with other scholars is a crucial component of psychological research progress moving forward. On the other hand, the discursive psychology method has some drawbacks, such as its constricting emphasis exclusively on human interaction and its attempt to downplay how prior encounters and experiences impact people's identities (Williams et al., 2020). This area of psychology maintains that language shapes ideas like memory, personality, and attitudes. This is constricting because it needs to pay attention to the multiple factors that could independently affect identity apart from social interactions and linguistic usage.

Furthermore, discursive psychology overlooks other relevant elements that may play a role in forming individual identities by focusing on communication and interaction with others. These include ideas like nature and nurture and brain function (Nigar, 2020). However, despite some criticism, discursive analysis is commonly considered an instrument for contesting the ethical and political ramifications of positivist psychology's study, theory, and application.

References

New Family Social (2021) *LGBT+ people still account for 1 in 6 adoptions in England in 2021, despite declining numbers [19 November 2021].* Available at: https://newfamilysocial.org.uk/General-News/12137140 (Accessed: 8 February 2022).

Nigar, N., 2020. Hermeneutic phenomenological narrative enquiry: A qualitative study design. *Theory and Practice in Language Studies, 10*(1), pp.10–18. http://dx.doi.org/10.17507/tpls.1001.02

Riley, S., Brooks, J., Goodman, S., Cahill, S., Branney, P., Treharne, G. J., & Sullivan, C. (2019). Celebrations amongst challenges: Considering the past, present and future of the qualitative methods in the psychology section of the British Psychology Society. *Qualitative Research in Psychology.* https://doi.org/10.1080/14780887.2019.1605275

Sandhu, H. S., Arora, A., Brasch, J., & Streiner, D. L. (2019). Mental health stigma: Explicit and implicit attitudes of Canadian undergraduate students, medical school students, and psychiatrists. *The Canadian Journal of*

Psychiatry, *64*(3), 209-217.

https://doi.org/10.1177/0706743718792193

Sundler, A. J., Lindberg, E., Nilsson, C., & Palmér, L. (2019). Qualitative thematic analysis based on descriptive phenomenology. *Nursing Open*, *6*(3), 733-739.

https://doi.org/10.1002/nop2.275

Walker, K. A. (2020). *The construction and impact of power in cross-sector partnerships: An interpretive phenomenological study* (Doctoral dissertation, Antioch University).

https://www.proquest.com/openview/9acd2f0b1a
ed9474aa242cdf970e6c4c/1?pq-
origsite=gscholar&cbl=18750&diss=y

Williams, V., Boylan, A.M. and Nunan, D., 2020. Critical appraisal of qualitative research: necessity, partialities and the issue of bias. *BMJ Evidence-Based Medicine*, *25*(1), pp.9-11.

http://dx.doi.org/10.1136/bmjebm-2018-111132

Chapter. 21

'Neuropsychology offers the only suitable way to study human memory.' Critically evaluate this statement, drawing on evidence from biological and cognitive psychology.

CONTENT

Neuropsychology and Human Memory

Introduction

The field of neuropsychology examines how the mind and brain interact. It lies at the intersection of cognitive, clinical psychology, and neurobiology. Several ideas have helped psychologists understand how memory functions by defining such processes' mechanisms and anatomical underpinnings. Studies in neuroscience have revealed dynamical brain changes as operational underpinnings of memory traces, whereas cognitive psychology tackles cognitive processes by dissecting them into modular compartments (Mallard et al., 2020). The debate over whether memory is organised into distinct systems that correlate to specific brain structures or if various processes convey it in a comprehensive and dynamic arrangement of brain function is regularly brought up. Clinical neuropsychology typically views memory activities as the culmination of integrated actions of various subsystems. The discovery of the twofold dissociation of cognitive diseases has promoted this notion of memory as different systems distinct in terms of their structural and functional characteristics (Petker et al., 2019). Due to the particular pattern of neuropsychology in the study of memory, the field has therefore been depicted as the best means of learning about memory. Therefore, this paper aims to evaluate if neuropsychology is the best way to study memory by drawing in cognitive and biological psychology concepts.

Biological Psychology

Neuropsychology is a therapeutic field that combines an interest in psychological diseases with knowledge of how neuronal cells in the brain, spinal cord, and body function biologically. The neuropsychologist connects behaviours to underlying typical and pathological biological processes of the brain using unbiased, scientific methodologies (Valler, 2020). Professional neuropsychologists examine unusual behaviour patterns to determine the biological anomalies causing or leading to abnormal behaviour. Neuropsychology, as it has been traditionally characterised, is the study of and the measurement, comprehension, and adjustment of brain-behaviour interactions. Neuropsychology aims to comprehend how the morphology and neural networks of the brain influence and create behaviour and mental functions such as emotions, personality, reasoning, learning and memory, problem-solving, and awareness. Disentangling fundamental differences can help move closer to comprehending memory's biology. Biological psychology helps prove the role of neuropsychology in studying memory by looking at the sophisticated intersection between brain structures. The hippocampus, which functions as a data preprocessor and elaborator, represents one of the most significant brain areas in explicit memory (Woods et al., 2019). The hippocampus aids in encoding information regarding spatial connections, the framework of events, and linkages between memories. The hippocampus also functions as a relay that temporarily stores the memory before sending it to other brain regions, like the cortex, for actual rehearsal, refinement, and long-term retention.

Other brain regions, including the cerebellum and amygdala, focus on tacit and dynamic memories, whereas the hippocampus manages explicit memory. According to research, the cerebellum is far more active during learning connections and priming tasks. Animals and people with cerebellar damage perform more poorly in trials of classical conditioning (Vallar, 2020). Clinical studies of individuals with amnesia, a memory illness characterised by forgetfulness, provide evidence for the significance of various brain areas in different types of memories. Amnesia can impair retrieving or encoding in forward or reverse directions, similar to effects on memory that interfere with memory (Petker et al., 2019). The amnesia may go backwards in people who have experienced brain trauma, such as a stroke or another type of trauma. Retrograde amnesia is a memory disease that results in the incapacity to recall past events before a specific time. Retrograde amnesia is typically quite profound for recent memories compared to older memories, showing that memory consolidation takes a while, and events that occurred recently may not be retrieved since they were not fully encoded.

When the hippocampus is damaged, an amnesia that moves forward prevents the encoding of new memories. Anterograde amnesia is the term for this condition. Anterograde amnesia is the failure to shift information from short-term to long-term memory, preventing new memory generation. A good example involved Molaison, who underwent hippocampal surgery to lessen severe convulsions before passing away in 2008 (Bilder and Reise, 2019).

Molaison experienced almost total anterograde amnesia after the procedure. He could recall most of everything that had transpired before the surgery, especially the early events in his life. However, he was no longer able to make new memories. It was claimed that Molaison read the same publications repeatedly without realising she had already seen them. Anterograde amnesia examples reveal the brain regions associated with various kinds of memory (Bilder and Reise, 2019). However, Molaison's implicit memory was unaffected because his cerebellum was unharmed, even though his hippocampus was injured. He learned how to outline shapes in a mirror, which calls for procedural memory, but he never explicitly remembered doing it or the individuals who gave him the task.

Even if some brain regions are more crucial than others in forming memories, this does not imply that all memories are kept in the exact location. Karl Lashley, a psychologist, proved this aspect, using rats trained to navigate mazes to examine where memories were held in the brain by lesioning various brain regions to see if the rats could still navigate the labyrinth (Mankin and Fried, 2020). Since this concept sounded simple, Lashley anticipated discovering that memory was kept in specific brain regions. Instead, Lashley concluded that memory is dispersed all through the brain instead of concentrated in one area after finding that the rats maintained at least some recall of the maze regardless of where he excised brain tissue. This evidence is an example of neuropsychological studies of memory, proving that neuropsychology is the best way to study memory.

Cognitive Psychology

The study of cognitive psychology focuses on the mind's inner workings, including perception, thought, memories, attentiveness, language, problem-solving, and learning. Despite being a relatively new area of psychology, it has swiftly gained popularity and is now one of the most well-known (Maillard et al., 2020). This cognitive study has several real-world implications, including helping people with memory problems, improving decision-making precision, discovering strategies to recover brain damage, treating learning disorders, and designing educational curricula to improve learning. In addition, psychologists can create new strategies for assisting individuals with psychological problems by learning more about how people think and process information. This aspect aids researchers in better understanding how the human brain functions.

Various cognitive psychological phenomena have helped in understanding human memory. One of the well-known examples is those studies involving children. Experiments of these children have helped in studying various aspects of human memory. Prominent research that looks at newborns' activity with mobiles at three months old looks at early indicators of recall memory (Mankin and Fried, 2020). In this experiment, a thread from a vibrant mobile was tied to the baby's foot part of the experiment so that when the baby kicked, the mobile would move, gratifying them. It was demonstrated that the newborns kicked to create movement a few days after the initial instruction. After a brief recall lesson during which they watched the mobile move, the baby commenced kicking two weeks later, even unattached to their foot. In this test, the mobile was recognised, and cued recall and recall after a week were also demonstrated. Two key memory components are recognition and recall; these are especially helpful in youngsters because the oral memory report might need to be present or trustworthy when evaluating very young children. When they are around nine months old, some children can imitate certain simple acts they see for up to 24 hours after seeing them (Lee et al., 2020). A contextual memory test used to determine the child's memory capacity involves reproducing activities like picking one thing over the other or continually placing an object in the exact location. Between 18 and 24 months, deferred imitation— the capacity to imitate behaviour without cues—

can be seen and tested—can be put to the test. Children's ability to recreate more complicated events improves as they get older.

Childhood development psychologist Jean Piaget did research evaluating toddlers' cognitive and memory skills. These experiments were performed utilising objects first shown to the youngster before being hidden from view. Infants, still highly young, may think the thing does not exist. However, around 8 to 12 months old, children will start searching for the lost object (Wojcik et al., 2019). This behaviour demonstrates memory and the understanding that the thing still exists even though it is invisible. Due to this, the hypothesis of object permanence was developed, showing that memory and cognitive function have advanced to the point of mental representation.

Facial recognition is another aspect of cognitive psychology that helps study human memory. A youngster might begin to imitate facial expressions as early as seven days old by protruding their tongues or lips or opening their mouth (Wang, 2021). Although the ability to replicate shows the newborns' capacity to encode and imitate the image, there is considerable controversy as to whether this is a choice or reflexive behaviour. In Face memory through longer delays can be observed in infants as young as 2-3 weeks favourable changes, like less crying and smiling, indicate that they see a familiar face. Habituation, the act of attending to a standard stimulus less in preference to a novel one, is another way to demonstrate recognition. This aspect can be observed in various ways, such as auditory and visual recognition, as early as five months old. In a study with infants aged 8 to 10 months, well-known and recently introduced items and people were displayed at periodic intervals and with varying time intervals (Pounder et al., 2021). In addition, initial looks and looking time were measured, and the results showed that habituation and memory recall was present. Perception is another aspect of cognitive psychology that helps in understanding human memory. This aspect is much more sophisticated than people might first think, much like all other aspects of cognition. According to studies, perception functions both top-down and bottom-up (Chandler et al., 2019). Neurons that participate in bottom-up processing light up in response to particular components of an image, such as the shape of a face or jawline. Top-down cognition considers how one's prior knowledge influences their current view. When two persons are exposed to identical stimuli, but their anticipation and previous knowledge differ, bottom-down cognition can aid in understanding. When little data is given, integrating bottom-up and top-down processing allows one to understand static and moving visuals. For example, one can monitor a person going through a crowd (Wojcik et al., 2019). The mirror neuron system is highly intriguing and valuable in scientific research into biological motion. Similar brain regions are engaged when an action is observed as when it is performed. The approach describes how people may replicate another person's activities, which is essential to learning. It is crucial to remember that cognitive psychology has several drawbacks that render it inappropriate or unpleasant for some people, particularly those with intellectual disabilities and more severe mental health conditions. Although the client and his capacity for change are the main emphases of this approach, some people could view it as being too focused, leading them to overlook significant factors, including personal history, family, and more general emotional disorders. Keep in mind that there is no room within this field of psychology for in-depth personal analysis and emotional exploration or for troublesome topics from multiple angles, all of which would necessitate a client to seek a different strategy, like counselling (Chandler et al., 2019). The tendency of cognitive psychology to overlook other crucial behavioural influences is one of its other flaws. Overall, cognitive psychology has several significant advantages for real-world applications but drawbacks. Further debate on the scientific nature of the method is necessary to decide whether it will benefit society.

Conclusion

Clinical research on patients with cognitive impairments will strongly impact how cognition is conceptualised and reflected in brain functioning. This phenomenon is especially true in clinical neuropsychology, where the theoretical underpinnings fundamentally justify the procedures and tools used. The present study described how a particular notion of clinical investigations has resulted from the significant effects of structural and anatomic-clinical concepts of memory. The above discussion shows that various aspect of biological and cognitive psychology helps in understanding human memory. For example, cognitive psychology, such as facial recognition, provides evidence of recalling memories. In addition, biological psychology evidence on how amnesia occurs also helps in understanding more about memory. This evidence proves that neuropsychology is the best way to study human memory.

References

Bilder, R.M. and Reise, S.P., 2019. Neuropsychological tests of the future: How do we get there from here? *The Clinical Neuropsychologist*, 33(2), pp.220-245. [Online]. Available at: https://doi.org/10.1080/13854046.2018.1521993[Accessed 09 Jan. 2023].

Chandler, C., Foltz, P., Cheng, J., Bernstein, J.C., Rosenfeld, E.P., Cohen, A.S., Holmlund, T.B. and Elvevåg, B., 2019, June. Overcoming the bottleneck in traditional assessments of verbal memory: Modeling human ratings and classifying clinical group membership. In *Proceedings of the Sixth Workshop on Computational Linguistics and Clinical Psychology* (pp. 137-147). [Online]. Available at: https://aclanthology.org/W19-3016/[Accessed 09 Jan. 2023].

Lee, H., Bellana, B. and Chen, J., 2020. What can narratives tell us about the neural bases of human memory? *Current Opinion in Behavioral Sciences*, *32*, pp.111-119. [Online]. Available at: https://doi.org/10.1016/j.cobeha.2020.02.007[Accessed 09 Jan. 2023].

Maillard, A., Cabé, N., Viader, F. and Pitel, A.L., 2020. Neuropsychological deficits in alcohol use disorder: Impact on treatment. In *Cognition and Addiction* (pp. 103-128). Academic Press. [Online]. Available at: https://doi.org/10.1016/B978-0-12-815298-0.00008-3[Accessed 09 Jan. 2023].

Mankin, E.A. and Fried, I., 2020. Modulation of human memory by deep brain stimulation of the entorhinal-hippocampal circuitry. *Neuron, 106*(2), pp.218–235. [Online]. Available at: https://doi.org/10.1016/j.neuron.2020.02.024[Accessed 09 Jan. 2023].

Petker, T., Owens, M.M., Amlung, M.T., Oshri, A., Sweet, L.H. and MacKillop, J., 2019. Cannabis involvement and neuropsychological performance: Findings from the Human Connectome Project. *Journal of Psychiatry and Neuroscience, 44*(6), pp.414-422.[Online]. Available at: https://doi.org/10.1503/jpn.180115[Accessed 09 Jan. 2023].

Pounder, Z., Jacob, J., Evans, S., Loveday, C., Eardley, A. and Silvanto, J., 2021. Individuals with congenital aphantasia show no significant neuropsychological deficits in imagery-related memory tasks. *PsyArXiv*, pp.1–22. [Online]. Available at: https://www.samuel-evans.co.uk/uploads/1/1/9/5/119533268/aphantasia_cortex_submission_zp_20.5.21.pdf[Accessed 09 Jan. 2023].

Vallar, G., 2020. Neuropsychological disorders of memory. In *Handbook of Clinical and Experimental Neuropsychology* (pp. 321–368). Psychology Press. [Online]. Available at: https://doi.org/10.4324/9781315791272-18[Accessed 09 Jan. 2023].

Wang, Q., 2021. The cultural foundation of human memory. *Annual Review of Psychology*, 72, pp.151–179. [Online]. Available at: https://doi.org/10.1146/annurev-psych-070920-023638[Accessed 09 Jan. 2023].

Wojcik, C.M., Beier, M., Costello, K., DeLuca, J., Feinstein, A., Goverover, Y., Gudesblatt, M., Jaworski III, M., Kalb, R., Kostich, L. and LaRocca, N.G., 2019. Computerised neuropsychological assessment devices in multiple sclerosis: A systematic review. *Multiple Sclerosis Journal*, 25(14), pp.1848-1869. [Online]. Available at: https://doi.org/10.1177/1352458519879094[Accessed 09 Jan. 2023].

Woods, S.P., Kordovski, V.M., Tierney, S.M. and Babicz, M.A., 2019. The neuropsychological aspects of performance-based Internet navigation skills: A brief review of emerging literature. *The*

Clinical Neuropsychologist, *33*(2), pp.305-326.
[Online]. Available at:
https://doi.org/10.1080/13854046.2018.1503332[
Accessed 09 Jan. 2023].

Chapter   22

'In psychology, studying personal experience should be more important than measuring traits and abilities.' Critically evaluate this statement, drawing on evidence from social psychology and the psychology of individual differences.

Introduction

This essay aims to analyse why in psychology, studying personal experiences should be more important than measuring traits and abilities. This essay will assess and critically evaluate existing fundamental aspects of personal experiences with the social psychology framework and why it should be prioritised over measuring traits and abilities. The study of personal experiences in psychology provides an in-depth insight into how social norms shape human feelings, thoughts and behaviour. Personal experiences then offer the premise that it is possible to identify the variables responsible for influencing human interactions. Based on the differences in individual experiences, aspects such as emotions are essential for understanding interpersonal relations in psychology. In instances where those in a relationship have been subjected to enduring love owing to factors attributable to emotions, behaviours and thought processes, it is possible to use personal experiences within the framework of the phenomenological approach.

On the other hand, measuring traits and abilities is an approach to the psychology of individual differences. It is equally essential when studying how people are unique in their approach to life. In addition, psychology has informed the concept of nature versus nurture of individual differences, which has been critical in understanding the abilities that make others more suitable than others in terms of their roles.

Main Body

Studying individual differences is essential in understanding how unique qualities apply to a social group and organisation. A typical example psychology of individual differences is when traits and abilities are used to measure quality, such as intelligence quotient. Arguably, the intellectual capabilities tests are designed to establish the level of the individual cognitive development that would then reveal the individual's progress in qualifying for the roles assigned to them or their personal cognitive development. For this reason, learning the traits and abilities is a significant scope of the broader psychology of individual differences and characteristics.

Also, the psychology of individual differences is vital when striving to compare the traits and abilities of different individuals to improve the same. The tests and experiments guided by the psychology of individual differences are essential to drawing comparisons among those tested to identify developmental milestones across the lifespan. Using factor analysis is a technique applicable to reducing many variables by grouping them according to a few factors. Factor analysis is an essential tool for identifying the traits and abilities that are unique to the individual, but it also provides insights where there are correlations (Taherdoost, Sahibuddin & Jalaliyoon, 2022, p 375). Using the explanatory factor analysis, it is possible to develop data collection tools such as questionnaires that accurately determine whether the device serves its intended purpose. The large sets of data and handling a large group of participants in a test provide researchers with the reduced variable used in comparing traits and abilities.

On the other hand, the social psychology framework that informs studying personal experiences regarding interests in forming relationships can be understood in terms of instrumentality. Ideally, instrumentality provides for people's motives when developing relationships (Roberson, Spielmann & Kopetz, 2020. p438). Arguably, people choose relationships based on how effective such relations can address their personal needs. Understanding the reason for having ties makes it possible to explain elements of human behaviour, mainly when they are in a relationship. The study of personal experiences then provides the premises for shaping interpersonal relations. When people are looking for a partner who is attractive to them, they are bound to look for one who has the qualities that are attractive to them and would fulfil what they lack (Kross & Giust, 2019, p 45). Social phenomenology is essential when it comes to understanding people's motives when forming relations meant to address the areas of life in which there are gaps. For example, a man who did not experience the love and affection of his parents would likely fall in love with a partner who is readily available to provide them with attention and affection. Using the model of instrumentality, people get into relationships with the underlying factors that are meant to make them stay in the relationship as long as they are bound to benefit.

Apart from assessing the motives that influence people to be part of a relationship, the study of personal experiences opens the conversation about family patterns and formations. The family's social interactions and power relations are dynamics that are explicable using personal experience. Because of the evolving family patterns and relations such as those of gay parenthood is entirely in terms of the relations, unlike that of the heterosexual traditional family units. Using the phenomenological approach to the study of human experiences, using semi-structured interviews effectively produces authentic experiences for the participants. Researchers in the field of social psychology can engage the participants without restricting their responses (Zerbini et al., 2020). Consequently, the participants can offer their experiences without limiting the experiences they should provide to the researchers. On the contrary, measuring traits and abilities are limited because participants who participate in such studies fully express their powers for the researchers to ascertain their variations among individuals. The use of semi-structured interviews when there is a need to collect the experiences of an individual has made it a more practical approach to the study of personal experiences. It is possible to provide a holistic understanding of human behaviour, emotions and thought processes to properly understand the factors that motivate a person's actions. With the opportunity for the participant to fully express themselves without manipulation from the researchers, then the level of accuracy of the results is guaranteed. Additionally, the researchers collecting the data cannot impose their views on the participant for them to provide experiences that would resonate with the researchers' motives. By doing so, the data collection methods for studying personal experiences provide the researchers with first-hand information about their experiences.

Another advantage of studying personal experiences is that the researchers need to be in a position to use bracketing meant to discourage the insights from the information provided by the participants. Notably, bracketing hinders the realisation of the participant's actual experiences when they are focused on sharing their unique ideas about their life or perspective towards a subject. Furthermore, the researcher is at risk of immersing themselves in the data produced by the participant if their experiences are relatable, which has the adverse effect of interfering with the study's accuracy (Jaques et al, 2019, p3040). Bracketing then becomes a threat to collecting data from the participants in social psychology. However, the problem of bracketing is even more elaborate and problematic when measuring traits and abilities using the framework of the psychology of individual differences.

The shortcoming of measuring individual traits and abilities is that it needs to allow the participants to elaborate on their abilities. The use of confirmatory factor analysis is limited in the sense it is used to test a hypothesis that is often limited in the sense that it does not provide an opportunity for the participant to explain or demonstrate their abilities (Sellbom & Tellegen, 2019, p 1428). Instead, the measurement is based on the observed traits possessed by the participants without considering an individual's abilities that are not observable. The limitation needs to make it possible for researchers to fully identify people's existing differences and capabilities when conducting the study on measuring the traits and skills. In addition, the confirmatory factor analysis is more complex in terms of reducing the variables that are to use to test for the characteristics and abilities of an individual. For this reason, using this approach to study traits and skills is a limitation to exploring an in-depth knowledge of the individuals.

Another limitation with measuring the traits and abilities is that the accuracy of the outcome is likely compromised when there is an array of variables to be reduced to specific identical factor for study among participants. Arguably, the tendency of bias when measuring the traits and differences is a problem that affects the accuracy of the outcome and the process of measuring the two factors. The method of assigning the variables to a factor that makes it possible for an accurate to provide the desired outcome measures traits and abilities problematic, mainly when there are numerous variables. Still, fewer factors are aligned with the same. However, social psychology is not limited to the traits and abilities of the participant taking part in a test. Instead, it opens up an opportunity for the individual participants to feel that they can take part in the process of sharing their experiences using the guidance of open-ended interviews that do not necessarily need the measurement of the abilities of the experiences that the individuals share (Buunk, Dijkstra & Van,2021). Therefore, the researcher using social psychology can produce accurate results since they cannot impose their worldview on the participants. Instead, the participants' personal experiences are recorded using the data collection method, such as the focus groups that are not limited to subjecting the participants to having the same view as the researcher. The qualitative data collection method used in social psychology is advantageous because it entails the participants' psychological processes to understand their personal experiences (Radburn& Stott, 2019, p 421). For this reason, the outcome of the research on social psychology assessing personal experiences can present human behaviour and an in-depth explanation provided by the participant.

The study of personal experiences using the social psychology framework provides for sociality, an essential element of understanding participants' relations with the people they interact with to influence action. The aspect of sociality offers the opportunity for the researchers to have a holistic approach to understanding the phenomena they study (Radburn& Stott, 2019, p 438). Therefore, the researchers should prioritise the use of sociality within the context of understanding the relations the participants have with the others they have socialised with throughout their life to identify how such concerns have impacted their experience (Pranee, 2019, p 391). In the same way, the interpretation of the personal experiences provided by the participant takes into consideration the question of spatiality when sharing personal experiences. The dimension of spatiality makes the studying of the individual experience elaborate in that it provides the researchers with an understanding of what factors within the identified spaces are attributable to the participants' experiences regarding the phenomenon under study (Lovakov&Agadullina, 2021, p 485).

For this reason, studying personal experiences ought to be an integral part of the psychological process in studies. Arguably, there is a sharp contrast between the measuring of traits and abilities and the studying of personal experiences in the use of spatiality to have a broader understanding of the factors that are influencing behaviour. The measure of individual traits and differences does not consider the more comprehensive view of a participant's social and spatial influences when studying a phenomenon. Consequently, personal experiences should be emphasised in measuring traits and abilities. As one way of reducing the problem of bias and the bracketing to distort the data collection process, using the information extrapolated from the participants is a practical approach allowing the personal experience to be part of studying the psychological phenomenon (Dörfler&Stierand, 2021 p778).

Additionally, studying personal experiences allows the researchers to immerse themselves in the data provided by the participants to fully understand their experiences to enhance the accuracy of the research outcome. On the other hand, there is minimal space for understanding external influences, such as the relationships that shape their traits and abilities. Therefore, measuring individual characteristics and differences does not provide for the in-depth analysis of the factors surrounding participants and their impact on the variables that are to be used in the study of the psychological aspect.

Conclusion

Conclusively, studying personal experiences provides an in-depth understanding of the psychological phenomenon being studied. As such, they are using it within the framework of social psychology, making it possible to understand how the influences in relations are attributable to behaviour. For example, the choice of ties is informed by an individual's needs, a phenomenon that is explicable using personal experiences. On the other hand, measuring traits and differences does not provide for the broader context of the influences that have contributed to behaviour or the phenomenon being studied. Therefore, there is a need to emphasise the study of personal experiences and avoid bracketing the researchers' experiences with those of the participants to ensure the accuracy of the study's outcome.

References

Buunk, A.P., Dijkstra, P. & Van Vugt, M., 2021. *Applying social psychology: From problems to solutions*. Sage.

Dörfler, V. & Stierand, M. 2021. Bracketing: a phenomenological theory applied through transpersonal reflexivity, *Journal of Organizational Change Management*, Vol. 34 No. 4, pp. 778-793. https://doi.org/10.1108/JOCM-12-2019-0393

Jaques, N., Lazaridou, A., Hughes, E., Gulcehre, C., Ortega, P., Strouse, D.J., Leibo, J.Z. and De Freitas, N., 2019, May. Social influence as intrinsic motivation for multi-agent deep reinforcement learning. In *International conference on machine learning* (pp. 3040-3049). PMLR.

Kross, J. &Giust, A., 2019. Elements of Research Questions in Relation to Qualitative Inquiry. *Qualitative Report*, 24(1) pp 45-67

Lovakov, A. &Agadullina, E.R., 2021. Empirically derived guidelines for effect size interpretation in social psychology. *European Journal of Social Psychology, 51*(3), pp.485-504.

Pranee Liamputtong 2019. *Handbook of Research Methods in Health Social Sciences.* Springer Singapore. pp. 391-410

Radburn, M. & Stott, C., 2019. The social psychological processes of 'procedural justice': Concepts, critiques and opportunities. *Criminology & Criminal Justice, 19*(4), pp.421-438.

Roberson, J., Spielmann, S.S. &Kopetz, C., 2020. When more means less: the impact of instrumentality dilution on evaluations of romantic relationships. *Comprehensive Results in Social Psychology, 4*(3), pp.345-359.

Sellbom, M. &Tellegen, A., 2019. Factor analysis in psychological assessment research: Common pitfalls and recommendations. *Psychological assessment, 31*(12), p.1428.

Taherdoost, H.A.M.E.D., Sahibuddin, S.H.A.M.S.U.L. &Jalaliyoon, N.E.D.A., 2022. Exploratory factor analysis; concepts and theory. *Advances in applied and pure mathematics*, *27*, pp.375-382.

Zerbini, G., Ebigbo, A., Reicherts, P., Kunz, M. & Messman, H., 2020. The psychosocial burden of healthcare professionals in times of COVID-19–a survey conducted at the University Hospital Augsburg. *GMS German Medical Science, 18.*

Chapter   23

The influence of epistemological beliefs on learning difficulties

Content

Introduction

Problem statement

Epistemological beliefs

Significance of the study

Methodology

Psychometrics

Validity and reliability of the questionnaire

Construct validity

Content validity

Criterion validity

Reliability

Test-retest

Internal consistency reliability

Interview process

Classroom observation

Data analysis

Discussion

The relationship between epistemological beliefs and interest

Effect of reflective thinking on the epistemological beliefs

Summary and conclusion

References

Introduction

A psych philosophical term known as an epistemological belief refers to a learner's belief about knowledge acquisition and teaching-learning. Five parameters are simple knowledge, specific knowledge, authority knowledge, quick learning, or fixed ability are examples of epistemological beliefs. Learners' epistemological ideas are based on their aptitude, motivation, and learning activities. For example, it could be simpler to acquire knowledge if someone believes it to be simple.

If they believe that knowledge is abstract, it will take time to learn, and this idea could cause issues with how knowledge is acquired. The individual's viewpoint on the teaching and learning process is known as their epistemological beliefs.

Few students believe that knowledge can be gained at different rates, while others believe learning quickly is preferable to learning slowly. Knowledge acquisition is primarily dependent on the abilities of the learners. Epistemological beliefs and academic success among students are correlated with gender, attitude, information source, justification of knowledge, and knowledge development.

The Indonesian educational system aims to create inclusive schools that can accept and educate a variety of pupils, including those with physical and learning disabilities. As a result, children with significant learning challenges who would have previously faced the possibility of being excluded from school are now allowed to enrol in mainstream, inclusive classrooms. However, these kids may have serious communication problems with their peers and instructors. Keyword signing has proven to be one strategy that works well in this situation.

Problem statement

Some evidence supports the idea that instructors' individual attitudes on the advantages and disadvantages of sign-supported communication for kids may restrict or encourage its usage in the classroom and throughout schools. Therefore, understanding the relationship between instructors' ideas about the impacts of signing, classroom practice, and their epistemological beliefs is crucial if Singalong Indonesia is to be used successfully.

Epistemological beliefs

Epistemological views are beliefs about knowing and knowledge, according to Berding et al. (2017). (p. 103). Others have worked to investigate the term belief has different definitions. According to Garmon (2004), beliefs can be compared to attitudes, ideas, and philosophies (Simmons et al., 1999). According to Kagan (1990), beliefs play a crucial role in the decision-making process that could result in a person taking a particular action. Both individuals and groups can describe their beliefs (Nespor, 1987). (Fishbein & Ajzen, 1975). Both teachers' (Speer, 2005) and students' (Pehkonen & Törner, 1996; Schoenfeld, 1983) explanations for the behaviours seen in the classroom have drawn the attention of researchers in education. "The main problem when defining beliefs is to select, based on what is being examined, which perspective is most acceptable for defining beliefs, the society or the individual, and then to be consistent within this one" sterholm (2010).

Epistemological views are beliefs about the nature of knowledge and learning, according to Ismail et al. (2013). Understanding a person's epistemological views is difficult because a person's epistemology is made up of many different beliefs (Schommer et al., 1992). Moreover, those epistemological ideas are dynamic and subject to change throughout time (Ismail et al., 2013); that is, a teacher who holds firm to a particular method of instruction may alter their views if the right circumstances allow them to do so. Understanding faculty members' epistemic perspectives can also be a tool for professional development (PD) resource mobilisation. In other words, it is simple to have a robust understanding of the type of PD required for a particular individual or group.

According to their custodial and humanistic orientations, Schramm-Possinger (2015) categorised instructor beliefs in one study. On the one side, teacher-directed activities that don't provide pupils with more learning autonomy are the main focus of the custodial ideas. On the other hand, humanistic techniques foster a demanding environment that encourages students to develop greater levels of independence, self-control, self-discipline, and engagement in their academic pursuits. Therefore, the opinions of the teachers regarding classroom interactions require more examination. The classification of teachers' epistemological ideas was expanded by Luft and Roehrig (2007) into five categories: traditional, informative, transitional, responsive, and reformed. The first two categories are beliefs held by teachers, whereas students have the final two.

It has been established that, concerning the connection between epistemological views and identity, these beliefs impact how that identity develops during identity formation (Krettenauer, 2005). Even though science identity is a domain-specific identity and a significant outcome of scientific learning, systematic research on the potential impact of epistemological beliefs on the shaping constructs of science identity to improve students' perceptions of science identity as a whole need to be completed. It's important to note that external validation highlights the social aspect of identity construction (Godwin & Potvin, 2017). On the other hand, epistemological views are a part of the cognitive system that mainly influences intra-individual variables (Bromme et al., 2009)

Students' comprehension of the learning task and the knowledge to be learned is primarily impacted by students' epistemological views, which influence the learning process and outcomes (Bromme et al., 2009). Therefore, it seems sensible to assume that epistemological beliefs enhance students' perceptions of their competence and performance rather than directly impacting external acknowledgement. As a result, we only cover the direct connection between interest, competence, performance views and epistemic beliefs below.

Significance of the study

The study examined how students' academic performance was impacted by their learning preferences and epistemological beliefs. Two types of trust have been identified in the literature: the first is that learning depends on effort, and the second is that understanding depends on aptitude. In addition, in comparison to female students, male students have more epistemic beliefs.

However, the epistemological perspective of future teachers directly affects performance. Similarly, a favourable association was established between high school students' scientific epistemological beliefs and their motivation to learn science. According to research, both formal and informal educational programs' relationships between meta-cognitive methods were influenced by epistemological beliefs. When understanding biology, epistemological beliefs constitute a significant predictor of self-efficacy.

Epistemological beliefs, age, gender, and ethnicity were discovered to be directly associated with achievement in the literature. Positive correlations were identified between students' gender, grade level, and epistemic attitudes and beliefs. Epistemological opinions have internal coherence rather than existing in isolation. Though there is a negative link between epistemological views and teaching anxiety in

Comment [Ma]:

mathematics, epistemological beliefs influence educational goals, principles, and teaching-learning methodologies.

Methodology

Research design

We applied a quasi-experimental post-test-only methodology for this study. The process comprised a mixed methods study that reported the same quantitative and qualitative interview data questionnaire.

Questionnaires

Questionnaires are the first prerequisite for gathering essential data for this investigation. The survey questions effectively convey the researchers' intended meaning. This was a problem with the participants and researchers needing a different language and culture. The questionnaires were piloted, and the initial responses were noted down. The analysis suggested links between the types of epistemological beliefs teachers hold, their attitudes towards inclusive education, and the use of keyword signing. The issue, as will be described later, was that the data did not initially support independent and social-constructivist beliefs.

This information from the questionnaire could help create teacher training on applying keyword signing in inclusive classrooms and institutions. However, it required more improvement in terms of its validity and reliability, as with all pilot questionnaires.

Acquiring precise and useable data is crucial when conducting questionnaire research; thus, the questionnaire must be valid and dependable. This is essential element of questionnaire design that psychometrics is a whole field of study devoted to it.

Psychometrics

A subfield of psychology called psychometrics is concerned explicitly with creating, administering, and interpreting questionnaires and scales that aim to categorise and gauge various facets of psychological aptitude and experience. To confirm Psychometric researchers subject thousands of subjects to rigorous testing to confirm the validity and reliability of current scales and measures point in your research career, undertaking such a time- and money-consuming approach would not be acceptable (or practicable).

Designing the questionnaire

One must go through five primary stages while researching to ensure your questionnaire design is sound.

1. Clearly define your research issue and the population (and, thus, the sample) you are interested in studying.

2. Describe the psychological concepts that your questionnaire will attempt to measure.

3. Develop your merchandise or inquiries (thinking about question-wording and suitable response options).

4. Test your questionnaire (removing or altering any problematic questions).

5. To complete your questionnaire, evaluate its validity and reliability.

Validity and reliability of the questionnaire

Any particular measures you want to employ in your research should be considered in the reliability and validity judgments. Any further analysis will only be worthwhile if your metrics are meaningful. It is essential to keep in mind that a questionnaire may be made to test a single construct, or it may be made to draw on a variety of constructs, beliefs, or behaviours. If so, it is essential to independently consider the dependability and validity of each unique notion (or variable).

Consider the reliability and validity of the questionnaire using the example of epistemological beliefs. Consider the fact and reliability of the sub-measures (innate ability, learning effort, authority/expert knowledge, and certainty knowledge), as you may wish to study the various sub-constructs independently.

Construct validity

Fundamentally, you must have faith in the construct validity of your measure, which means that it assesses the psychological construct it intends to measure. There are numerous techniques to examine the construct validity. One way is to determine if the measure appears to participants and researchers to reflect the relevant notion. Does the test appear to be measuring what you believe it to be measuring? Face validity is the term used to describe this arbitrary assessment of validity. A measure's apparent validity is not a guarantee of its reliability. Face validity, however, can be crucial for participants. They can feel as though they are being questioned needlessly and refuse to fill out the questionnaire if they think the test being conducted lacks face validity.

Content validity

This relates to whether a test addresses every aspect, or content domain, of the relevant construct. For instance, a general intelligence test will not be content validity. It excludes verbal intelligence and addresses mathematical intelligence. It is easy to establish whether a measure has content validity in some situations where the content domain of the construct is evident, but it is more challenging in others (such as creativity, about which you will learn more next week)

Criterion validity

Examining the correlation between the measure's scores and some other outcome or criterion is required. There are numerous subtypes of criterion-related validity, including:

Research occasionally aims to forecast future behaviour. In these situations, we evaluate predictive validity by examining the correlation between our measure and a future behaviour criterion. In the case of a job application, for instance, psychometric tests might be administered. Companies use these particular exams because they have predictive validity or the ability to predict future job performance accurately.

As an alternative, we can examine the connection between the measure and a related standard (i.e. something measured at the same time or concurrently). The term "concurrent validity" refers to this.

A concept known as convergent validity is connected to concurrent and predictive validity. Measures intended to evaluate the same construct should be related to one another. Measurements of the same or comparable constructs should, in other words, "converge." There should be a correlation between various intelligence tests and relevant variables (e.g. academic attainment).

On the other hand, but no less crucially, we must ascertain whether our measure is separate from different standards with which it should not be associated. Discriminant validity is the name for this kind of validity. Although it may seem bizarre and excessive, it is crucial to understand that our measure is unique compared to measurements of other constructions and that we can distinguish between them. A measure of a conceptually distinct construct like self-esteem shouldn't have a strong correlation with a measure of a construct like IQ, for instance.

Reliability

A measure's consistency and stability are referred to as reliability. Why this is such a crucial attribute for psychological tests should be pretty evident. If a metric yield different finding each time you apply it, what's the point? In a perfect world, psychological assessments accurately reflect a participant's performance on the relevant variable. Although measurement error is expected in the actual world, we strive to keep it to a minimum.

Test-retest reliability, internal consistency reliability, and inter-rater reliability are some distinct ways to evaluate reliability. The latter often entails computing a coefficient that represents the reliability's strength.

Test-retest

When determining test-retest reliability, a measure is given at two different times, and the correlation between the two results is examined. Correlation is used for this. Hopefully, you are now comfortable with correlational analysis. Correlations enable you to explore the relationship between two variables measured at the interval or ordinal level, as you discovered on DE100 and DE200. Correlation directly compares one variable's scores with those of another to determine whether there is a relationship between two variables. There is high test-retest reliability if participants score similarly on both occasions, as indicated by a strong correlation. Conversely, test-retest reliability is low if the scores are dissimilar, as there will be little association between them.

Internal consistency reliability

Naturally, it's only sometimes possible to gather information from participants on two separate occasions; thus, researchers frequently have to assess dependability based on data collected on a single event. Since psychological tests often consist of several items (or questions), researchers can compare participants' responses to other test items intended to evaluate the same psychological concept. Internal consistency dependability refers to how trustworthy a measure is within itself.

Split-half reliability is one type of internal consistency reliability. In this scenario, a questionnaire's items are randomly divided into two groups. The results of the participant's performance on the survey's two halves are then determined and compared using correlation. Their ratings on both sets of items should be remarkably similar and highly associated if a scale is exceptionally dependable. Conversely, the metric could be more trustworthy if significant differences exist between the results.

Interview process

Interviews were used to determine faculty epistemological beliefs. The respondents were made to describe and define various views held by pre-service. During the interviews, 13 faculty members (including the five who were interviewed before and after PD)

Classroom observation

A variety of steps were taken during the observations. In the first stage, we watched the required training videos, gave them ratings, and compared our ratings to the recommended ratings to get ready for use. Next, the two researchers simultaneously observed five courses during the second training phase, evaluating each observation independently to allow for comparisons. Finally, the disparities were explored using the training video to achieve more accurate ratings of the RTOP. The remaining classes were then watched and graded by individual researchers.

Data analysis

Two analysis methods were used to analyse the data from the questionnaire. The methods were:

Correlation reveals the degree of association between two variables and their direction and statistical significance.

Simple linear regression: You may model the relationship between two variables using simple linear regression and then make predictions utilising that model.

Simple linear regression was typically more advantageous than multiple linear regression because it enabled you to identify the type and importance of the relationship between your variables and to forecast the behaviour of one variable based on another. However, suppose one is still constrained by the fact that one can only look at two variables simultaneously, just like with correlation. The issue is that because humans are complex beings, things rarely happen to them in isolation, as we know from everyday experience. Therefore, it is improbable that you could successfully model human experience or behaviour with just two variables. As a result, focusing on the relationship between two variables may lead to oversimplification, reducing the analysis's applicability.

Discussion

The relationship between epistemological beliefs and competence/performance beliefs

Students' judgments of the likelihood that they will comprehend domain content knowledge and their capacity to complete domain activities are known as competence/performance beliefs (Verdun, 2021). However, more research needs to specifically examine the connection between competence/performance beliefs and epistemological beliefs. Although self-efficacy and self-concept are two concepts closely related to competence/performance beliefs, it has been thoroughly shown in various contexts that epistemological views significantly impact self-efficacy and self-concept.

In terms of the connection between competence/performance beliefs, self-efficacy, and self-concept, some researchers contend that self-efficacy (i.e., self-perception about the capacity to complete a particular task) and self-concept (i.e., the overall perception of self-competence in a discipline) are included in competence/performance beliefs (Robinson et al., 2020; Scherer, 2013). Other researchers concur that self-efficacy and self-concept are similarly organised to competence/performance beliefs (Verdun, 2021). Either understanding argues that an explanation of the connection between epistemological beliefs and competence/performance views could be supported by the impact of epistemological beliefs on self-efficacy or self-concept.

The relationship between epistemological beliefs and interest

Interest is a relatively stable motivational trait in a particular learning domain defined by pleasant feelings and personal significance, while epistemological beliefs are crucial for comprehending students' motivational conceptions (Choung et al., 2020; Kizilgunes et al., 2009). Numerous research has shown a favourable relationship between curiosity and epistemological beliefs. Students who hold advanced epistemological ideas are more motivated by studying themselves than by receiving accolades from their professors or degrees (DeBacker & Crowson, 2006). Those who emphasised rules of inquiry and evidence evaluation were more likely to be interested in the learning domain (Terms & Brent, 2009). They regard themselves as architects of knowledge and anticipate finding evidence to support or refute their ideas through classroom investigation. Similarly, Kapucu and Bahçivan (2015) discovered that high school student's understanding of the value of physics in their lives and society increased along with their interest in the study of physics, depending on how complicated their epistemological beliefs were.

Effect of reflective thinking on the epistemological beliefs

According to Bromme et al. (2009), epistemological beliefs only significantly influence learning in the latter stages of self-regulation learning when reflective thinking is fully engaged. Reflective thinking is frequently cited as a crucial skilled student should have (Sabariego Puig et al., 2020). John Dewey initially articulated reflective thinking in 1933, and according to him, one of the main goals of education should be to develop students' reflective thinking (Hong & Choi, 2011). Reflective thinking is actively, continuously, and thoughtfully revaluating any belief or assumed knowledge in light of underlying assumptions and held tendencies (Dewey, 1933; Hong & Choi, 2011).

Summary and conclusion

This study looked at connections between epistemological views, reflective thinking, and science identity was the main goal of the study. Therefore, it makes sense to imply that epistemological beliefs and reflective thinking both favour students' identity formation in light of the theoretical analysis discussed above (Engelbertink et al., 2020.)
But epistemological convictions and identities are context-specific (Hofer, 2006; Robinson et al., 2019). The empirical examination of the strong connections between high school students' epistemological ideas, reflective thinking, and

identity within the science area is absent from the prior studies. Therefore, the main objective of this study is to determine whether or not students' epistemological ideas about science and their reflective thinking while learning science are related to their sense of science identity. Additionally, other studies have demonstrated that an individual's complicated epistemological beliefs more strongly predict the level of reflective thinking. It follows that a second hypothesis that reflective thought mediates the relationship between epistemological views about science and scientific identity is a logical conclusion. The second goal of this research is to determine whether reflective thinking may help explain how epistemological ideas about science can indirectly influence science identity.

References

Abd-El-Khalick, F., Boujaoude, S., Duschl, R., Lederman, N. G., Mamlok-Naaman, R., Hofstein, A., Niaz, M., Treagust, D., Tuan, H., & I. (2004). Inquiry in science education: International perspectives. Science Education, 88(3), 397–419. https://doi.org/10.1002/sce.10118

Akpur, U. (2020). Critical, reflective, creative thinking and their reflections on academic achievement. Thinking Skills and Creativity, 37, 100683. https://doi.org/10.1016/j.tsc.2020.100683

Alake-Tuenter, E., Biemans, H. J. A., Tobi, H., Wals, A. E. J., Oosterheert, I., & Mulder, M. (2012). Inquiry-based science education competencies of primary school teachers: a literature study and critical review of the American National science education standards. International Journal of Science Education, 34(17), 2609–2640. https://doi.org/10.1080/09500693.2012.669076

Alhaji, A. (2021). Individual and contextual effects on science identity among American ninth-grade students (HSLS:09): Hierarchical linear modelling. Research in Science & Technological Education. https://doi.org/10.1080/02635143.2021.1972959

Bakeman, R., & Robinson, B. F. (2014). Understanding statistics in behavioural science. Psychology Press.

Berzonsky, M., & Kuk, L. S. (2000). Identity status, identity processing style, and the transition to university. Journal of Adolescent Research, 15(1), 81–98. https://doi.org/10.1177/0743558400151005

Bowen, T. (2016). Becoming professional: Examining how WIL students learn to construct and perform their professional identities. Studies in Higher Education, 43(7), 1148–1159. https://doi.org/10.1080/03075079.2016.1231803

Boyes, M. C., & Chandler, M. (1992). Cognitive development, epistemic doubt, and identity formation in adolescence. Journal of Youth and Adolescence, 21(3), 277–304.

Brandmo, C., & Bråten, I. (2018). Investigating relations between beliefs about the justification for knowledge, interest, and knowledge across two socio-scientific topics. Learning and Individual Differences, 62, 89–97. https://doi.org/10.1016/j.lindif.2018.01.010

Bromme, R., Pieschl, S., & Stahl, E. (2009). Epistemological beliefs are standards for adaptive learning: A functional theory about epistemological beliefs and metacognition. Metacognition and Learning, 5(1), 7–26. https://doi.org/10.1007/s11409-009-9053-5

Browne, M. W., & Cudeck, R. (1993). Alternative ways of assessing model fit. In K. A. Bollen & J. S. Long (Eds.), Testing structural equation models (pp. 136–162). Sage Publications.

Burke, P. J., & Stets, J. E. (2009). Identity theory. Oxford University Press.

Burns, R. A., Crisp, D. A., & Burns, R. B. (2018). Competence and affect dimensions of self-concept among higher education students: A factorial validation study of academic subject-specific self-concept. European Journal of Psychology of Education, 33(4), 649–663. https://doi.org/10.1007/s10212-018-0369-x

Carlone, H. B., & Johnson, A. (2007). Understanding the science experiences of successful women of colour: Science identity as an analytic lens. Journal of Research in Science Teaching, 44(8), 1187–1218. https://doi.org/10.1002/tea.20237

Chan, N.-M., Ho, I. T., & Ku, K. Y. L. (2011). Epistemic beliefs and critical thinking of Chinese students. Learning and Individual Differences, 21(1), 67–77. https://doi.org/10.1016/j.lindif.2010.11.001

Chemers, M. M., Zurbriggen, E. L., Syed, M., Goza, B. K., & Bearman, S. (2011). The role of efficacy and identity in science career commitment among underrepresented minority students. Journal of Social

Issues. https://doi.org/10.1111/j.1540-4560.2011.01710.x

Chen, J. A., & Pajares, F. (2010). Implicit theories of the ability of Grade 6 science students: Relation to epistemological beliefs and academic motivation and achievement in science. Contemporary Educational Psychology, 35(1), 75–87. https://doi.org/10.1016/j.cedpsych.2009.10.003

Chen, S., & Wei, B. (2020). Development and validation of an instrument to measure high school students' science identity in science learning. Research in Science Education. https://doi.org/10.1007/s11165-020-09932-y

Chen, S., Binning, K. R., Manke, K. J., Brady, S. T., McGreevy, E. M., Betancur, L., Limeri, L. B., & Kaufmann, N. (2021). Am I a science person? A strong science identity bolsters.

Chapter 24

Influence of Media on Behavior

The media has become an increasingly powerful tool in our society, tremendously impacting how people behave. The media significantly influences our attitudes, beliefs, and behaviours, from the news we watch to the music we listen to. The media can inform, educate, and entertain, but it can also be used to manipulate and control. Studies have found that media can positively and negatively affect behaviour, depending on how it is used. This paper discusses the influence of media on behaviour.

The media is essential in setting social norms and expectations by influencing people's thoughts and actions. Through television, films, newspapers, magazines, social media, and other forms of media, people learn about societal expectations through the stories and messages they are exposed to. The press can reinforce existing norms and expectations or create new ones by highlighting certain behaviours or values as desirable or acceptable (. Ferguson,2013). For example, media reports can focus on respecting differences, promoting diversity, and tolerating others. Similarly, the media can also portray certain behaviours as inappropriate or socially unacceptable. This can lead to a shift in social norms and expectations as people strive to conform to what they see in the media.

The media can shape public opinion and, therefore, can reinforce stereotypes. This can be done by perpetuating negative stereotypes in films, television shows, advertisements, and other forms of media. These stereotypes can further marginalise certain groups of people and lead to real-world implications, such as discrimination and prejudice. Additionally, the lack of representation of particular groups of people in the media can further reinforce stereotypes. For example, the lack of female representation in the media can perpetuate the idea that women are incapable of specific roles or jobs.

Still, the media promotes consumerism through various methods, including advertising, product placement, and endorsements. Advertising is the most apparent form of media promotion, as companies use multiple forms of media, such as television, radio, and print, to reach potential consumers. Product placement is another form of media promotion, which involves placing a product in a show or movie to encourage viewers to purchase it. Endorsements from celebrities, athletes, or other influencers are also common, as these people have high levels of credibility and can influence many potential buyers (Anderson & Bushman,2001). Finally, social media is another platform used to promote consumerism, as companies can use it to reach a broad audience and create hype around their products.

The media can expose individuals to new ideas by presenting them with different perspectives and stories from around the world. News outlets, documentary films, and streaming services can provide individuals with various views and reports they may not have had access to before. By exposing individuals to different ideas, the media can help them to become more informed, open-minded citizens. Additionally, the media can be used to promote positive messages and advocate for social change. For example, the media can be used to discuss issues such as racial justice, religious freedom, and gender equality. Through the media, individuals can explore these topics and better understand each issue's complexities. The media can foster a more informed and tolerant society

 by exposing individuals to new ideas.

The media can unite people to share common interests, experiences and values. For example, social media has connected people worldwide in a way that was never possible before. This has allowed people to form online communities to discuss topics, share opinions and support one another. Additionally, television and radio programs often provide a platform for people to come together and discuss their views, which can help strengthen their sense of community

(Tukachinsky & Cohen,2013). Finally, local newspapers and magazines can foster a sense of community by informing people about what's happening in their area. All of these outlets can help create a sense of belonging and connection, strengthening community ties.

Again, the media has an immense power to shape public opinion, influence political discourse and mould general beliefs. Through the lens of television, radio, newspapers, magazines, and the internet, the public is bombarded with messages that can substantially impact their beliefs and attitudes. The media can be a powerful force in reinforcing existing beliefs and prejudices. First, the media helps to sustain existing biases and prejudices. Media coverage of specific issues often reinforces existing beliefs and prejudices, such as racial and gender stereotypes. For example, media coverage of people of colour often perpetuates harmful stereotypes, such as portraying them as criminals or violent. This type of coverage can lead to widespread negative beliefs about people of colour that can be difficult to challenge. Similarly, news stories about women often reinforce gender stereotypes, such as portraying them as weaker or less capable than men.

Second, the media can be used to spread false information and propagate dangerous ideas. For example, the internet is rife with incorrect information and conspiracy theories that can be used to spread fear and hatred. This type of media coverage can be used to reinforce existing biases and prejudices, such as racism and xenophobia. The spread of false information and conspiracy theories can lead to dangerous beliefs and attitudes that are difficult to challenge (. Ferguson,2013). Also, the media can be used to manipulate public opinion. For example, certain news outlets can be used to spread propaganda and distort facts to sway public opinion. This media coverage can reinforce beliefs and prejudices, such as political or religious views. By manipulating public opinion, the media can sustain certain assumptions and biases that may not be reality-based.

Media has always been a powerful tool for normalizing violence and aggression. The media significantly impacts how we perceive our environment and the people around us. It can be argued that it has been used to normalize violence and aggression in various ways. One way the media normalizes violence and aggression is by portraying violence as a "normal" part of life. This can be seen in television shows, movies, and video games, where violence is often described as a necessary or acceptable way to solve conflicts. This can lead to viewers or players becoming desensitized to violence, making it seem more pleasing in their own lives. It also can create a culture where violence is seen as an acceptable way to solve conflicts.

Another way that the media normalizes violence and aggression is by making it seem glamorous. This is often seen in movies or television shows, where the "tough" or "cool" characters use violence as a way to get what they want (Anderson & Bushman,2001). This conveys that violence is a viable option for achieving goals and can encourage people to use violence to get what they want. Still, the media can normalize violence and aggression by portraying it as a "necessary evil." This is often seen in war movies or television shows where violence is described as a necessary part of a mission or a "justified" form of punishment. This conveys that violence is an essential part of life rather than an aberration that should be avoided.

The media plays a significant role in our lives, providing entertainment and escapism. It can be seen as a tool to help us relax, escape from the pressures of everyday life and just let go of our worries. From the latest blockbuster movie to the newest trending video game, the media offers us a way to escape reality and indulge in something different. The media provides us with entertainment and escapism, from movies and television shows to video games and social media. While these media outlets often provide us with news and information, they also offer us a way to relax and enjoy ourselves. We can watch a movie with friends or family, play a video game with friends, or scroll through social media to see what's new. These activities can give us a much-needed break from the stresses and pressures of everyday life.

The media also offers us a chance to experience something different. We can explore new worlds in movies, travel through other times and places in television shows, or explore different cultures in video games. We can learn about different people and places, helping us better understand the world around us. This can be especially helpful for those feeling isolated or disconnected from their surroundings. Finally, the media can also provide us with a sense of community. We can connect with people worldwide through social media, creating a strong sense of belonging and a feeling that we're not alone. We can also explore different forms of media and find people who share the same interests as us, forming meaningful relationships and creating a sense of belonging that can be hard to find in real life.

In conclusion, the media plays a significant role in influencing behaviour. Through the constant bombardment of messages, people are more likely to act in specific ways and make confident decisions. In addition, media messages can be used to encourage positive and discourage negative behaviour and can help shape a person's attitudes and beliefs. Ultimately, the media can shape the behaviour of individuals, groups, and even entire societies

References

. Ferguson, C. J. (2013). Media and adolescent mental health: The impact of media on body image, aggression, and addiction. Clinical Psychological Review, 33(8), 1060-1070.

Anderson, C. A., & Bushman, B. J. (2001). Effects of violent video games on aggressive behaviour, aggressive cognition, aggressive affect, physiological arousal, and prosocial behaviour: A meta-analytic review of the scientific literature. Psychological Science, 12(5), 353-359.

Tukachinsky, R., & Cohen, A. (2013). Media and adolescent behaviour: A systematic review of longitudinal studies. Journal of Adolescent Health, 52(3), 331-339.

Chapter 25

Influences of Social and Personality Development During Childhood

Most personality characteristics are carried from infancy to adolescence. Social and personality development in childhood is influenced by their biological maturations, social interactions, and the children's representation of the self and environment. To understand social and character development, an individual must look at children from several perspectives that mould the story. Firstly, one should look at the social context in which every kid grows and, more so, the relationship that gives them guidance, security, and knowledge. Secondly, they should assess biological maturation, which aids in developing emotional and social skills that impact their temperamental personality. Thirdly, individuals should look at the kids' advancing representations of their social context and themselves. Most psychologists describe social and personality maturation as the sustained interconnection between the biological, social, and characterisation of psychological advancement elements. This paper discusses two major theories of social and personality development in childhood, various social and character development influences, and the approaches used to research personality development and findings.

Some major personality theories of personality development are the behaviourist and the social cognitive theories. For instance, behaviourists connect personality with the external environment's effects on the responses. The criteria applied in the behavioural aspect analysis are referred to as behavioural theories. One of the significant behaviourists' perspectives is the strong emphasis on experimentation and scientific thinking. This belief was developed by Skinner, who created a model that insists on the mutual interaction of organisms with the environment. Skinner maintained that children will always do wrong things if they learn that the behaviour creates attention and acts as a reinforcer. (Lamb & Bornstein,2013). For example, he said infants cry because their previous crying resulted in attention. The child's crying is the response, while the attention they are given is the consequence. According to this tenet, people form behaviour based on the environmental impacts on their answers.

Another perspective addressing the issue of personality development is social cognitive theories. According to this theory, behaviour is determined by the cognitions such as expectations about the world and more so about other individuals. Cognitive concepts, therefore, emphasize mental processes like thinking and judging. In this theory, Albert Bandura held that the forces of memory and feelings were highly dependent on environmental influences. Bandura was famous for the 'Bobo doll experiment.' Bandura videotaped his friend kicking and abusing the bobo doll in the experiment. He then ensured that the kindergarten children watched the video before going out to play. After getting into the playroom, they saw bobo dolls and the hummers. Individuals that observed the kids play saw them beating up the beauty. He referred to this experiment and the findings as observational learning. According to this theory, most children's social and personalities are amplified by their social contexts (Lamb & Bornstein,2013).

Several factors influence social and personality development in childhood. For instance, the heredity of particular parental character traits dictates children's social behaviour. Schmidt et al. (2016) retain that about 66% of children's personalities are inherited from their parents. This means that some parental character traits can be passed across generations with the strong gene allele's aid, which carries the parents' genetic makeup. Thus, the acquired characteristics affect the children's physical, psychological, and social attributes as they grow. For instance, in several cases, parents with undesirable social features like shyness, dishonesty, and theft have given birth to children who eventually possess these personalities. Again, the idea of children being introverts or extroverts solely depends on whether their parents owned the two attributes. Many theorists have also argued that some leadership traits like courage, charisma, and empathy can be inherited from parents to support their claim that leaders are usually born (Montessori, 2015). Generally, heredity highly impacts social and personality development in childhood.

Family relationships influence the social and personality development of children in various ways. Dunkel et al. (2019) maintain that 80% of children naturally establish a significant emotional attachment with their care providers while in infancy. The relationship between the infants and their parents determines how the babies behave in social contexts. Caregivers motivate children to stay close to them by attending to their needs at the right time and appropriately. Parents also make children feel secure warm, and provide them with guidance while growing, and boost the kids' intimate relationships. The children's security in their development stages differs based on the care providers' reinforcements upon their confidence and the kind of support provided. Thus, kids feel satisfied if care providers give adequate care and support.

In contrast, infants become insecure whenever parents give inconsistent care, or they ignore their needs. In response, the infant may cry. If the caregivers continue ignoring them, they may learn that their environment is not favourable for them, developing negative attitudes towards their social contexts. This implies that the caregivers' behaviour towards the infants will positively or negatively affect their psychological or emotional development. Children will always cling to their caregivers whom they perceive as friendly but behave strangely, exhibiting agitating behaviour toward the ones they believe to be unfriendly. The children's reactions to their care providers can tell their attachment to them (Dunkel et al. 2019).

Security attachment is an essential factor that dictates social and personality development among children. Valkenburg & Peter (2009) holds that Infants who receive secure attachments are more likely to relate well with peers as they experience more established emotional attachment, making them better understand their social environment. These children become more aware of their environment and develop a positive self-concept. Such attachments mould the children's personalities and determine how they interact with others.

The secure and insecure concepts in early childhood influence children's adolescent social relationships. The caregiver-child relationship changes with the biological growth of the child. Maturity is associated with various social realizations as children develop cognitively. These kids may change their preferences hence colliding with their parent's expectations. The parent-child misunderstanding may result in conflict between the two parties. The approach used by the parent to address such a situation will significantly affect the quality of the relationship with the kid. If there is excellent and friendly communication, a strong relationship will exist between parents and the kids in their early childhood. Such children develop self-confidence that eventually moulds their behaviour (Dunkel et al. 2019).

Additionally, parental roles dictate the children's social and personality development. This is because the children's moral growth, academic, and other life activities solely depend on parental guidance. The parent's authority impacts the children's autonomy and social competencies. For instance, mothers make demands on girls that differ from those of boys. They provide both males and females with the exact instructions, but boys will be given more autonomy than girls. Mothers also hold their daughters with more accountability standards in case of failure than their sons. The difference in independence between children of the two sexes makes girls exhibit exceptional behaviour standards in their later developmental stages (Valkenburg & Peter,2009)

The type of family relationship shapes the social and personality development of children. Children brought up in a family where the two parents are co-operative and loving will likely have desirable social and character traits. On the other hand, children from divorced families may experience anger and confusion. They are likely to be very demanding, uncooperative, and usually show aggressive behaviour. Research has shown that divorce interferes with children's ability to separate themselves emotionally from their parents. In single-parenthood cases, children may lack confidence because such families produce a lack of male figures for boys in the absence of their father. Girls living with single mothers after their parents' divorce negatively perceive men, negatively affecting their adolescent and adult life (Dunkel, van der Linden, & Kawamoto, 2019).

Family social status is another aspect that can influence children's social and personality development. Generally, families from humble backgrounds survive in more unfavourable environments and are highly stressed as they have limited social and psychological resources than those from well-to-do families. Therefore, parents living in poverty treat their children differently from wealthy parents. They spend less time with their children, talk to them less, provide inadequate age-appropriate toys, and are less friendly. These parents also provide irregular intellectually stimulating activities and are usually stricter and prefer applying physical punishment while instilling discipline in their children (Valkenburg & Peter,2009). Such parental behaviour is attributed to depression associated with particular demands of surviving in poverty.

In most cases, the emphasis on obedience and the poor parents' striker discipline may be perceived as the logical response to the realities of the environment in which they live. However, children from humble backgrounds are different from their better-off peers at all levels of development. For instance, children born in low-income families experience early disabilities and have higher congenital disability rates. Poor children often fall sick and tend to be undernourished during their growth and development. These lower-income children may record lower average IQ scores and perform lower in classwork and social activities like games, as affirmed by Piaget's cognitive development stages (Dunkel et al.2019).

Besides, children from low-income families show more behaviour problems than peers from well-to-do families. The negative implications of poverty are also exhibited in children growing up within an environment with street gangs, drug pushers, street violence, and overcrowded homes. According to Valkenburg & Peter (2009), 50% of primary and secondary school students have experienced a violent social crime in their life history. Children who witness such crimes or are victimized have increased chances of suffering from emotional challenges, unlike their peers who fail to undergo these encounters. This explains why the social and personalities of children from different social and economic statuses differ across various developmental stages.

Children's personality is highly dictated by the interaction of temperament characteristics with their immediate social environment. According to Schmidt et al. (2016), temperaments are the inborn traits that organize and influence the child's response to the world. These traits are usually stable from birth, and they are lifelong characteristics that cannot be generalized as good or bad. The child's temperaments count whether they will be difficult or easy to raise. The way the child perceives himself and others are based on how his temperaments fit in the environment and the reaction of the people forming the social environment.

Parents' understanding of their children's temperaments enables them to stop blaming themselves for natural and normal problems for the kid's temperaments. Generally, some children are more cuddy and with more regular sleeping patterns than others. Some kids also tend to be noisier than their peers. When parents learn how their children respond to particular situations, they adopt appropriate approaches to address issues that may pose difficulties. Parents may prepare kids for such cases and sometimes avoid environmental circumstances that may cause problems for the children. This enables them to realize that not all children's behaviour associated with temperament traits requires attention (De Fruyt et al.2006).

Schmidt et al. (2016) also argue that the more the parents understand their children's unique personalities, the more they feel effective and supportive. When the children's temperament becomes compatible with the people's expectations, it is said to be 'goodness of fit.' In case of incompatibility, there is what is termed 'personality conflict.' In the early stages of childhood, the parent can put up with the infant's temperament traits instead of opposing them. Nevertheless, as the child matures, the caregiver can support the child to adopt and appreciate the world by accommodating temperament characteristics.

Social and personality development among children is also shaped by their increased understanding of their social contexts. The relationship between the child and their parents and peers triggers their crucial social and emotional skills while growing. Children respond to their social contexts during infancy by reacting to their care providers. These children consciously learn that individuals have emotions and attitudes that impact their state of mind. This case becomes evident when infants look at their parents' faces whenever they undergo strange situations. Slobodskaya (2021) refers to this condition as social referencing. When the caregiver seems calm and reassuring, the infant feels safe and responds positively. However, if the mother looks uncomfortable, the child reacts negatively. The idea of social referencing emphasizes that infants are aware of their caregivers' emotional appearances allowing them to distinguish between the safe and the strange situations.

Through the responsiveness of their immediate environment, children learn other individuals' emotions, motives, and attitudes that impact their mental states, hence determining how they behave when they undergo various environmental situations in the future. As the kid's mind develops, their understanding and interpretation of their social contexts grow. Their response to their social environment eventually shapes attitudes and social behaviour while interacting with others (Schmidt et al. 2016).

Culture is a critical factor that affects children's social and personality development in early childhood. Montessori (2015) insists that Parents and siblings in various cultures have a significant role in shaping children's thinking and behaviour. Parents prepare children to interact with society in their early life stages. Children learn social and cultural rules, taboos, and humanity's expectations from their parents and siblings, thus determining how they behave in other people's presence. For example, the culture dictates the parents' conversational styles and other family members, which the children eventually imitate.

Research has revealed that European American cultures have long self-narratives promoting personal autonomy and preferences. The interaction approaches in these cultures emphasize respect and turn-taking during a conversation. On the other hand, Chinese and Korean children's discussions usually are relationally oriented, brief, and exhibit a significant intensive concern with authority. They also assume more passive roles in communication. Additionally, cultural variations in the interaction between children and adults determine how children behave socially. In the Chinese culture, where parents are rigorous and assume absolute authority over kids, parents bring up their children in a more traditional way. Children in these demanding environments tend to accept their parents' demands even when unwilling to do so (Motessori,2015).

The children's peers influence their social and personality development in middle childhood. The peers can act as fellow adventurers, classmates, and confidants. Slobodskaya (2021) claims that friends support one another in developing self-esteem and improving the sense of competency in their social world. In middle childhood, boys and girls enjoy group activities like riding bikes, skating, building forts, and playing house. This implies that conformity and popularity become an aspect of concern and worry. It is worth noting that friendship is founded on similarity in same-age peers and may rarely be affected by racial, ethnic, or other social differences. However, intolerance for peers who may not be similar triggers prejudice about the ones who are different. Even though friends and peers may promote prejudicial stereotypes, most kids become flexible in thinking about their friends, showing varying personalities from diverse backgrounds.

Schmidt et al. (2016) attest that 45% of peer pressure negatively impacts children's personalities. Those kids who are highly subject to peer pressure experience low esteem and may adopt group behaviour to improve their self-esteem. When they cannot resist their friends' destructive influence, and more so in ambiguous circumstances, they retain undesirable personalities such as dishonesty, drunkenness, and arrogance, as exhibited by their peers.

Social media is another critical source of information and entertainment that amplifies social and personality development among children, especially adolescents. Some significant media influences in the modern era include Facebook, you Tube, What sap, Instagram, and telegram. Children can use gadgets like computers or smartphones to access these social media platforms. In addition, other entertainment content can be accessed through televisions and the radio. De Fruyt et al. (2006) have revealed that 90% of school-aged children in America use smartphones or computers regularly, and 60% depend on the internet.

Over-dependency on media and social media platforms have positive and negative implications for children's social and personality development. For example, spending time online enables children to be socially competent in their digital era, easily fitting into the broader society and acquiring the current generation's social competencies. It has been discovered that social media make children more empathetic, relationship-oriented, and considerate. Children with electronic gadgets can become open and express their emotions by liking videos and pictures or commenting on their peers' updates (Montessori,2015).

Children retain lifelong friendships with others through online connections, although they don't meet face to face. In most cases, youngsters' virtual empathy is positively received by their distressed peers on social media. These platforms boost their moods and behaviour and enable them to develop a problem-solving culture. It is through social media that most modern youngsters learn to be compassionate (Slobodskaya,2021).

Social media helps children interact with individuals in various parts of the world and expose them to ideas and cultures that enable them to attain a broader general attitude about people and life. Additionally, social media helps introverted children to open up through the internet, which boosts their confidence. After interacting with people through social media platforms, youngsters can communicate with them in person confidently (Montessori,2015).

Nevertheless, social media can negatively impact children's social and personality development. Schmidt et al. (2016) testify that these platforms create addiction effects, as features like shares and likes to stimulate the brain's reward centre. This makes the reward circuity more sensitive during adolescence, which explains why teenagers are more highly addicted to social media than adults. The reward circuitry features continue affecting their moods. Eventually, the youngsters' social behaviour is amplified, and their lives become centred on social media.

Teens with social media addiction tend to spend more time watching photos and videos posted on their preferred accounts. Such dependence negatively affects their productive activities like learning, work, and sports. They, therefore, waste their substantial time, thus getting poor grades. When it comes to attention that some of the kids have wasted their time, leading to failure in classwork or social activities, they develop negative moods and defeatist attitudes. A recent study has revealed that children who spend more than three hours in the day on social media have higher chances of suffering from poor mental health. Their regular immersion in the virtual world reduces their social and emotional development rate. It can also result in antisocial personalities among teens due to cyberbullying, social comparisons, and reduced face-to-face interactions (Slobodskaya,2021).

Montessori (2015) has observed that reliance on Facebook can reduce adolescents' subjective well-being. The more they rely on Facebook, the more they become dissatisfied with life. At times teens may suffer from depression associated with social networking sites, thus becoming anxious and moody as they perceive their friends to be better than theirs. This may hinder real-life relationships and the development of social skills among children and teens. In addition, when the in-person interaction among children is reduced, they grow up with poor learning and interpreting skills, facial expressions and non-verbal cues, which may cause them to be non-empathetic. Consequently, these children and teenagers have poor verbal and non-verbal communication.

Posting endlessly on social media accounts cause an obsession with the self among youngsters. Their moods end up depending on whether their photos get appreciated on social media or not. The teens may get disappointed when they realize they rarely receive the expected attention. Sometimes teenagers and some children may have social media pages, thus becoming self-centred. Therefore, vulnerable children grow up believing everything revolves around them and eventually develop dysfunctional emotional conditions that cause them no empathy for others (Slobodskaya,2021).

Having analysed factors that determine the children's social personalities across all developmental stages, it was necessary to discuss some of the various psychologists' research methods in their experiments and their results. For instance, in predicting whether the way children behave in their early stages determines their behaviour during adolescence, some researchers used the preserved data acquired from the Colorado Adoption Project. They also observed how children reacted to the people around them and the strangers. Using self and unique personality ratings, the researchers concluded that how children behave in their strangers' presence dictates their personality at twelve years and above. This implies that most personality characteristics are carried from infancy to adolescence (Dunkel et al., 2019).

In conclusion, social and personality development are uninterrupted processes from infancy to adolescence and may extend to adulthood. Biological, social, and representative impacts determine these processes. Even though these changes exist, children develop and depict their self-concepts through social behaviours and personalities. Among the theories that explain personality development among children are behaviourists and social-cognitive approaches. Behaviourists connect the character with the external environment's effects on the responses. Simultaneously, the social cognitive theory retains that behaviour is determined by the cognitions such as expectations about the world and more so about other individuals. Several factors influence social and personality development in childhood, ranging from genetics to environmental factors such as peers, society, culture, and social media.

References
De Fruyt, F., Bartels, M., Van Leeuwen, K. G., De Clercq, B., Decuyper, M., &Mervielde, I. (2006). Five types of personality continuity in childhood and adolescence. Journal of Personality and Social Psychology, 91(3), 538–552. https://doi.org/10.1037/0022-3514.91.3.538

Dunkel, C. S., van der Linden, D., & Kawamoto, T. (2019). Early childhood social responsiveness predicts the general factor of personality in early adolescence. Infant and Child Development, 28(2), e2123. https://doi.org/10.1002/icd.2123

Lamb, M. E., & Bornstein, M. H. (Eds.). (2013). *Social and personality development: An advanced textbook*. Taylor & Francis.

Montessori, M. (2015). The Education of the Individual. The NAMTA Journal, 40(2), 15–28.

Schmidt, L. A., Tang, A., Day, K. L., Lahat, A., Boyle, M. H., Saigal, S., & Van Lieshout, R. J. (2016). Personality Development Within a Generational Context: Life

Course Outcomes of Shy Children. Child Psychiatry & Human Development, 48(4), 632–641. https://doi.org/10.1007/s10578-016-0691-y

Slobodskaya, H. R. (2021). Personality development from early childhood through adolescence. Personality and Individual Differences, 172, 110596. https://doi.org/10.1016/j.paid.2020.110596

Valkenburg, P. M., & Peter, J. (2009). Social Consequences of the Internet for Adolescents. Current Directions in Psychological Science, 18(1), 1–5. https://doi.org/10.1111/j.1467-

Chapter 26

Legal Issues in Psychology and Counselling

Legal issues in counselling are essential to ensure that the rights of both the counsellor and the client are respected. Counsellors must know the laws and regulations governing the profession and how to apply them in their practice. This includes understanding the rights of the client, the counsellor's responsibilities, the limits of confidentiality, and the legal implications of any decisions made during counselling. This paper will provide a brief overview of legal issues in counselling and their consequences to the counsellor, client, and profession.

Chemical reliance counsellors have a legal and ethical obligation to safeguard their customers. They had a responsibility to safeguard patients from injuring themselves and protect other partners against the customers. Their fundamental aim is to ensure that the commitment to defend the customer's rights has to be respected (Appelbaum, 1985). Most imposed regulations require advisors to break confidentiality to protect customers and alert them of potential dangers throughout counselling. Clients are informed about the design of all facilities offered by counsellors. They train customers on themes like the purposes, targets, procedures, constraints, possible threats, and service rewards. Therapists take progression to ensure that clients are aware of the hindrance of treatment and how tests and results will be used.

The responsibility to safeguard the client from harm usually arises when the sufferer is susceptible to others' choices or relies heavily on another for their physical health. Individuals that require assistance frequently cannot prevent themselves from harming themselves and consequently depend on the psychologist for aid. Furthermore, a responsibility to safeguard doesn't only apply to the customer but also to some clients that are perceived as susceptible victims. A therapist who delivers therapy to a customer who later considers suicide can break the confidentiality agreement after consulting with an approved provider and assessing the applicable legislation.

Therapists and their customers work together to develop therapeutic strategies with a reasonable opportunity for achievement, and these are appropriate for their customers' temperament, abilities, progressive class, and circumstances. Therapists and clients revise counselling strategies regularly to ensure their continued viability and effectiveness while respecting customers' right to choose. The counsellor must also draft an informed agreement highlighting the mentoring practice parameters (Appelbaum, 1985). Before beginning treatment, the psychotherapist and customer should go over the contract. If the therapist defines that the customer poses a vital risk to other members, the psychotherapist should take suitable precautions to safeguard the patient. In addition, the responsibility to protect constitutes involving security men in certain situations, informing the appropriate healthcare organ, and using supervision.

The chemical reliance therapist is critical in shielding customers and adhering to the

American Counselling Association's moral code and targets. The American Counselling Association's main stipulation is that the counsellor should respect the secrecy of future and existing clients and bid the private data from those customers when it is only essential to the psychotherapy course (American Counselling Association B.1.b). In addition, the therapist is supposed to share confidential data with customers' understanding or lack of legal validation (American Counselling Association B.1.c).

      At the beginning and during the therapy process, therapists tell clients of the constraints of secrecy and check to recognize circumstances in which privacy must be broken. There are also exceptions where there should be a requirement to safeguard the customer from likely future damages that may necessitate information exposure. A therapist should consult with a therapist if they are unsure whether such exceptions are valid. For example, section B2 (b) states that if a client informs their therapist of suffering from a fatal disease that is lethal, the therapist is warranted in reporting the data only to the considerable partners. This must be completed if the therapist knows they are a potential threat of getting the disease.

There are also some professional capabilities for counsellors as stipulated by the ACA Code of Ethics. Therapists only function in the parts where they have skills explained by their training, practice, practical exercise, national and government professional credentials, and appropriate practical training. Counsellors learn information, self-understanding, sensitivity, and abilities relevant to being a cultural competency counsellor in dealing with a varied client group. In contrast, multicultural counselling competency is necessary across all counselling specializations (American Counselling Association C. 2. a). According to section C5, Counsellors should not tolerate or participate in discriminatory practices against potential or existing clients, employees, students, or researchers according to age, culture, religion, disability, gender, race, marital class, language partiality, socio-economic status, immigration class, or any other legally protected basis. In addition to this, Sexual assault is not permitted by counsellors. Sex assault takes the part of a lone, severe occurrence or a sequence of continuous acts (American Counselling Association C. 6. a).

Section D of the American Counselling Association explains how therapists should relate with employers, colleagues, and employees. Counsellors recognize the skills of other professional assemblies, and they work to create and reinforce interactions with associates from the other corrections to best work for clients. They need help to make agreements with bosses concerning satisfactory criteria of client caution and professional behaviour that enable changes in institutional strategy conducive to clients' progress and expansion. They warn their recruiters of poor policies and practices and try their best to bring changes to these policies through productive action in an institution, including transfer to suitable certification, approval and national licensing of organizations, or charitable cancellation of employment. Therapists are not supposed to insult an employee or colleague or discharge a worker that acted responsibly and adequately to reveal unsuitable employer strategies and practices.

The term project has been used by American Counselling Association several times to highlight how important it is for therapists to evade any damage to their customers. It has also been used to ensure that the Code of Ethics of ACA is appropriately interpreted well by the therapists, and they should execute their duty in the ethical and law.

One of the most significant legal issues in the future of counselling in the US is the issue of informed consent. Informed consent is the process by which a client is made aware of the potential risks and benefits of treatment before they agree to receive it (Miller,2019). In the past, this process was relatively informal, with the counsellor simply discussing the pros and cons of the treatment with the client. However, in the future, more formal processes and documentation will likely be required to ensure that the client is fully aware of a treatment's potential risks and benefits before they agree to receive it.

Another legal issue that is likely to arise in the future of counselling in the US is the issue of confidentiality. Confidentiality is a cornerstone of the counselling profession, and counsellors need to protect the confidentiality of their client's information. Currently, many states have laws to safeguard the confidentiality of counselling records. Still, as technology evolves and more data sharing becomes commonplace, these laws will likely need to be strengthened and refined to ensure that the client's confidentiality is maintained.

In addition, the legal issue of professional liability will likely become increasingly important in counselling in the US. Professional liability is the potential for a counsellor to be held financially responsible for any harm their client may suffer due to their counselling services (Miller,2019). Currently, most states have laws that protect counsellors from professional liability, but these laws may need to be strengthened to ensure that counsellors are adequately protected from potential legal claims.

In conclusion, Legal issues in counselling constantly evolve, and practitioners must stay informed on the latest developments and changes in the laws and regulations. Knowing the legal parameters of the profession is essential to providing ethical counselling services and can help protect both the counsellor and the client. It is necessary for practitioners to be aware of their moral and legal responsibilities and to take action to ensure their practice complies with the applicable laws.

References

American Counseling Association. (2014). American Counseling Association ethics. *Alexandria, VA: Author.*

Appelbaum, P. S. (1985). Tarasoff and the clinician: problems in fulfilling the duty to protect. *The American journal of psychiatry.*

Miller, P. (2019). Legal Issues in Counseling. American Counseling Association. Retrieved from https://www.counseling.org/knowledge-center/legal-issues-in-counseling

Chapter   27

The "angry black women" myth

The "Angry Black Women" myth is one of the most dominant beliefs in contemporary American society. This belief asserts that Black American women are angrier than European American females. Black women are believed to exhibit unjustified anger and irrationality whenever they directly express their rage to the individuals or circumstances that annoyed them. This paper aims to refute this myth because it is based on the negative images and attitude of subordination of African American women. Still, it is not based on empirical research.

The mythology of angry black women originated in the American culture back in the slavery era in the United States. It is mainly famous within pop culture and is currently spread through popular television shows, films, books, and sometimes in politics. The pop traditions associated the Black females' anger with personality instead of tracing it from the inciting situations. The myth perceived these women as hostile, illogical, aggressive, ill-tempered, and acting ignorant without provocation. The mental clinicians emphasized the myth and retained that they received more aggression cases among black females than white women to make matters worse.

Anger is a universal emotion that cuts across all ages, sexes, and ethnicities, and it is experienced throughout the entire human lifespan. Anger makes humans aggressive, thus seeking to cause pain or harm to other individuals. According to social psychology, two forms of aggression comprise instrumental and hostile attacks. Instrumental aggression aims to achieve a goal without necessarily having the intention to cause harm, while feelings of anger trigger hostile aggression to cause damage (Spielman et al., Page.453). The perspective of evolutionary psychology retains that human males are more likely to exhibit aggression than females. Women express their aggression and frustrations mainly through communication that undermines the social perspectives of others. It is, therefore, surprising to note how the myth of angry black women limits anger to females of one ethnic group.

The myth has created a negative stereotype against African Americans in America. Spielman et al. (Page.447) define a stereotype as an assumption made about a particular group of people, despite their characteristics. Such a belief is then generalized and used to describe all group members. Many Black American men use the stereotype to justify domestic violence in contemporary society. Many American women are thus suffering intimate partner violence due to this myth.

African American women become angry mainly due to external stressors like racism and the economic disadvantage they experience in biased American culture, not due to their personality, as the myth claims. The victims feel they are not treated with the respect they deserve (Wingfield, Page.203). They lament the insult and signs of disrespect they see from the Whites. For instance, Whites usually question black women's integrity, ethics, values, decisions, knowledge, and judgment. They suffer from distrust and use anger to show displeasure whenever they are mistreated to protect themselves from a sexist, classist, and racist society. However, this means they display more intense anger than White females.

In an empirical test to determine the myth's validity, a sample of young adult black American women was taken to examine the experience and the expression of anger among the stereotyped group. First, the respondents were asked to fill in questionnaires containing standard measures of anger. These forms comprised a fifty-seven-item scale with two primary scales of trait anger and a subscale that aimed to evaluate particular aspects of a given "state and trait anger and anger expression index containing anger expression and anger control scales" (Walley-Jeans, Page.78). The subscales assessing state anger measured the intensity of the annoying feelings and the degree to which current feelings are associated with physical or verbal expression of anger. On the other hand, the subscales measuring trait anger measured angry temperament and reaction; they examined how often angry emotions are experienced in a given time without a particular provocation and in circumstances that triggered frustrations.

The anger control scales were also used to measure how anger could be regulated by suppressing anger emotions by calming down when angered or avoiding the outward expression of anger towards annoying people, situations, or objects. It still measured how anger was felt, but it could not be expressed. In exploring how anger was experienced and expressed in the selected sample, the participants' scores were compared to the reference group. The reference group was the normative sample, comprising 977 women (Walley-Jeans, Page.77). Some normative sample members were healthcare professionals, managerial and clerical personnel, and students. The current sample had seventy-six Black American female university students recruited from institutions in the Southeastern United States. Participants ranged from eighteen to twenty-eight years.

The procedure for this study started with collecting data to investigate interpersonal aggression. Respondents were mainly students taking the introduction to psychology course. After getting permission from the tutors, researchers visited specific classes to mobilize the volunteers to participate in the study (Walley-Jeans, Page.78). A t-test was undertaken to distinguish between the current sample and the normative sample's mean to analyze the data collected.

The results of this study disagreed with the widespread myth of angry and aggressive Black American women. Surprisingly, African American females had reported experiencing less frequent angrier emotions when they were disrespected, criticized, and evaluated negatively. According to the study, women between 18 and 19 tended to suppress their feelings of anger instead of expressing them verbally or physically. African American women are likely to be suppressing their anger due to the low social class they occupy in American society (Walley-Jeans, Page.82). Although it was pleasing to note that African American women could experience anger and fail to express it, such unexpressed emotions could cause depression, psychosomatic conditions, and low self-esteem in the victims. The respondents between 20–and 29-year-old would quickly calm down upon getting angry. This stereotype causes Black American women to become non-threatening while socializing with various ethnic communities. Not only does the result of the study disconfirm the negative stereotype that these women experience higher frequencies of anger and more tendency to engage in physically and verbally aggressive behaviour as they mature, but it also shows that Black Americans are susceptible to their angry emotions and therefore improve in finding solutions to such emotional problems.

The stereotype of angry black women in the United States has several implications. Spielman et al. (Page.447) maintain, "As a result of holding negative beliefs and negative attitudes about a particular group, people tend to treat the target of prejudice poorly." The myth discourages the typical 'Black girl' behaviour, like assertiveness, as it is misinterpreted as aggressiveness, which could undermine the affected girls' academic potential. Additionally, considering that some mental health specialists believe in this stereotyping image of Black American women, their psychological health problems may be overlooked, thus being handled or treated poorly and with more contempt.

Besides, some domestic violence shelters deny housing facilities to Black American women victims claiming that the latter sound either too strong or fails to sound fearful enough. The shelter workers decide that the people receive mental health and safety support concerning the stereotype. This study projects that the belief that African American women are just aggressive by nature will continue jeopardizing the lives of black women in the future if the myth is not eradicated. Many black women will be held accountable for their problems and perceived as less needy. They will be less considered for critical interventions, leaving them at an increased risk of further assault (Walley-Jeans, Page.83). Generally, the predominant misguided misperception of the angry, aggressive black American women has adverse implications on this population.

In conclusion, the current research gives scientific support to refute the myth that black American women are angrier and expresses anger more uncontrollably than female Whites. This erroneous and problematic label significantly undermines black females' interpersonal and social interactions. It also prevents them from benefiting from essential resources inappropriate ways. All Americans are responsible for evaluating all their beliefs to determine whether they can be proven scientifically or are just traditional biased claims aimed at intimidating a specific individual or a group of people. Furthermore, society should be aware that the emotion of anger is universal and is not limited to gender or ethnicity. Therefore, a consistent investigation of the experience of anger among African American women is essential to help society treat every human equally and empathetically

Reference

ROSE M et al. *Psychology 2e* (2015) https://openstax.org/books/psychology-2e/pages/1-1-what-is-psychology

Walley-Jean, J. Celeste. "Debunking the myth of the "angry Black woman": An exploration of anger in young African American women." *Black Women, Gender & Families* 3.2 (2009): 68-86.

Wingfield, Adia Harvey. "The modern mammy and the angry Black man: African American professionals' experiences with gendered racism in the workplace." *Race, Gender & Class* (2007): 196-212.

Chapter 28

Observation and Planned Experience Child Portfolio

The children were in the science laboratory, experimenting with handling and treating a baby patient from the observation. Their caregiver's name is Rosemary, and the name of the three children is Dulce, Aubra, and Maricella; the latter will be the child of my focus. Before coming for a group experiment, the children had come from a 10.00 tea break, where they had taken tea and some snacks.

Maricella measured the quantity of medicine to give the sick baby(toy). Then, she sucks the drug into the syringe and injects the patient. She also provides the patient with some chocolate and wipes the spilt medicine on the patient's face. After opening the first aid kit, she takes a container with some liquid mixture and puts it into another syringe, ready to inject the baby again. On the other hand, Dulce holds the baby carefully as Maricella measures its temperature. Aubra, though a passive learner, is very attentive and keeps cracking a jock that she wants to give the patient some cheese. However, Rosemary puts up with her and tries to create a good relationship with all the kids, irrespective of their personalities and behaviour. She believes that her attachment to them will influence their future learning and development, as Bowlby argued in the attachment theory (Bowlby& Ainsworth,2013).

The observation showed that although the caregiver, Rosemary, is very social with the children, she does not do all the tasks for the children while in the experiment. Instead, she applies the learner-centred approach, where the kids do the lab activities themselves. If the children encounter difficulties while undertaking the task, Rosemary helps to understand the procedure. She always regards the early-year Australian learning framework that requires all children's learning experiences to develop the aspects of being, becoming, and belonging to build their future academic success (Cheeseman et al.,2014).

The learners-centred instruction method applied by Rosemary is meant to instil courage among the learners, as they are politely corrected whenever they make mistakes. Also, an experiment in a group enables children to learn from each other, as Bandura attests in his social learning theory, which states that new behaviour can be attained through observation and imitation (Nabavi,2012).

To promote the children's learning, I would give the bright learners slightly more advanced tasks like Mericella to sharpen their creativity and retain her active throughout the group work session. I also ensure passive learners like Aubra participate in the experiment activities to attain the intended learning outcome at the end of the lesson. I also encourage learners to feel free even after making mistakes to ensure their self-esteem is always high and that none of them feels downcast, shy, or annoyed upon making mistakes. Lastly, I would reward all the learners who perform best in the experiment and those who exhibit outstanding improvement in the learning activities (Goldstein et al., .2016).

The experiment's learning focus was to help Mericella actively carry out the medical investigation with her fellow friends to boost her practical capabilities and social skills. From the observation, Miricella is a very determined and active 4-year girl who is always quiet in a formal classroom set-up. On the other hand, although she keeps saying she wants to become a physician when she grows up, Marcella is timid, affecting her relationship with her classmates. Therefore, the teacher prefers having Mericella do most of her experiments in threes to boost her social relations with her colleagues.

Even though the experiment experience is physically active, it is also socially interactive. The activity entails children acting in the roles of doctors in a social set-up. In this experiment, the caregiver is part of the activity, as she not only directs the kids on how to undertake the training but also does some of their tasks. The caregiver's engagement in the experiment motivates the children, and Mericella, who undertakes most of the group work.

I plan for this experiment to ensure learners can interrelate what they learn in class with real-life situations. For instance, as observed, having discussed with the kids in the class about physicians' roles in providing health care, it was necessary to take the kids to the lab to see the tools and equipment doctors use to treat them. I will also apply the group experiment approach to learning in cases where some learners are introverts to develop the habit of sharing ideas with others. A good example is Mericella, who takes all her time doing her class activities without socialising with others. However, her interaction skill has improved since Rosemary persuaded her to work in groups.

Considering that my children's learning activities will comprise a basic medical experiment, I will use a baby toy that acts as the sick baby, measuring tape, thermometers, syringes, and tissue paper to wipe the spilt chemicals. I will also require a first aid kit containing triangular bandages, disposable sterile gloves, safety pins, scissors, and various syllabi and painkiller tablets. Besides, a long table will be necessary to place the patient (toy)while receiving the treatment and give the kids somewhere to put their tools (Duban,2019).

I take several precautions to ensure that the experiment meets health and safety requirements. First, I will list potentially dangerous chemicals and undertake regular stock checks. Second, I will maintain high-security standards by immediately securing hazardous chemicals and reporting any missing chemicals. Third, I will ensure that all my learners put on shoes with a good grip while entering the laboratory to ensure that none of them slide and fall. Finally, I will ensure that safety clothing and equipment are appropriately used where necessary.

Additionally, I shall ensure that the first aid kit is available for my learners' safety and contains all necessary tools and medicine, like bandages and eyewash facilities. Furthermore, my laboratory will be adequately cleaned, and I will always provide adequate warm water, soap, and towels. Lastly, I will ensure that all chemical spills are wiped immediately, all equipment is stored after use, and wastes are correctly disposed of (Duban,2019).

The best time for a medical experiment is after the 10.30 tea break. The kids feel energetic and motivated to participate in various learning activities after taking some snacks and tea. This experiment is best carried out in the laboratory, where different types of equipment are required during the exercises. The security of the children from the rain and hot weather is ensured. As a caregiver, I should ensure that each learning group comprises at least three kids of different sexes. The children should have varying learning abilities to enable slow learners to benefit from their bright group members.

I will use various teaching techniques to sustain the scaffolded learning of my children. Where the children need help remembering what they learned previously, I will provide them with hints that could be pictures, gestures, and verbal to help them complete the assignment. I will also offer the kids straining to undertake the task several suggestions to connect what they already know with what they are trying to learn. I will avail all the appropriate learning resources to the kids. For example, if my learners cannot draw cats' pictures, I can ask them whether they can find cats in other places, like toys or drawings that their fellow first learners have drawn.

Besides, I will use models and demonstrations to boost my children's learning. This will include directing the kids on how to solve problems through demonstrating or modelling. Using models in teaching will enable them to develop crucial social skills such as sharing and expressing their ideas. Again, I will provide the kids with adequate support and feedback. I shall positively react to wrong and correct answers because such actions will encourage participation. I shall praise the best performers and all the kids who attempt the tasks (Goldstein et al., .2016).

Additionally, I will pose open-ended questions to the children to enable them to apply their imagination skills. An example of such a question is: "Do you have any other idea…?" Furthermore, I shall break the learning activities into small steps to help the stuck learners. Lastly, I will divide the children into groups of different sexes and with learners of all academic abilities to learn from each other.

To follow this experience, I will apply diverse teaching strategies to continue supporting the kids. For instance, I will develop literacy skills among the children using language-rich activities such as reading a book loudly to the learners every day to improve their reading compression. I will also incorporate tasks that teach basic mathematics concepts, like counting physical objects such as coloured fruits or tiles, to relate them to written numbers. Lastly, I will introduce creative and art activities that comprise singing, drawing, and movements to enable the children to express emotions and articulate other movement experiences to abide by the psychomotor domain of learning (Sönmez,2017).

As a future caregiver of pre-schoolers, I have benefited a lot from this experience. I have learned to create a strong relationship with my learners by empathising with them and applying teaching approaches catering to their academic needs. In addition, through this experience, I have also understood the significance and application of Bowlby's Attachment theory, which maintains that early children's relationships with their caregivers are critical in their development and continue affecting their social relationships even in the later stages of life (Van Rosmalen,2016).

Reference

Bowlby, J., & Ainsworth, M. (2013). The origins of attachment theory. *Attachment theory: Social, developmental, and clinical perspectives*; 45.

Cheeseman, S., Sumsion, J., & Press, F. (2014). Infants of the knowledge economy: the ambition of the Australian Government's Early Years Learning Framework. *Pedagogy, Culture & Society*, 22(3), 405-424.

Duban, N., Aydogdu, B., & Yüksel, A. (2019). Classroom Teachers' Opinions on Science Laboratory Practices. *Universal Journal of Educational Research*, 7(3), 772-780.

Goldstein, H., Kelley, E., Greenwood, C., McCune, L., Carta, J., Atwater, J., ... & Spencer, T. (2016). Embedded instruction improves vocabulary learning during automated storybook reading among high-risk preschoolers. *Journal of Speech, Language, and Hearing Research*, 59(3), 484-500.

Nabavi, R. T. (2012). Bandura's social learning theory & social cognitive learning theory. *The idea of Developmental Psychology*, 1-24.

Sönmez, V. (2017). Association of Cognitive, Affective, Psychomotor, and Intuitive Domains in Education, Sönmez Model. *Universal Journal of Educational Research*, 5(3), 347-356.

Van Rosmalen, L., Van Der Horst, F. C., & Van der Veer, R. (2016). From secure dependency to attachment: Mary Ainsworth integrates Blatz's security theory into Bowlby's attachment theory— *history of Psychology*, 19(1), 22.

Chapter   29

Psychology Of Motivation and Emotion

The psychology of motivation and emotion is a field of psychology that studies the behaviour and mental processes associated with motivation and emotion. Motivation refers to the desire or willingness to engage in an activity, while sentiment refers to the mental state or feeling associated with an experience. This field of psychology examines how these two concepts interact and influence each other and the various factors that affect them. This essay will discuss the psychological aspects of motivation and emotion, focusing on the theories and research conducted in this area.

Intrinsic and extrinsic motivation are two different types of motivation. Intrinsic motivation is an internal drive to achieve something, while extrinsic motivation is an external reward or punishment that drives an individual to act. According to Deci & Ryan (2000), intrinsic motivation is often considered the most effective form. It comes from within and is more likely to be sustained over an extended period. Intrinsic motivation is often driven by personal interests and goals and is, therefore, more likely to be sustained over a more extended period. It can be seen as a form of self-motivation, as the individual is driven to act by their internal motivators, such as a desire to learn a new skill or to improve at a task. Intrinsic motivation is often seen as more powerful than extrinsic motivation, as it positively affects an individual's performance and well-being.

On the other hand, extrinsic motivation is driven by external rewards and punishments. This can include prizes such as money, praise, or recognition and disciplines such as failure or criticism. Extrinsic motivation is often less effective than intrinsic motivation, as it is more likely to be short-lived and can lead to a lack of intrinsic motivation (Reeve,2018). Nevertheless, intrinsic and extrinsic motivation is essential in achieving desired goals and outcomes. Intrinsic motivation is often seen as the more effective form of motivation. It is driven by the individual's interests and objectives and is more likely to be sustained over a more extended period. However, extrinsic motivation can also help achieve goals and be used in conjunction with intrinsic motivation to achieve desired outcomes. To understand how motivation works, it is essential to understand the different theories of motivation. The first theory of motivation is Maslow's Hierarchy of Needs. This theory suggests that humans are motivated by a hierarchy of needs. Physiological needs such as food, water, and shelter are at the base of the order. As these needs are met, humans move up the hierarchy to safety needs, then social needs, esteem needs, and finally, self-actualisation needs. Maslow argued that higher-level needs could only be met if the lower-level requirements had been completed first.

The second theory of motivation is the Expectancy Theory. This theory suggests that an individual's explanation is based on their belief that their effort will result in a desired outcome. Individuals are more likely to be motivated if they believe their endeavours will produce a desired reward. As such, this theory suggests that individuals will be more motivated if offered tips or incentives for completing tasks. The third theory of motivation is the Goal-Setting Theory. This theory suggests that individuals are likelier to be motivated by a clear goal. This theory acknowledges that plans help individuals focus their efforts and create a sense of direction (Deci & Ryan,2000). Goals also help individuals measure their progress and success.

 The fourth theory of motivation is the Theory of Self-Determination. This theory suggests that individuals are more likely to be motivated if they have a sense of autonomy and control (Ryan & Deci, 2000). In addition, this theory suggests that individuals need to feel a sense of ownership and a sense of purpose to be motivated. The fifth theory of motivation is the Cognitive Evaluation Theory. This theory suggests that individuals are more likely to be motivated if they receive positive reinforcement for their efforts. This theory suggests that positive feedback helps individuals feel validated and encourages them to continue their efforts.

Notably, Emotions are an essential part of the human experience, and for centuries, scientists and psychologists have attempted to identify how we experience and express emotions. Consequently, scholars have devised several theories of emotions. For instance, the James-Lange theory of emotion, proposed by psychologist William James in 1884, states that emotional experiences result from physiological reactions in the body (Reeve,2018). According to James, when we experience something, our body responds with physiological arousals, such as increased heart rate and perspiration. The brain interprets this arousal as an emotional response, such as fear or anger. For example, if a person sees a bear in the woods, their body will respond with increased heart rate and perspiration, and the brain will interpret this as fear.

The Cannon-Bard theory of emotion, proposed by Walter Cannon and Philip Bard in 1929, states that emotional experiences and physiological reactions coincide. According to the Cannon-Bard theory, dynamic response and physiological arousal coincide when we experience something. For example, when a person sees a bear in the woods, they will simultaneously experience fear and increased heart rate and perspiration. The Schachter-Singer theory of emotion, proposed by Stanley Schachter and Jerome Singer in 1962, states that emotional experiences result from a cognitive appraisal. According to Schachter and Singer, when we experience something, we interpret the situation and assign an emotional response to it. For example, if a person sees a bear in the woods, they may analyse the situation as dangerous and post a reply of fear to it.

 Finally, the Lazarus Theory of Emotion, proposed by psychologist Richard Lazarus in 1984, states that emotional experiences are composed of cognitive appraisal and physiological arousal. According to Lazarus, when we experience something, we interpret the situation, assign an emotional response to it, and experience physiological arousal. For example, suppose a person sees a bear in the woods. In that case, they may interpret the situation as dangerous and assign a response of fear to it, while also experiencing an increase in heart rate and perspiration.

The connection between motivation and emotions is strong and multifaceted. Motivation is the driving force that encourages us to pursue our goals and aspirations. It is a powerful force essential for success and can be influenced by various factors such as our environment, experiences, beliefs, and emotions. On the other hand, emotions are the mental states and feelings we experience in response to certain stimuli. They are essential for our survival and well-being and can be either positive or negative. Motivation is directly affected by our emotions. Positive emotions, such as happiness, joy, and excitement, increase our motivation to pursue our goals. We are likelier to take risks and invest our effort in tasks when we feel positive emotions. Conversely, negative emotions, such as anger, fear, and sadness, can lead to demotivation, making us feel helpless and unable to take action. Our emotions, in turn, are heavily influenced by our level of motivation. When motivated to pursue a goal, we experience a range of positive emotions, such as anticipation, excitement, and enthusiasm. On the other hand, when we lack motivation, we tend to experience negative emotions, such as sadness, disappointment, and frustration.

Ultimately, the connection between motivation and emotions is reciprocal. Our feelings can influence our level of inspiration, and our group of reason can control our feelings. Recognising this connection and using it to our advantage is essential. We can use our emotions to motivate ourselves and to stay focused on our goals and aspirations. Conversely, we can use our motivation to manage our feelings and stay optimistic.

In conclusion, the psychology of motivation and emotion is a field of psychology that studies the behaviour and mental processes associated with motivation and emotion. This essay has discussed the various theories and research relating to motivation and emotion and how the two concepts influence each other. It is clear that reason and emotion are closely related and that understanding these concepts can help us to understand better and predict human behaviour.

References

Deci, E. L., & Ryan, R. M. (2000). The "what" and "why" of goal pursuits: Human needs and the self-determination of behaviour. Psychological Inquiry, 11(4), 227-268.

Reeve, J. (2018). *Understanding motivation and emotion*. John Wiley & Sons.

Ryan, R. M., & Deci, E. L. (2000). Self-determination theory and the facilitation of intrinsic motivation, social development, and well-being. American Psychologist, 55(1), 68-78.

Chapter   30

Psychology of Suicide

The psychology of suicide is studied because individuals choose to end their lives. It examines the psychological factors contributing to suicidal behaviour, including depression, hopelessness, impulsivity, and stress. It also looks at the psychological impact of suicide on family members and society. This paper discusses the causes of suicide, its consequences, and how to prevent suicide cases in the organisation.

When stress becomes overwhelming, it can lead to feelings of hopelessness and despair. These feelings can be so intense that the person feels that suicide is the only way to escape the pain. People experiencing stress often feel like they don't have anyone to talk to or that no one will understand what they're going through (Anestis,2018). This can lead to feelings of isolation and hopelessness. When these feelings become too intense, the person may see suicide as an avenue of escape.

In addition to the mental and emotional strain caused by stress, it can also have a physical effect. People who are under a lot of stress may find it difficult to sleep, or they may become ill more often. This can lead to a feeling of exhaustion and despair, which can, in turn, lead to a desire to end it all. Finally, stress can lead to feelings of worthlessness and self-loathing. People who feel like they are not good enough or a burden to society may see suicide as a way to end their suffering.

In its most severe form, depression can lead to thoughts of suicide. When a person suffers from depression, they may feel overwhelmed by their emotions and unable to cope with the feelings they are experiencing. They may feel they are a burden to those around them or have nothing left to live for. As the depression continues, the person may become isolated, withdrawn, and unable to see hope for the future. This can lead to thoughts of suicide as a way to escape the pain and suffering and end the cycle of despair.

Depression can also lead to suicide by causing changes in a person's physical and mental health. For example, people who are depressed may have difficulty sleeping, become easily fatigued, and experience changes in appetite (Oquendo & Mann,2012). They may also experience changes in their thinking and behaviour, such as difficulty concentrating, making decisions and a lack of interest in activities that once provided joy. These changes can cause a person to feel that life is no longer worth living and that suicide is the only way to end their suffering.

In addition to changes in physical and mental health, depression can lead to suicide by causing a person to feel hopeless and helpless. Those who are suffering from depression may feel as though their situation is beyond repair and that there is no other way out. They may also feel they have no control over their lives and that they can do nothing to improve their situation. This sense of hopelessness and helplessness can lead to thoughts of suicide as a way to regain control and end their suffering.

It is worth noting that impulsivity is a trait that affects many individuals and can lead to various adverse outcomes, including suicide. O'Connor (2008) claims that impulsivity describes an individual's tendency to act without thinking of the potential consequences of their actions. More impulsive individuals may be more likely to act on suicidal thoughts without considering the consequences of their actions. Impulsivity can be a significant contributing factor to suicidal thoughts and behaviours. More impulsive individuals may often have difficulty controlling their emotions, including those associated with suicidal ideation. Impulsive individuals may also be less likely to consider their actions' long-term consequences or seek help for their mental health issues. As a result, they may be more likely to act on their suicidal thoughts without considering the consequences of their actions. Impulsive individuals may also be more likely to engage in risky behaviours that may increase their risk of suicide. For example, they may be more likely to use drugs and alcohol, which can increase their risk of suicide by impairing their judgment and making them more likely to act on suicidal thoughts.

 Impulsive individuals may also be more likely to engage in self-harm, such as cutting or burning, which can increase their risk of suicide by providing an avenue for acting on suicidal thoughts. Impulsive individuals may also be more likely to experience extreme emotional states, such as depression or anxiety, which can increase their risk of suicide. This is because powerful emotional states can lead to impaired judgment and an increased likelihood of acting on suicidal thoughts.

Suicide has a devastating and lasting effect on family members. When a family member commits suicide, it often leaves survivors with a range of emotions, including guilt, anger, shock, and sadness. Responsibility is often the most difficult emotion to cope with, as survivors may feel they could have done something to prevent death. They may also think they are to blame for the dying, despite knowing it was their loved one's choice. This guilt may lead to helplessness and confusion, as survivors may not understand why the death occurred or why their loved one did not seek help.

 Anger is another typical response to a loved one's suicide. Survivors may feel angry that the death occurred and that it was out of their control. They may also feel mad at the deceased for not seeking help or taking such a drastic step. Shock is also a typical response, as the sudden death often leaves family members stunned. The sadness that accompanies a family member's suicide can be profound. Survivors may feel overwhelmed by the sorrow and unable to process the death. This can lead to isolation, as the survivors may feel that no one else can understand their pain.

The economic costs of suicide can be significant. Suicide is estimated to cost the U.S. $52 billion yearly in direct medical expenses, lost productivity, and quality of life (Nock & Borges,2008). This cost can be exceptionally high in rural areas, where the lack of resources and social support can make it difficult to access mental health services. The social costs of suicide can be even more devastating. Suicides can lead to an increased stigma around mental illness, making it more difficult for individuals to access mental health care. It can also lead to an increase in fear and mistrust in communities, as well as an increase in risky behaviours such as substance abuse. Additionally, it can lead to a decrease in the sense of community and an increase in feelings of isolation.

There are several ways to prevent suicide and help those struggling with suicidal thoughts. The first step in preventing suicide is to recognise the warning signs. These warning signs may include talking about feeling hopeless, withdrawing from activities and social situations, displaying a sudden change in mood or behaviour, exhibiting reckless conduct, or talking about suicide or death. If someone is showing any of these warning signs, taking them seriously and supporting them is essential.

Another way to prevent suicide is to talk openly and honestly about it. The stigma surrounding suicide can make it difficult to talk about, but being open and honest about it is essential. Discussing mental health issues and suicide openly can help create a safe and supportive environment for struggling (Aseltine &

Gore,2010). It is also essential to provide resources to those struggling with suicidal thoughts. This can include providing access to mental health services, such as therapy or counselling, and support from friends and family. Additionally, many crisis hotlines are available for those who require immediate help. Finally, it is essential to be supportive of those who are struggling with suicidal thoughts. This can include providing emotional support, listening without judgment, and offering hope for the future. Additionally, it is crucial to ensure that those struggling with suicidal thoughts have access to the resources and support they need to get through their current struggles.

In conclusion, the psychology of suicide is a complex and multifaceted subject. It is a difficult topic to understand and a challenging experience to process. Suicide is a complex and often tragic experience. Still, it is essential to recognise that the individual considering suicide is likely in great pain and distress. Therefore, it is necessary to provide support, resources, and understanding to those in crisis and those who have lost a loved one to suicide. With proper support and understanding, those considering suicide can find hope and healing.

429

References

Anestis, M. D. (2018). A contemporary conceptualisation of suicide and suicidal behaviour. Annual Review of Clinical Psychology, 14, 447-473.

Aseltine, R. H., & Gore, S. (2010). An ecological model of suicide risk. Clinical Psychology Review, 30(4), 304-315.

Nock, M. K., & Borges, G. (2008). Suicide and suicidal behaviour. Epidemiologic reviews, 30(1), 133-154.

O'Connor, R. C. (2008). Theories of suicide: A systematic review. Suicide and Life-Threatening Behavior, 38(3), 241-262

Oquendo, M. A., & Mann, J. J. (2012). The neurobiology of suicide. Nature Reviews Neuroscience, 13(9), 663-672.

Chapter   31
Sleep Insomnia

Sometimes, we sacrifice our time for sleep working, claiming that we can survive without sleeping, provided that we generate lots of money to meet our basic needs and luxuries. However, we must realise that sleep is crucial to our health and equally necessary to a healthy diet and physical exercise. However, whatever our reason for lack of sleep, insomnia has adverse physical and mental implications. In this paper, I will discuss the different types of insomnia, the symptoms, diagnoses, causes, preventions, treatment, and the impacts of insomnia on the lives of the victims.

Insomnia is a sleep disorder that makes a person have difficulties falling or remaining asleep. The illness can be short-lived or a long-term problem. Acute insomnia takes one day to a few weeks, while chronic insomnia occurs when the condition consistently lasts more than three nights in three months. The two major types of insomnia comprise primary and secondary disorders. Primary insomnia is when the individual's health problems do not cause sleep problems. In contrast, secondary insomnia is a state in which the sleep challenge is triggered by health conditions such as pain and discomfort at night (Ratini& Melinda,2020)

Individuals experiencing insomnia are likely to depict various signs and symptoms. The victims cannot fall asleep during the night or keep waking up after sleeping. They wake up very early before dawn, having not rested during the night sleep, and usually undergo daytime sleepiness and fatigue. They also suffer from irritability, anxiety, and depression, which make it difficult to pay attention and focus on critical tasks or to remember. Sometimes, the insomnia patient needs clarification due to worries about sleep and often makes careless mistakes.

The medical practitioner may also evaluate the person's medical history and sleeping history to diagnose insomnia disorder. They may advise the victim to keep a sleep record for about two weeks to assess sleeping patterns and how the victims feel during the day. At times, the doctors may intend to discuss the quality of their sleep with the patient's bed partners. If the causes of insomnia are unclear or the insomnia patients show signs of other sleep disorders,the victims may be advised to spend at least one night in the sleep centres. Tests are then carried out to monitor and determine various body activities while sleeping, such as heartbeats, breathing, body movements, eye movements, and brain waves (Brown et al. .1336)

There are several causes of insomnia. Stress associated with health, school, work, finances, and marital affairs can keep our minds active throughout the night, resulting in difficulty falling asleep. Traumatizing life situations like illness or the death of loved ones, separation, divorce, and loss of jobs can also result in insomnia.

Long-distance travelling and an altered work schedule can result in insomnia disorder. This is because our circadian rhythms are the internal clock, controlling the sleep-wake cycle, body temperature, and metabolism. Therefore, interrupting our circadian body rhythms can lead to sleep issues. In this case, insomnia is caused by jet lag associated with travelling across different time zones and frequent changes in work shifts.

Poor sleeping habits such as inconsistent bedtime schedules, naps, uncomfortable sleeping environments, or using our beds for working, watching television and eating can cause insomnia. In addition, using computers, smartphones, video games, TV and other screens immediately before bedtime can disrupt our sleep cycle.

Eating many heavy food and beverages in the evening poses sleep challenges. Therefore, we are advised to take light meals before bedtime because consuming too much food results in physical irritation while sleeping. Also, most people undergo heartburn, and backflow of food and acid from the stomach into the gullet after eating, thus remaining awake while in bed at night.

Additionally, medications and medical conditions escalate the chances of suffering from insomnia. Several prescribed drugs, such as antidepressants and medicines for blood pressure and asthma, interfere with sleep. Again, over-the-counter pills like painkillers, cold medications, and weight loss substances contain stimulants, such as caffeine, that cause sleeping difficulties. Some of the medical conditions that can trigger insomnia are heart disease, chronic pain, asthma, cancer, diabetes, Alzheimer's disease, gastroesophageal illness, and sleep-related disorders like apnoea (Ratini, Melinda,2020)

There are diverse lifestyle habits that can be practised regularly to prevent insomnia. People should consistently maintain their sleeping and waking time every day, whether on a weekday or weekend. They should also get involved in regular activities like physical work and exercises to promote quality night sleep. Whenever individuals are not active during the day, they should avoid naps but reduce the amount of caffeine and alcohol and reject the idea of consuming nicotine because it negatively affects sleep. If the patients have been prescribed medication, they are responsible for examining whether the drugs can result in insomnia.

Again, people should avoid taking heavy meals and excess beverages before sleeping.

Instead, they can embrace eating light, easily digested meals before bedtime. Regular bathing and listening to soft music can also promote quality sleep. However, individuals should avoid daily activities in their bedrooms, like reading and watching movies. The bedrooms should only be dedicated to sleep and sex among married couples.

Even though embracing good habits like stress management, physical exercises, and appropriate medication can restore quality sleep and control insomnia, the approach does not always work for all people with insomnia. Therefore, medical treatment is necessary to heal the disorder. The doctor can recommend sleeping pills to enable the victim to fall and stay asleep. However, doctors do not advise people to rely on sleeping drugs for long due to their adverse side effects. Instead, they recommend applying diverse approved medication types to address insomnia disorder (Brower& Kirk,419).

Medical practitioners may also recommend cognitive behavioural therapy for people living with insomnia. Counselling is meant to eradicate negative thoughts or actions that awake people during bedtime. In addition, the approach helps people change beliefs that deter them from sleeping. The therapy is preferred in the first stages of insomnia treatment.

Over-the-counter sleep aids are also crucial in the treatment of insomnia. For instance, non-prescription sleep drugs contain antihistamines, making people tired, though they are not for regular use. However, insomnia patients should consult their doctors before taking antihistamine pills because they may cause several adverse side effects like confusion, dizziness, daytime sleepiness, a decline in cognitive ability and difficulty urinating, more so among the aged.

Although every person is easily predisposed to insomnia disorders, a specific group of individuals are at high risk of experiencing the condition. For instance, during the menstrual cycle and menopause, women experience hormonal shifts that cause hot flashes and night sweats, interrupting sleep. In addition, pregnancy is another critical factor that puts women at a higher risk of getting insomnia.

Again, the risk of getting insomnia increases with age. As one approaches 60 years, the sleep pattern changes. Noise and other environmental distractors quickly awaken the person. Also, as age progresses, the internal clock system advances, making the aged experience fatigue in the evening and wake up very early in the morning. The change in daily activities as someone ages predisposes them to a high risk of insomnia. This is because older adults are rarely active, both socially and physically. They take a daily nap during the day, interfering with sleep at night (Hirshkowitz et al., .41).

Additionally, as people grow old, their health changes. They experience persistent pain like arthritis, back problems, and distress, interfering with their sleep. They also undergo health complications like bladder problems that make them keep urinating at night, thus interrupting their sleep. In addition, older people desperately partake in medication more than youths, which increases the probability of insomnia due to drugs. Though in rare cases, sleep problems may be an issue for teenagers and children. Nonetheless, some teenagers and children undergo challenges in having regular bedtime due to their delayed internal clocks. They prefer sleeping late at night and waking up late in the morning.

There are various implications of insomnia. People who have insomnia perform very poorly at school and work. They have slowed reactions while operating dangerous machines or driving and are likely to cause fatal accidents. Insomnia can also lead to anxiety and drug and substance abuse among the youth. Consequently, the disorder increases the severity and risks of other chronic illnesses or conditions like heart disease and hypertension.

The recent and most reliable statistics on insomnia reveal that about 25 per cent of Americans experience insomnia yearly. Out of the 30% of American adults with insomnia, more than 10% have chronic insomnia. Research has depicted that 83% of the individuals that suffer from anxiety and depression also show symptoms of insomnia and that three-thirds of all women experience sleep problems during pregnancy. Additionally, more than 27% of the most hardworking American women experience insomnia disorders, compared to only 20% of hardworking men. Sadly, research has shown that insomnia is a vital factor in deaths caused by motor vehicle accidents in America and beyond the continent (Insomnia. *Mayo Clinic, 2016)*.

In conclusion, quality sleep is critical for our health, as it controls other physical and mental health complications associated with insomnia. Therefore, there is a need to embrace good lifestyle habits that can help prevent insomnia disorder. Again, older people should be taken care of, as they are highly predisposed to deaths associated with insomnia than the youths. Suppose individuals realize that they experience symptoms linked to insomnia. In that case, they should seek medical checkups and treatment on time before the condition becomes a chronic problem, resulting in various negative implications on the victims' lives.

Reference

Brower, Kirk J. "Assessment and treatment of insomnia in adult patients with alcohol use disorders." *Alcohol* 49.4 (2015): 417-427.

Brown, Kelly M., and Beth A. Malow. "Pediatric insomnia." *Chest* 149.5 (2016): 1332-1339.

Hirshkowitz, Max, et al. "National Sleep Foundation's sleep time duration recommendations: methodology and results summary." *Sleep Health* 1.1 (2015): 40-43.

Insomnia. *Mayo Clinic*, Mayo Foundation for Medical Education and Research, 15 Oct. 2016,

Ratini, Melinda. "Insomnia: Definition, Symptoms, Causes, Diagnosis, and Treatment." *WebMD*, WebMD, 4 Jan. 2020,

Chapter   32

The Roles Of Technology In Human Development

The role of technology in human development is undeniable. In the modern world, technology has become an integral part of our lives, from communication and transportation to medicine and education. Technology has transformed the way we interact with each other, the way we work and the way we access information. It has also enormously impacted human development, from improving the quality of life and increasing access to resources and services to advancing our knowledge and understanding of the world. Technology has enabled us to create a more sustainable and equitable future for all and to better prepare for the challenges of the future. This paper will discuss the roles of technology in human development.

Technology has made vast strides in improving health and well-being in recent years, and its potential to do so is seemingly unlimited. For example, medical professionals can use technology to diagnose and treat ailments more efficiently and accurately. In addition, technology has enabled individuals to monitor their health and well-being better, providing them with the means to take control of their health.

One of the most notable ways technology has improved health and well-being is by developing electronic health records (EHRs). EHRs allow medical providers to quickly and easily access patient data, enabling them to make more informed decisions about diagnosis and treatment (Krogstie & Janssen,2006). EHRs also provide a centralised patient medical history record, making tracking and managing chronic conditions easier. Furthermore, EHRs allow for better provider communication, leading to better care coordination.

In addition to improving the effectiveness of medical care, technology has positively impacted patients' quality of life. Wearable technology, such as fitness trackers, has enabled individuals to monitor and manage their health, allowing them to make informed decisions about their well-being (Rajan, L., & Kurian,2016). Smartphones, tablets, and other devices have allowed individuals to access health information and resources from virtually anywhere, making it easier to stay informed and take action when needed. Finally, technology has also improved mental health and well-being. Apps and websites have enabled individuals to connect with others in similar situations, providing them with a source of support. Additionally, artificial intelligence (AI) has allowed medical providers to identify better and treat mental health issues, providing more effective treatment options for patients.

In today's world, technology has become an integral part of education and learning. Technology has changed the way students learn and how educators teach. Technology is everywhere in the education system, from online classes to online resources. Technology has enabled students to learn more effectively and efficiently while giving educators the tools to deliver effective instruction.

Technology has had a positive impact on learning in many ways. One of the most notable is the ability to access information quickly and easily. With the rise of the internet, students can access a wealth of knowledge and resources at their fingertips. This has opened up a whole new world of educational opportunities for students, allowing them to explore new topics and expand their knowledge. Additionally, students can use technology to collaborate with others and access resources worldwide. From online discussion boards to video conferencing, technology has made it easier for students to engage in meaningful conversations and share ideas.

Technology also allows educators to deliver more effective instruction. Teachers can use technology to create engaging and interactive lessons for their students. Technology can help teachers create an immersive learning experience for students, from videos and podcasts to interactive whiteboards. Additionally, technology can be used to track student progress and provide feedback (Lazear,2015). This helps educators personalised instruction and ensure that students learn the material effectively. In addition, technology has enabled students to take a more active role in their learning. With the rise of online learning, students can learn at their own pace and on their own time. This allows students to pursue their passions and explore topics of interest. Additionally, technology has made it easier for students to stay organised and manage their time effectively.

 In today's world, technology has become an integral part of our lives. It has revolutionised how we communicate with one another in ways that were unimaginable even a few decades ago. Technology has made it easier to stay in touch and keep up with family, friends, and colleagues no matter where they are. One of the most notable ways technology has facilitated communication is through the rise of social media and messaging apps. These platforms allow people to stay connected with their loved ones and even reconnect with people from their past. For example, many people use Facebook and Instagram to stay updated with their friends and

family lives. Social media has also allowed us to stay connected with people from different cultures and backgrounds, giving us a better understanding of different lifestyles and beliefs.
 Another excellent example of technology facilitating communication is the widespread use of video conferencing. This type of technology has made it easier for people to stay in touch with their loved ones living farther away. Video conferencing allows people to have face-to-face conversations regardless of their location. This technology has also enabled businesses to hold meetings with colleagues and customers worldwide without having to travel.

Technology has also made it easier to share information quickly and efficiently. For example, email has become one of the most popular ways to send messages and documents. Not only is email an efficient way to communicate, but it is also a great way to store important information for future reference. Additionally, the rise of cloud computing has made it possible for people to store and share data with others regardless of their location.

Technology has revolutionised the way we communicate and connect. Technology has drastically changed how we communicate and stay linked, from a simple text message to a video call. One of the most popular ways to communicate is through social media platforms like Facebook, Instagram, Twitter, and Snapchat. Social media has made it easier for people to stay connected with friends and family. People can share pictures, videos, and stories about their lives through social media. This allows people to instantly connect with those they may not have had the chance to.

Another way technology has improved communication is through video calls. With the help of apps like Skype, WhatsApp, and Facetime, people can quickly connect virtually anywhere in the world. This allows people to communicate face-to-face regardless of the distance between them. Technology has also made it easier for people to share ideas and collaborate on projects. With the help of cloud computing, people can work together on the same document or project regardless of location. This makes working together in teams much more straightforward and eliminates the need for physical meetings. Finally, technology has made it easier to stay informed about worldwide events. People can get up-to-date information about world events and news through news websites, blogs, and social media. This makes it much easier for people to stay connected and informed about what is happening in their local area or worldwide.

Today's technology has profoundly impacted transportation, making it faster, easier, and more efficient than ever before. Technology transforms how people travel and commute, from developing self-driving cars to implementing high-speed rail networks (Mishra & Koehler,2006). The most significant contribution of technology to transportation is the development of self-driving cars. Automated vehicles have the potential to revolutionise the way people get from point A to point B, as they can drive themselves without requiring a human driver. This technology has the potential to drastically reduce traffic congestion and provide a safer, more efficient way of getting around. In addition, self-driving cars can be used for various other applications, such as transportation for the elderly or disabled or delivery services.

High-speed rail networks have also been made possible by advances in technology. These networks can provide fast, efficient transportation over long distances, allowing people to travel between cities in a fraction of the time. This technology has made it easier and more affordable to travel long distances, making it a viable option for many people who cannot afford air travel or who do not have the time. Besides, technology has also made it easier and more convenient to purchase tickets for transportation. Many companies now offer online ticketing systems that make buying tickets and checking schedules easy. This has made planning trips and travel between destinations much more uncomplicated, eliminating the need to stand in line to purchase tickets.

Technology has become an integral part of modern life, revolutionising how we work, live, and play. With the rapid advancement of technology, it has become increasingly important to understand how technology enhances productivity. Technology has the potential to make us more productive, efficient and organised in our daily tasks. The most apparent advantage of technology is the ability to automate tasks. By using automation, businesses can drastically reduce the amount of time spent on mundane, repetitive tasks. This frees employees' time to focus on critical customer service and innovation tasks. Automation also increases data entry accuracy, leading to fewer mistakes and more efficient production.

 Another way in which technology enhances productivity is through the use of artificial intelligence (AI). AI can quickly process large amounts of data and identify patterns to help businesses make better decisions. By leveraging AI, companies can promptly analyse customer data to identify trends and make more informed decisions about product development or marketing strategies.

Technology can also increase productivity by streamlining communication. With the rise of digital communication tools such as email, chat, and videoconferencing, teams can quickly and conveniently collaborate on projects without having to be in the same room. This enables teams to work more efficiently and produce better results in less time. It also has the potential to improve the customer experience. By leveraging technology such as customer relationship management (CRM) software, businesses can better understand customer needs and create customised experiences. This leads to higher customer satisfaction, leading to increased sales and profits.

The world has become increasingly interconnected in the past decade, and with this increased connectivity comes greater vulnerability to cyber-attacks. From large-scale data breaches to individual identity theft and everything in between, it is clear that security is a significant concern in today's digital age. Fortunately, technology is helping to enhance security in a variety of ways.

 One of the most critical advances in security technology is the increased use of encryption. Encryption is scrambling data to be unreadable without the appropriate key. This means that even if a malicious actor were to obtain access to a system, the data it contains would remain secure. Encryption is used across various systems, from banking systems to corporate networks and individual devices. This added layer of security is essential in preventing unauthorised access.

Another security advancement is the use of biometric authentication. This involves using physical features such as fingerprints and facial or voice recognition to verify someone's identity. This type of authentication is much more secure than traditional methods, such as passwords, as it is virtually impossible to duplicate a person's biometric data. Biometric authentication has become increasingly popular for unlocking smartphones, logging into online accounts, and entering secure areas. Still, artificial intelligence (AI) is increasingly vital in enhancing security (Lazear,2015). AI can detect patterns of malicious activity, such as unusual login attempts or data breaches, and alert security personnel. AI can also detect malicious code and malware and take action to prevent it from spreading.

In conclusion, technology has become an integral part of human development. As technology evolves, its role will become even more critical. Technology can help us solve problems, increase efficiency, and improve our quality of life. Technology has enabled us to do impossible things before and has allowed us to access information and resources that would otherwise be inaccessible. Technology has helped to revolutionise how we interact with each other, making us more productive, efficient, and connected. Technology has become an essential part of our lives, and we must continue to use it to its full potential.

References

Krogstie, J., & Janssen, M. (2006). The Role of Technology in Human Development: A Systematic Review. The Information Society, 22(3), 231-249.

Lazear, E.P. (2015). Technology, Human Capital, and Economic Growth. Journal of Economic Perspectives, 29(1), 3-22.

Mishra, P., & Koehler, M. (2006). Technological Pedagogical Content Knowledge: A Framework for Teacher Knowledge. Teachers College Record, 108(6), 1017-1054.

Rajan, L., & Kurian, V. (2016). Technology and Human Development: Exploring the Role of Technology in Enhancing Human Development. International Journal of Development Research, 6(2), 62-68.

Chapter   33

Impact Of Sleep Deprivation on Mental Health

Sleep deprivation is a severe issue that significantly impacts one's mental health. Sleep deprivation can lead to anxiety, irritability, depression, and difficulty concentrating. It can also lead to an inability to make decisions and an increased risk of developing certain physical illnesses. Furthermore, it can increase the risk of developing psychiatric disorders, including bipolar disorder and schizophrenia. This paper will explore the impact of sleep deprivation on mental health.

Sleep deprivation can enormously impact a person's mental health, particularly anxiety. Anxiety is characterised by worry, fear, and uneasiness, which can be exacerbated by a lack of sleep (Braley & Troxel,2019). When an individual is a night sleep deprived, it can lead to an increase in anxiety due to several factors. First, sleep deprivation can lead to physical exhaustion and cognitive impairment. When a person suffers from physical fatigue, they are more likely to be irritable, have difficulty concentrating, and be more prone to feeling overwhelmed. This can leave the individual feeling anxious and overwhelmed by the tasks that they have to do. In addition, when a person is cognitively impaired due to lack of sleep, they may be more likely to misjudge situations or become overly concerned with small details, exacerbating their anxiety.

 Second, sleep deprivation can increase stress hormones, such as cortisol and adrenaline. These hormones are responsible for triggering the body's fight-or-flight response, which can lead to feelings of fear and panic. When a person is a sleep deprived, their body is more likely to be in a state of heightened arousal, making them more likely to feel anxious or panicked in certain situations. Third, sleep deprivation can lead to increased negative thinking and rumination. When an individual is sleep deprived, they are more likely to view conditions in a negative light and become stuck in a cycle of negative thinking. This can lead to an increase in anxious thoughts and fears, leading to a rise in anxiety. Finally, sleep deprivation can lead to an increase in impulsive behaviour. When a person is sleep deprived, they may be more likely to act impulsively without considering the consequences of their actions. This can lead to feelings of guilt and regret, which can further increase anxiety levels.

Sleep deprivation is a major problem in modern society, and its effects on cognitive function can be significant. Sleep deprivation has been linked to various cognitive impairments, including difficulty concentrating, memory problems, decreased alertness, and difficulty making decisions. It can also lead to an increase in risk-taking, as well as reduced creativity and problem-solving skills. The long-term effects of sleep deprivation on cognitive function can be particularly damaging. Studies have found that chronic sleep deprivation can lead to permanent mental impairment (Gupta & Gupta,2018). These impairments can include memory problems, decreased ability to process information, and decreased ability to learn and recall new information.

Additionally, research has shown that lack of sleep can increase the risk of developing neurodegenerative diseases such as Alzheimer's and Parkinson's. The short-term effects of sleep deprivation can also be significant. Studies have found that even one night of sleep deprivation can lead to substantial decreases in attention and concentration and difficulty making decisions and solving problems. Sleep deprivation can also lead to increased irritability, anxiety, and depression. Studies have shown that sleep deprivation can lead to an increased risk of depression. For example, one study found that people who slept six hours or less per night were three times more likely to develop depression (Nofzinger. et al.,2004). Another study found that people who slept less than six hours per night were more likely to suffer from depression than those who slept seven to nine hours per night. Studies also suggest that poor sleep can worsen the symptoms of depression, making it harder to manage.

Several steps can be taken to reduce the risk of depression associated with sleep deprivation. The first is to maintain a regular sleeping and waking schedule. Going to bed and waking up at the same time each day helps to regulate the body's natural circadian rhythm and can help ensure you get the sleep you need. Limiting exposure to screens and other electronic devices before bed is also essential, as the blue light from screens can disrupt your sleep. Additionally, avoiding caffeine late in the day can help you fall asleep more easily. Finally, creating a calming bedtime routine can also help relax the mind and body before sleep and can help improve sleep quality.

Memory loss is one of the most pervasive effects of sleep deprivation, as it can significantly impede day-to-day functioning. When a person is deprived of sleep, their ability to retain and process information is quite impaired (Reite & Short, 2020). Sleep plays a critical role in consolidating and storing information in long-term memory. The brain cannot effectively keep the newly acquired knowledge without adequate sleep, leading to memory problems. Furthermore, the brain cannot access previously stored information without enough sleep, leading to further memory issues.

Sleep deprivation also affects one's ability to focus and concentrate, further impairing memory. With adequate rest, it is easier to stay focused and attentive, leading to difficulty retaining newly acquired information. As a result, the ability to recall previously stored data can be significantly affected. Sleep deprivation can also lead to physical and psychological exhaustion, further reducing memory ability. When a person feels fatigued, they are less likely to be able to focus or concentrate, which can lead to difficulty remembering information. Furthermore, fatigue can lead to decreased motivation, further impairing one's ability to recall previously stored data.

Sleep deprivation has a significant impact on moodiness. It is a fact that people who don't get enough sleep tend to be more irritable and prone to negative emotions. Studies have found that people who are sleep deprived are more likely to experience mood swings, increased anxiety, lower levels of motivation, and depression. One reason why sleep deprivation affects mood so significantly is that it affects the way the brain works. Studies have found that sleep deprivation impairs the ability of the brain to regulate its emotions (Nofzinger. et al.,2004). When the brain is not able to properly regulate emotions, it can lead to feelings of irritability, a short temper, and difficulty controlling emotions.

 Sleep deprivation also affects the body's ability to produce chemicals that regulate emotions. For example, serotonin and dopamine are two chemicals that are important for regulating mood. When people are sleep deprived, their bodies cannot produce enough of these chemicals, leading to feelings of depression and anxiety (Gupta & Gupta,2018). In addition, sleep deprivation affects the body's ability to regulate its hormones. When hormones are not controlled properly, it can lead to increased stress hormone levels, making people more prone to feeling negative emotions. Finally, sleep deprivation has been linked to higher cortisol levels, a hormone released during stress. High cortisol levels can lead to fatigue, irritability, and difficulty focusing. Again, lack of sleep has been linked to an increased risk of psychosis, including schizophrenia and bipolar disorder. Sleep deprivation has been found to increase the risk of psychotic symptoms, including hallucinations and delusions, and impair cognitive function. Studies suggest that people who are sleep deprived have a higher risk of experiencing psychotic symptoms, such as paranoia and delusions, compared to those who get enough sleep. Sleep deprivation can also make people more vulnerable to developing psychotic disorders. It has been suggested that the lack of quality sleep can cause an imbalance in the brain's neurotransmitter systems, leading to psychotic symptoms. Additionally, people who suffer from sleep deprivation may struggle to cope with stress, leading to psychosis.

Besides, sleep deprivation has a profoundly negative effect on the immune system. It has been linked to impaired natural killer cell activity, decreased production of cytokines, and increased inflammation. It can also impair the body's ability to respond to vaccinations, making fighting off infections and viruses more difficult. Sleep deprivation can also lead to a weakened immune system, making it more difficult for the body to fight disease and illness (Braley & Troxel,2019). In addition, sleep deprivation can increase levels

of cortisol, a stress hormone that can further weaken the immune system. These effects make a person more vulnerable to illnesses and can even worsen existing medical conditions.
In conclusion, sleep deprivation has a significant impact on mental health. It can lead to mood swings, anxiety, and depression and cause long-term brain damage. In addition, lack of sleep can lead to impaired memory, difficulty concentrating and increased risk of mental illnesses. Therefore, it is essential to ensure you get enough sleep every night to maintain good mental health.

References

Braley, K. E., & Troxel, W. M. (2019). Sleep deprivation, mental health, and health-related quality of life. Sleep Medicine Clinics, 14(2), 161–169. https://doi.org/10.1016/j.jsmc.2018.12.009

Gupta, N. A., & Gupta, A. P. (2018). Sleep deprivation and mental health. Indian Journal of Psychiatry, 60(4), 441–445. https://doi.org/10.4103/psychiatry.IndianJPsychiatry_169_18

Nofzinger, E. A., Buysse, D. J., Germain, A., Price, J. C., Meltzer, C. C., Miewald, J. M., & Kupfer, D. J. (2004). Functional neuroimaging evidence for hyperarousal in insomnia. American Journal of Psychiatry, 161(11), 2126–2133. https://doi.org/10.1176/appi.ajp.161.11.2126

Reite, M., & Short, K. (2020). Mental health implications of sleep deprivation. Psychology & Health, 35(1), 1–20. https://doi.org/10.1080/08870446.2019.1618039

Chapter   34

The Impact of Stress on Mental Health

Stress is a part of life, but it can have several adverse effects on mental health. Stress can cause anxiety, depression, and other psychological issues. It can also lead to physical symptoms such as headaches, insomnia, and fatigue. Stress can even impact our ability to focus, make decisions, and interact with others. Understanding the effects of stress on mental health is essential to develop strategies to cope with and reduce stress.

One of the significant mental health issues caused by stress is depression. This is a severe mental disorder that affects millions of people around the world. It is a complex condition that is characterised by feelings of sadness, helplessness, and hopelessness (American Psychological Association,2020). Depression can have serious and long-lasting impacts on a person's life, including their physical, emotional, and social functioning. Depression can manifest in many different ways. People may constantly feel down, struggle to concentrate, and lose interest in activities that used to bring them joy. They may also experience changes in appetite and sleep, irritability, and physical symptoms such as headaches or stomachaches. Depression can be so severe that it interferes with someone's ability to function in school, work, or relationships.

The physical impacts of depression can be significant. People with depression are more likely to suffer from other illnesses and chronic pain. They are also more likely to engage in unhealthy behaviours like smoking and substance abuse. People with depression also face an increased risk of suicide. The emotional impacts of depression can be devastating. People with depression may feel worthless and helpless and may struggle to form and maintain relationships. They may also feel anxious and overwhelmed and have difficulty finding pleasure in activities.

The social impacts of depression can also be severe. People with depression may struggle to work, attend school, or participate in social activities. They may also have difficulty maintaining relationships with family and friends and may become isolated. Depression is a severe condition that can profoundly impact a person's life (National Alliance on Mental Illness,2020). It is essential to recognise the signs of depression and seek help as soon as possible. Treatment for depression can include psychotherapy, medications, and lifestyle changes. With treatment, people with depression can learn to manage their symptoms and lead fulfilling lives.

Anxiety is characterised by tension, worried thoughts, and physical changes like increased blood pressure. People with anxiety disorders usually have recurring intrusive thoughts or concerns. They may avoid certain situations out of worry. They may also have physical symptoms such as sweating, trembling, dizziness, or a rapid heartbeat. Although it is normal to feel anxious in certain situations, anxiety can become problematic when it interferes with daily activities such as work, attending social events, or forming relationships (Thoits,2013). It can also negatively impact physical health, such as the increased risk of heart disease, high blood pressure, and other medical conditions.

 Anxiety can have a variety of impacts on people's lives. It can lead to feelings of helplessness, hopelessness, and low self-esteem. People with anxiety may experience difficulty concentrating and sleeping and may also have trouble in social situations. Anxiety can lead to physical symptoms such as headaches, nausea, and digestive problems. It can also increase the risk of developing depression or other mental health issues.

The good news is that anxiety is treatable. Cognitive-behavioural therapy is a type of psychotherapy that can help people learn how to manage their stress. Medications such as antidepressants and anti-anxiety drugs can also treat anxiety. It is essential to seek help from a mental health professional if you think you may be suffering from an anxiety disorder. Stress can significantly impact a person's life, but it is possible to manage it with the help of a mental health professional. With the right treatment, people can learn how to cope with their anxiety and lead a healthy and fulfilling life.

Post-traumatic stress disorder, or PTSD, is a mental health disorder that can manifest after a person has experienced a traumatic event. This can include physical and/or psychological trauma, such as military combat, sexual assault, or a natural disaster. The symptoms of PTSD can vary from person to person but generally include recurring intrusive thoughts, flashbacks, nightmares, and physical symptoms such as increased heart rate, sweating, or muscle tension. People with PTSD may also experience feelings of guilt, shame, or fear and have difficulty sleeping or concentrating ((National Alliance on Mental Illness,2020). People with PTSD may feel like they are living in constant fear or tension, and they may avoid people or situations that remind them of the trauma they experienced. This can cause complications with work, family, and social relationships.

Fortunately, there are treatments available for PTSD. Cognitive behavioural therapy (CBT) is one of the most common treatments for PTSD. This type of therapy focuses on helping the patient understand and manage their symptoms and learn skills to cope with their distress. Other treatments for PTSD may include medications, such as antidepressants, anti-anxiety medications, or antipsychotics. These medications can help to reduce symptoms, such as intrusive thoughts, depression, and anxiety. Alternative treatments for PTSD include yoga, meditation, and mindfulness. These treatments can help to reduce stress and improve overall wellbeing.

Stress can cause bipolar disorders. Bipolar disorder is a mental health condition that affects a person's mood, energy, and ability to think clearly (American Psychological Association,2020). It can cause extreme shifts in mood, ranging from periods of mania or extreme highs to periods of depression or extreme lows. People with bipolar disorder can have difficulty managing their emotions, and this can lead to a range of issues, such as relationship difficulties, work problems, and financial difficulties. The exact cause of bipolar disorder is unknown, but it is thought to be related to a combination of genetic, environmental, and psychological factors. People with a family history of bipolar disorder are more likely to develop the condition. Additionally, some people may be more vulnerable to developing bipolar disorder if they have experienced a traumatic event or stressful life experience. The symptoms of bipolar disorder can be extremely disruptive to a person's life. People with bipolar disorder may experience periods of intense energy, sleeplessness, racing thoughts, and a sense of grandiosity. During these periods, they may also engage in reckless or impulsive behaviors, such as spending sprees, taking risks, or engaging in risky sexual behaviors. On the other hand, people with bipolar disorder may also experience periods of prolonged sadness, fatigue, difficulty concentrating, and thoughts of suicide. These symptoms can significantly interfere with a person's functioning, making it difficult to manage their daily activities.

Bipolar disorder can significantly impact a person's relationships, work, and finances. People with bipolar disorder may experience difficulty maintaining relationships, as their mood swings can make it difficult to interact with others. They may also find it challenging to keep a steady job, as their moods may interfere with their ability to perform their job duties.

Additionally, people with bipolar disorder may be more likely to engage in impulsive behaviours, such as spending sprees, which can lead to financial difficulties.

Treatment for bipolar disorder is available and typically includes medication, psychotherapy, and lifestyle changes. Medication can help to stabilise a person's mood, while psychotherapy can help a person to understand their condition and learn how to manage their symptoms. Additionally, lifestyle changes can help improve a person's overall mental health and wellbeing. Examples of lifestyle changes include regular exercise, eating a healthy diet, getting adequate sleep, and managing stress.

Stress causes insomnia, a sleep disorder characterised by difficulty falling asleep, staying asleep, or both. When people are stressed, their minds can be filled with worries and concerns, and it can be hard to shift into a relaxed state and drift off to sleep. Stress can also lead to nightmares, further disrupting the sleep cycle and making it difficult to get a good night's rest (American Psychological Association,2020). It causes mood swings which can range from mild to extreme. When we are stressed, our bodies release stress hormones, such as adrenaline and cortisol, which can cause us to become irritable, anxious, and easily overwhelmed. These feelings can quickly turn into anger, sadness, or even depression if they are not addressed. Again, stress can lead to difficulty concentrating. When our minds are racing and we feel overwhelmed, it can be hard to focus on tasks and stay on track. We may find ourselves easily distracted and unable to perform even the most basic tasks. In conclusion, stress can have a significant impact on mental health. The severity of the effects can vary depending on the individual and the amount of stress they are experiencing. Finding healthy ways to cope with stress is essential to maintain good mental health and wellbeing.

References

American Psychological Association. (2020). Stress Effects on the Body. Retrieved from https://www.apa.org/helpcenter/stress-body

National Alliance on Mental Illness. (2020). Stress. Retrieved from https://www.nami.org/About-Mental-Illness/Related-Conditions/Stress

Thoits, P. A. (2013). Self, identity, stress, and mental health. *Handbook of the sociology of mental health*, 357-377.

Chapter   35

The Psychology of Stress and Coping

Stress is a common everyday phenomenon and an inevitable part of life. Stress is reacting to a situation or event perceived as a threat or challenge. It is a psychological and physical response to a perceived challenge or demand. The psychology of stress and coping is the scientific study of how individuals, groups, and organisations cope with stressful conditions. It examines how people perceive, appraise, and respond to stress. This essay will provide an overview of the psychology of stress and coping, including the psychological theories of stress, the effects of stress on mental and physical health, and different coping strategies.

 There are several different psychological theories of stress. One of the most prominent is the transactional model of stress or the transactional approach. This approach views stress as a transaction between an individual and their environment. In other words, stress results from a person's perception of a situation and reaction to it (Taylor,2006). In addition, the transactional approach emphasises the role of cognitive appraisal in stress, which is the process of evaluating a situation and determining its meaning.

The cognitive-behavioural approach to stress also emphasises the role of cognition in anxiety. This approach focuses on how an individual's thoughts and beliefs about a situation can affect emotional and physical reactions. For example, individuals may experience more stress if they believe a situation is dangerous or threatening. This approach also emphasises the importance of learning to change unhelpful thinking patterns to reduce stress. Finally, the psychodynamic approach to stress focuses on the unconscious factors that can lead to anxiety (Krohne,2002). This approach emphasises the role of unconscious processes and conflicts in the development of stress. It suggests that unconscious processes, such as unresolved conflicts, can influence an individual's thoughts and behaviours, leading to stress.

The causes of stress can be divided into three main categories: external or environmental, internal or personal, and lifestyle factors. External or environmental factors are usually out of our control, including natural disasters, financial problems, and job loss (Mayo Clinic,2020). These kinds of events can be complicated to cope with and can lead to prolonged periods of stress. Internal or personal factors may include low self-esteem, perfectionism, and unrealistic expectations. These kinds of issues can create an internal struggle that causes us to feel overwhelmed, anxious, and stressed. Finally, lifestyle factors are the things we do that can impact our stress levels. These include a poor diet, lack of exercise, sleep, and substance abuse. These activities can all contribute to an increase in stress levels.

Physical signs and symptoms of stress can vary widely, but they all have one thing in common: they are the body's way of responding to a perceived threat or challenge. Stress can be caused by anything from a change in routine to a traumatic event, and the physical signs and symptoms of stress can result from acute and chronic stress. For example, one of the most common physical signs and symptoms of anxiety is an increase in heart rate and breathing rate. This is the body's way of preparing for a potential fight-or-flight response, as the sympathetic nervous system sends messages to the body to prepare for action. As a result, people may experience a racing heart, increased sweating, and even trembling or shaking.

Another common physical symptom of stress is muscle tension, which can manifest as headaches, back pain, and jaw clenching. This is the body's way of preparing to meet the challenge of a stressful situation, and it can lead to physical discomfort and even pain. Stress can also lead to changes in appetite, sleep patterns, and fatigue. People may eat more or less than usual or need help falling asleep or staying asleep. Again, this is the body's way of coping with the stress it is experiencing, but it can harm overall physical health. Finally, stress can also cause changes in physical health, such as an increased risk of heart disease, a weakened immune system, and digestive problems. These physical signs and symptoms of stress can be pretty serious, and finding ways to manage and reduce stress to protect one's physical health is essential.

Psychologically, stress can manifest in a variety of ways. It can cause feelings of anxiety, depression, and irritability. People feeling stressed may also experience difficulty concentrating, decreased motivation, thoughts of self-doubt, and feelings of isolation. Stress can also lead to unhealthy coping mechanisms like substance abuse and self-harm. Therefore, it is essential to recognise the signs and symptoms of anxiety to address it before it becomes a bigger problem. Various effective stress management methods include exercise, yoga, mindfulness, and talking to a professional. Taking time to relax and unwind can also be beneficial for reducing stress levels. Practising self-care and Prioritising healthy habits such as getting enough sleep, eating a balanced diet, and engaging in positive activities

are also important.

It is essential to understand the effects of stress to manage it effectively. Physically, chronic stress can lead to a weakened immune system, putting individuals at risk for various illnesses. Stress can also cause headaches, digestive issues, and fatigue. In addition, research suggests it may also affect heart disease, obesity, and diabetes (McEwen,2016). Mentally, chronic stress can lead to depression, anxiety, and other mood disorders. It can also lead to difficulty concentrating, making decisions, and remembering things. In addition, it can cause insomnia and difficulty sleeping, which can significantly impact overall health.

On a social level, stress can cause individuals to withdraw from friends and family and may even lead to the development of addictions. It can also lead to unhealthy coping mechanisms such as overeating, smoking, drinking, or using drugs. Recognising the signs of stress and taking steps to manage it is essential. Taking breaks throughout the day, getting enough sleep, exercising regularly, and eating a healthy diet can all help to reduce stress. In addition, talking to a therapist can be beneficial in managing stress and reducing its effects.

Although it can be challenging to cope with, it is an integral part of life and can even help motivate us to achieve our goals. However, when stress becomes too much, it can harm our mental and physical health. That's why learning how to cope effectively with stress is essential to maintain our wellbeing. The first step to dealing with stress is to identify its source. This could be an external factor, such as an upcoming deadline or a complicated relationship, or an internal factor, such as worrying thoughts or negative self-talk (Krohne,2002). Once you have identified the source, it is essential to take action to help reduce it. This could involve changing your life, such as taking on fewer commitments or seeking support from friends and family. It could also include developing healthy coping strategies such as mindfulness, deep breathing, and problem-solving.

Another important way to cope with stress is to take care of your physical health. Regular exercise can help to reduce stress levels, as can getting enough sleep and eating a balanced diet

(Mayo Clinic,2020). Additionally, taking frequent breaks throughout the day and making time for activities you enjoy is essential. Doing something fun can take your mind off stressful situations and improve your overall wellbeing. Finally, it's important to practice self-compassion. Learning to be kind and understanding to yourself is essential to managing stress. This could involve positive self-talk, setting boundaries, and making time for self-care. Practising self-care can reduce stress levels and improve your overall wellbeing. In conclusion, the psychology of stress and coping is an important area of research that has helped to improve our understanding of how individuals deal with difficult experiences. Stress is a part of life and is necessary for growth and development, but too much stress can be damaging. Knowing more about how individuals cope with stress can help us develop strategies to manage difficult situations better. Research into the psychology of stress and coping has helped to identify ways to reduce negative impacts and enhance our ability to cope with stressful situations. Understanding the psychological aspects of stress and coping can also allow us to create an environment that encourages healthy coping strategies.

References

Krohne, H. W. (2002). Stress and coping theories. *Int Encyclopedia of the Social Behavioral Sciences [cited 2021]*.

Mayo Clinic. (2020). Stress: Causes, Symptoms and Treatment. Retrieved from https://www.mayoclinic.org/healthy-lifestyle/stress-management/in-depth/stress/art-20046037

McEwen, B. (2016). Allostasis and allostatic load: Implications for neuropsychopharmacology. Neuropsychopharmacology, 41(1), 3-12.

Taylor, S. E. (2006). Tend and befriend: Biobehavioral bases of affiliation under stress. Current direction in Psychological Science, 15(6), 273-277.

Chapter   36
   Theories Of Stress and Coping

Theories of stress and coping describe how individuals manage stressful situations and the psychological and physiological responses to stress. Stress is unavoidable, and how we cope with it is essential in determining our overall well-being. Different theories have been developed to explain our reactions to stress and our strategies to manage it. These theories emphasise the role of individual coping strategies, the importance of social support, and the impact of psychological and physiological responses to stress. Understanding these theories can help us better handle stressful situations and improve our health.

The Cognitive Appraisal Theory of stress and coping is an influential psychological theory that examines the relationship between thoughts, feelings, and behaviours in stressful situations. This theory posits that how we interpret or appraise a situation affects our reaction to it. According to this theory, stress is a product of how we cognitively evaluate a situation and our ability to cope with it (Edmondson & Cooper,2016). The theory suggests that how we appraise a situation determines our response. When faced with a potentially stressful situation, we use our cognitive processes to evaluate it. This evaluation involves assessing the potential threat, our ability to cope with the problem, and its potential rewards. Depending on how we assess the situation, we will respond differently. If we perceive the situation as threatening, we will experience stress. If we perceive the situation as manageable, we may take action. In either case, our appraisal will influence our response.

The Cognitive Appraisal Theory of stress and coping also insists that our ability to cope with a situation can be improved through various strategies. These strategies include developing a positive mindset, increasing self-efficacy, and identifying helpful coping strategies. For example, having a positive attitude can help us look at the situation more constructively. Increasing self-efficacy can help us feel more confident in handling the case. And identifying helpful coping strategies can help us effectively manage our stress (Taylor,2006). Overall, the Cognitive Appraisal Theory of stress and coping provides us with an understanding of how our thoughts and beliefs about a situation affect our behaviours. By understanding the way, we appraise a problem and the strategies we can use to cope with it, and we can better manage our stress and lead healthier lives.

The Transactional Theory of Stress and Coping is a psychological theory that examines the relationship between stress, coping techniques, and how individuals perceive and respond to stressful events. This theory was developed by Richard Lazarus and Susan Folkman in 1984 and has been widely used in research and clinical settings. The theory proposes that people perceive and respond to stressful events differently, depending on their characteristics and the context of the situation. By understanding how different people cope with stress, we can better understand why some people are more successful in managing their stress than others. The Transactional Theory of Stress and Coping suggests that stress is created by a person's appraisal of a situation, followed by their coping responses. Examination refers to interpreting a problem and how the individual evaluates it. One's appraisal of a problem can be positive or negative. In addition, it can be based on various factors, such as the perceived severity of the event, the individual's resources and abilities, and their past experiences. Once the individual appraises the situation, they will select a coping response (Holahan & Moos, 2009). This can be either problem-focused, which involves addressing the source of the stress, or emotion-focused, which involves managing the emotional and psychological responses to the pressure.

In addition to understanding how people appraise and respond to stress, the Transactional Theory of Stress and Coping also looks at how people adjust to stressful situations over time. This is referred to as adaptation, which is the process of learning to deal with stressful events and managing the emotions that arise from them. It is important to note that adaptation is an ongoing process and is not a one-time event.

The Transactional Theory of Stress and Coping is a valuable tool for understanding how individuals perceive and respond to stressful events. It is also helpful in developing effective coping strategies that can help individuals manage their stress positively and effectively. Understanding how individuals appraise and cope with stressful events can create better strategies for managing stress and improving well-being.

The behavioural approach to stress and coping emphasises the role of learning and conditioning in how an individual responds to a stressor. According to this approach, an individual's responses to stressors are shaped by their experiences, such as the reinforcement of certain behaviours or the punishment of others. This means that if an individual has been rewarded for responding to a stressor in a particular way, they are more likely to use that same response in the future. Similarly, if they have been punished for responding to a stressor in a particular way, they are more likely to avoid using that response in the future.

Another essential concept in the behavioural approach to stress and coping is the idea of reframing. Reframing is looking at a stressful situation differently and finding new, more positive ways to respond. Reframing involves changing one's perception of a problem by identifying its positive aspects and focusing on those rather than the negative ones. This can help individuals refocus their energy on things that are within their control rather than those that are out of their control.

The behavioural approach to stress and coping can help individuals manage their stress more effectively. Through understanding the role of learning and conditioning, individuals can better understand why they respond to stressors in specific ways and can use cognitive and behavioural strategies to cope with them. Additionally, by reframing stressful situations, individuals can find new, more positive ways to respond to them and focus their energy on things within their control. By using the behavioural approach to stress and coping, individuals can be better equipped to manage their stress and improve their overall well-being.

The biopsychosocial approach is one of the most popular and widely used approaches to understanding and managing stress and coping with it. This approach, first developed by George Engel in 1977, looks at the physiological, psychological, social, and environmental factors that affect an individual's experience and response to stress. It focuses on the body's physical response to stress. This includes the release of hormones such as cortisol, adrenaline, and epinephrine, which are responsible for the body's fight-or-flight response. The body's physical reaction to stress can cause headaches, muscle tension, digestive issues, and fatigue.

The psychological aspect of the biopsychosocial approach looks at the mental and emotional responses to stress. This includes thoughts, feelings, and beliefs that can lead to emotional distress, such as fear, anxiety, and depression. It also consists of the individual's appraisal of the stressful situation, influencing how they cope.

The social aspect of the biopsychosocial approach focuses on the individual's relationships with others and how these relationships can control their stress level. For example, social support from friends and family can help buffer stress's effects. On the other hand, social isolation can increase stress levels.

The environmental aspect of the biopsychosocial approach looks at the external factors that can contribute to stress, such as overcrowding, noise, and air pollution. These environmental factors can have a direct impact on an individual's stress level, as well as their ability to cope with it.

Overall, the biopsychosocial approach is an effective way to understand and manage stress. By considering the physiological, psychological, social, and environmental aspects of stress, an individual can better understand their unique experience and develop coping strategies.

The Unconscious Mind Theory of stress and coping is a psychological theory suggesting that the unconscious mind plays a significant role in coping with stress. According to this theory, the unconscious mind can process and store information that is not accessible to conscious thought. This information can be used to aid in the process of coping with stressful situations. The Unconscious Mind Theory suggests that the unconscious mind can recognise patterns in stressful situations. By identifying these patterns, the individual can better understand the source of the stress and how to respond to it. For example, suppose an individual experiences a stressful situation similar to an experience. In that case, they can use their expertise to find a better way of dealing with stress.

The Unconscious Mind Theory also proposes that the unconscious can regulate emotional responses to stressful situations. By recognising patterns and controlling emotional responses, the individual is more likely to be able to cope with stress effectively. For example, if an individual becomes overwhelmed in a stressful situation, they may be able to recognise this pattern to take steps to manage the situation better.

The Unconscious Mind Theory of stress and coping is a fundamental psychological theory as it suggests that the unconscious mind has a significant role in coping with stress. By recognising patterns and regulating emotions, the individual can more effectively cope with stressful situations. Therefore, this theory is essential when considering stress management and how to best respond to stressful events.

The Coping Process Model Theory of stress and coping is a psychological model that explains how individuals interact with their environment and handle stressful situations. This model, developed by Dr Richard Lazarus in the late 1960s, suggests that an individual's ability to cope with stress is determined by their appraisal of the situation, their coping strategies, and the outcomes of their coping strategies (Holahan & Moos,2009). The model is based on the idea that individuals must first appraise the situation as either a threat or a challenge before choosing an appropriate coping strategy.

When individuals appraise a situation as a threat, they are more likely to use defensive coping strategies such as avoidance or denial. Conversely, when individuals appraise the case as a challenge, they are more likely to use problem-focused coping strategies such as actively seeking information or problem-solving. The model also suggests that individuals' ability to cope with stress is influenced by their resources, such as social support and self-efficacy.

The Coping Process Model Theory of stress and coping can be applied to various situations, including work-related, relationship, and health-related anxiety. This model can help individuals understand how their appraisal of a situation influences their coping strategies and how they can ultimately help them manage their stress (Folkman & Moskowitz,2000). For example, suppose an individual feels overwhelmed by their workload. In that case, they can use the model to assess the situation as a challenge and then choose a problem-focused coping strategy, such as delegating tasks or breaking the workload into smaller parts. This strategy can help the individual manage their stress and complete their work.

In conclusion, the Coping Process Model Theory of stress and coping is a useful psychological model that can help individuals understand how their appraisal of a situation influences their coping strategies and how their coping strategies ultimately help them to manage their stress. By using this model, individuals can better understand how to cope effectively with different types of anxiety and be better prepared to handle future stress.

References

Edmondson, D., & Cooper, C. L. (2016). Theories of stress and its relationship to health. Oxford: Oxford University Press.

Folkman, S., & Moskowitz, J.T. (2000). Positive effect and the other side of coping. American Psychologist, 55(6), 647-654.

Holahan, C.J., & Moos, R.H. (2009). Coping and adjustment to stress Theory, research, and applications. New York: Springer.

Taylor, S.E. (2006). Health psychology (5th ed.). Boston: McGraw-Hill.

Chapter   37
There Is More to Life Than Being Happy

In today's modern world, happiness is often seen as the ultimate goal. From advertisements to social media, we are constantly bombarded with images and messages that tell us that happiness is the key to success and that life is meaningless without it. The truth, however, is that there is much more to life than being happy. While happiness is important and can bring great joy to our lives, it alone is not enough to fulfil us.

The first thing to recognise is that happiness is fleeting. It comes and goes and is rarely a permanent state. Therefore, while striving to find moments of joy and contentment, we must understand that it is not a reliable source of lasting satisfaction. Instead, we should focus on finding purpose and meaning in our lives. This means looking beneath the surface of our daily routines and identifying what brings us a sense of satisfaction not just in the moment but throughout our lifetime. This could be anything from pursuing a passion or hobby to volunteering in our community to spending quality time with friends and family.

It is also important to remember that life is not all about pleasure. We must endure moments of struggle and hardship to grow and develop. However, rather than viewing these moments as unfavourable, we should embrace them as opportunities to learn and build resilience. Life is not meant to be easy, and we should be thankful for the challenges that help us become better and more well-rounded individuals.

Again, it is essential to understand that life is about more than just us. We should strive to make an impact on the world, whether it is through our actions, our words, or our deeds. Through this, we can find purpose and significance beyond our happiness. We can also find a sense of connection with others and a feeling of joy from knowing that we have made a positive difference in the lives of those around us.

The first potential disadvantage of focusing on happiness is that it can lead to unrealistic expectations. When people focus too much on being happy, they may develop unrealistic expectations about how their lives should be. For example, they may expect things to go perfectly or to always be in a good mood. When these expectations are not met, they may become frustrated or even depressed. This can lead to dissatisfaction with life and an inability to enjoy happy moments.

Another potential disadvantage of focusing on happiness is that it can lead to superficial relationships. When people focus too much on being happy, they may prioritize relationships with people based on external factors such as looks or money. This can lead to shallow relationships based on something other than genuine feelings of connection and affection. In addition, focusing on happiness can lead people to overlook the importance of meaningful connections and conversations with others.

Living a meaningful life isn't necessarily easy; it requires effort, commitment, and a strong sense of purpose. It is a journey, and while it may seem daunting, it is ultimately rewarding. To make this journey easier, it is helpful to identify a few key pillars that can serve as a foundation for meaningful living. The first pillar of living a meaningful life is cultivating positive relationships. Building solid relationships with family and friends helps us feel connected to something larger than ourselves. We can learn from others, share experiences, and be comforted by their presence. When we feel supported by our relationships, we are more likely to have the courage to take risks, the confidence to succeed, and the resilience to move forward when we fail. Positive relationships can also bring joy and a sense of belonging, enriching our lives and allowing us to feel more connected to the world.

The second pillar of living a meaningful life is being present at the moment. In today's world, getting caught up in technology and the fast pace of life is easy. However, we are often so focused on the future that we must remember to appreciate the present. To truly live a meaningful life, it is essential to be mindful and enjoy the beauty of the present moment. This can be done through meditation, yoga, or simply savouring a cup of coffee. Taking a few moments to be still and appreciate what is around us can help us be more grateful and mindful of our lives and relationships.

The third pillar of a meaningful life is developing a sense of purpose. A strong sense of purpose can help us stay focused on our goals, even when faced with obstacles. It can also motivate us to make positive changes in our lives and the lives of others. Finding a sense of purpose can be complicated, but it is essential for living a meaningful life. It can be helpful to reflect on what is important to you and what values you want to live by. Once you have identified these values, finding ways to live them out in your everyday life can be more manageable.

The fourth pillar of living a meaningful life is practising mindfulness and self-care. Taking the time to be mindful and care for ourselves is essential for a meaningful life. Mindfulness allows us to be aware of our thoughts and feelings, and self-care will enable us to nurture our physical, mental, and emotional wellbeing. Mindfulness and self-care can help us become more aware of our needs and wants and can also help us cope with difficult emotions. By nurturing ourselves, we can be better equipped to take on life's challenges and live more meaningfully.

The fifth pillar of living a meaningful life is engaging in meaningful work. Having a job that we are passionate about can bring us a sense of purpose and fulfilment. It can also help us make a difference in the world and use our skills to help others. Whether it is a full-time job, a side hustle, or volunteering, engaging in meaningful work can give us a sense of accomplishment and help us positively impact the world.

The sixth pillar of a meaningful life is giving back to the community. Giving back can take many forms, from donating money to volunteering time. It can help us feel more connected to our community and give us a sense of purpose. Giving back can also help us develop a sense of empathy and understanding for others. Giving back can make a positive difference in the world and enrich our lives.

In conclusion, it is essential to recognise that there is much more to life than being happy. Therefore, while happiness is integral to life, it should not be our sole focus. Instead, we should focus on finding purpose and meaning in our lives, learning from our struggles, and impacting the world. Through this, we can find satisfaction and fulfilment beyond our happiness.

Toddlerhood

Toddlerhood is the age between the first and the third year of a child's growth and development. During this stage, the physical increase decreases compared to its rapid growth in the first year. Still, it becomes more rapid compared to the later stages of development (National Institute of Child Health and Human Development,2021). This case applies to both physical growth and brain development. In addition, toddlers experience changes in motor development and sleep patterns.

Physical growth

Body growth is very swift among toddlers. The average boy is moderately heavier and taller throughout toddlerhood than an average girl. Toddlers lose some of infancy's body fat and start becoming learners as they become longer. They do not require much fat to maintain their constant body temperature. Again, the head, initially a quarter of the neonate's length, becomes one-fifth of the two-year-old kid's height. The other body parts continue to develop more swiftly than the head. By the time such a kid attains adulthood, the charge is usually one-eighth the total size of the whole body.

Toddlers in developed nations grow more rapidly and swiftly than those raised in developing countries. Usually, at birth and for the first six months, the kid's growth rate is similar in both developed and third-world countries because most cultures depend on breast milk and infant formula; they also take a small amount of solid food (American Academy of Pediatrics,2020). Nonetheless, as they approach six months and start taking solid food as the primary source of their diet, toddlers in developing nations acquire less protein, and the growth rate reduces. Based on the World Health Organization data, more than one-fourth of toddlers globally receive a diet that is poor in proteins, especially in developing nations.

Brain Development

The rate of brain growth continues to increase at the toddler stage. However, it should be noted that it is not the generation of brain cells that stimulates the toddler's brain development. Instead, the synaptic density is the number of the neurons' synaptic connections that differentiate early brain development. The multiplication of these connections is rapid in the first three years. At the toddlerhood stage, the production of the new synapses is at a peak in the frontal lobes, the section of the brain that comprises human cognitive qualities like creativity, planning, and reasoning. The synaptic density reaches its peak towards the end of the third year.

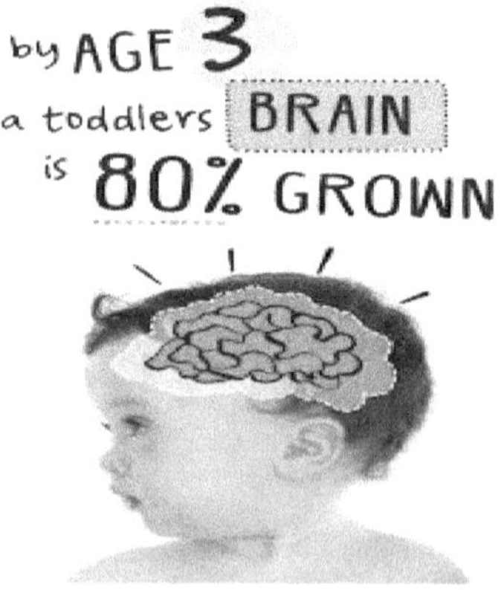

The long process of synaptic pruning starts immediately after the peak of synaptic density. The neurons' connections decrease inside the synoptic pruning, though they become more efficient. Those synapses that are used develop more while those that are unused die. During synaptic pruning, approximately one-third of synapses, the neurons' connections are removed from the frontal context. Various approaches are used to evaluate brain activity, giving evidence of the swift development of the brain in toddlerhood. A good example is an electroencephalogram that measures most electrical activities of the brain's cerebral cortex. Such a research techniques on toddlers has rapidly increased general cortical activities from one and a half to two years.

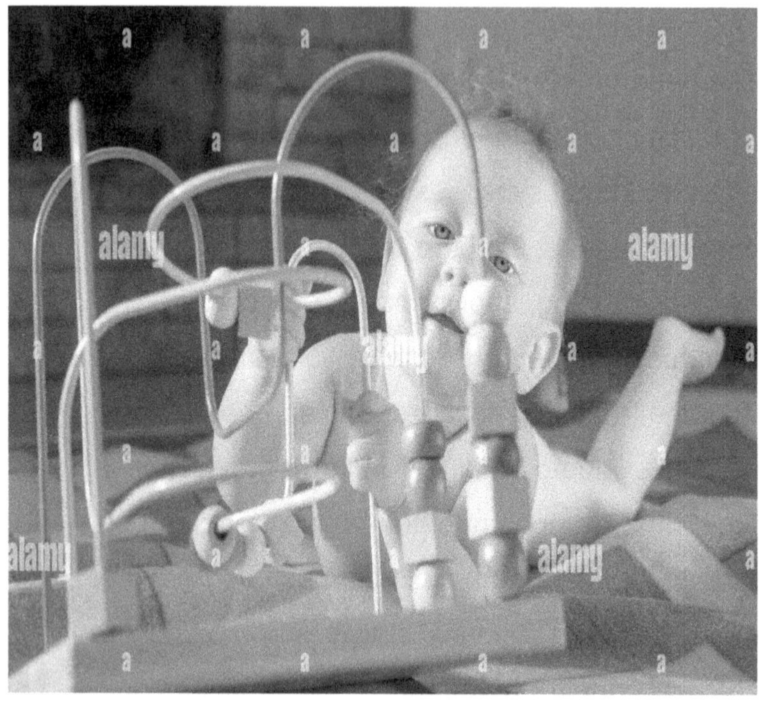

Sleep and teething

Several changes occur in the sleeping arrangement and the sleeping patterns of toddlers. Sleep duration decreases from 16 to 18 hours daily in the neonate to almost fifteen hours daily by the first year and twelve to thirteen hours by the second year.

The toddler sleeps less than the infant, takes more hours sleeping at night, and remains awake during the day for more time than the infant. Most toddlers take one nap, unlike infants, who may take more than two naps in a day.

Nevertheless, not all toddlers sleep throughout the night consistently, as the frequency of waking at night increases from 18 to 24 months. The resurgence of teeth among toddlers between 13 to 19 months explains the primary factor contributing to their waking. It is when molar starts to develop, which are large and more painful than the other types of teeth that appear during infancy.

Again, the kid creates a more definite sense of themselves and the social environment at the end of the first year; for example, if they sleep in different rooms with their parents, the toddlers become aware of this intentional separation and may find themselves in their parents' room. Toddlers in traditional cultures may continue sleeping alongside their mothers until they reach two years or start sleeping with their fathers or elder siblings when the mother becomes pregnant.

Motor development

Toddlerhood is associated with more advances in motor development, such as standing, walking, jumping, running, and climbing. Toddlers start by placing small items in the vast object, holding a spoon or cup, and forming a tower of blocks.

Motor development from toddling to running, jumping, and climbing

When toddlers start walking, they spread their feet apart and make small steps. While waking, the toddlers shift their weight from one leg to another. An average infant starts to walk during the eleventh month before getting to toddlerhood. But some variations occur where some children walk at nine months while others start walking when they are approaching 17 months.

At fifteen months, toddlers can stand for a while on one leg and climb on objects; however, they find it difficult to climb down things. For example, most toddlers can climb up the stairs but may climb down different stairs. By eighteen months, most children can run but with a stiff-legged posture. At twenty-four months, the toddler's running becomes more flexible, and they can throw small items and even kick a ball.

All About
Gross Motor Skills

They can climb up and down the stairs, squat for some time, and quickly jump up and down during this stage. As they approach the third year, toddlers attain more balance and flexibility. They also become less likely to fall because they can use visual information to cope with the movements in response to various surfaces. Children in traditional cultures are supported while making walking advances until they can properly stand and walk independently without falling. These cultures restrict children's movements to keep them safe.

From scribbling to building with blocks
After the first year of toddlerhood, children can hold on to objects while performing a different action with the other hand. Some toddlers can hold a spoon and try feeding themselves. They also learn to scribble with crayons, turn a book's page, and form a tower of about four blocks. In the 2nd year of toddlerhood, the kids' scribbling is more skillful, and some of them can even draw a semi-straight line; they can also build a tower of up to ten blocks (Verhoeven. et al.,2007)
Toilet training

During toddlerhood, children are trained on how to control their defecation and urination. As a result, most toddlers show signs indicating readiness for toilet training at eighteen and thirty months.

Some of these signs include drying for more than two hours during the day when the kids insist, they want to wear underwear, not diapers, and when they directly demand to use the toilets.

Weaning

Traditional cultures believe children should be breastfed for two to three years. Then, in case the breastfeeding takes some weeks and stops, the child should be introduced to the bottle, sucking gradually and smoothly. For some children, breastfeeding continues up to late toddlerhood, but some cultures may force the separation of the mother and the toddler when the latter attains two years to stop them from breastfeeding.

Conclusion

Toddlerhood is an exciting and fantastic growth, development, and discovery period. It is a time of rapid physical growth, motor development, and cognitive, language, and social development. It is a time of exploration and learning as toddlers explore their environment, begin to form relationships, and develop their unique personalities. During this time, parents and caregivers play an essential role in helping toddlers reach their full potential. With love, patience, and understanding, parents can help guide their toddlers through this rewarding stage of life.

References

American Academy of Pediatrics. (2020). Baby and Toddler Health: Growth and Development. Retrieved from https://www.healthychildren.org/English/ages-stages/toddler/Pages/Growth-and-Development.aspx

National Institute of Child Health and Human Development. (2021). What is Toddler Development? Retrieved from https://www.nichd.nih.gov/health/topics/toddlerdevelopment

Verhoeven, M., Junger, M., Van Aken, C., Deković, M., & Van Aken, M. A. (2007). Parenting during toddlerhood: Contributions of parental, contextual, and child characteristics. *Journal of Family Issues*, *28*(12), 1663-1691.

Chapter   39

Unhealthy Emotional Relationships with Food

The humans' relationship with food is both deep-rooted and complex. They use food to express love, celebrate, and nurture relationships. However, food can also act as a source of emotional stress for some people. An unhealthy relationship with food can result in various issues like overeating, purging, binging, and emotional eating. Such patterns of behaviour should be recognized to prevent lifelong health impacts. In this paper, I will address various unhealthy eating habits triggered by emotions and strategies to overcome them.

One of the groups highly affected by unhealthy emotional eating habits is the students. Caso. et al. (2020) maintain that whenever students become stressed, their bodies produce hormones such as adrenaline and cortisol, which increase their appetite. Students may therefore engage in poor eating habits as they start eating junk food to cater to their cravings. Junk food generally comprises a high amount of sugar, salt, and fat, which can trigger weight gain and other health complications such as cardiovascular diseases.

Consuming excess junk food can also cause a shortage of nutrients because these meals have few minerals and vitamins. Poor diet causes students not to concentrate appropriately in the classroom resulting in poor academic performance. Many learners turn to meals as a source of comfort hence overeating (Caso. et al.,2020). Eating due to stress can adversely affect the learner's psychological health leading to emotions like shame and guilt.

The young working class is another group of people affected by stress-eating. Lopes. et al.(2021) attests that young working groups are over-relying on ultra-processed food to manage stress. Such foods have high amounts of fat and sugar, which increases the energy levels in their bodies that are difficult to regulate. In addition, these foods contain artificial flavours, preservatives, and colours, adversely impacting their health. Consequently, eating ultra-processed foods can increase the victims' perceived stress.

An experiment with poor pregnant women revealed that women who are obese and those that suffer from advanced depression are more likely to eat junk food compared to women who do not have stress. Furthermore, lopes. et al.(2021) claim that the research on the lifestyles and diet of volunteers who were not suffering from depression showed that individuals who consumed more fast foods had a 48% increase in developing depression compared to people who did not take these foods.

It is worth noting that stress-eating behaviour and heavy consumption of alcohol are associated with social, cultural, and emotional aspects of the youths' lives. According to Scott. et al. (2020), unhealthy feeding habits cause a person to develop low self-esteem, negative self-image, and stress, resulting in increased alcohol abuse. In addition, heavy drinking can lead to increased social isolation, thus contributing to more unhealthy eating behaviour. Again, the youths' culture is characterized by alcohol as a social lubricant, which further improves harmful feeding behaviour.

Still, the challenge of an unhealthy relationship with food affects older adults. Molnar. et al. (2015) attests that one of the most common causes of unhealthy emotional relationships with food among the elderly is loneliness. Loneliness often results from losing a loved one or a reduction in social interactions due to physical or mental health issues. It can lead to overeating or the consumption of unhealthy foods in an attempt to fill the void. Another cause of unhealthy emotional relationships with food among the elderly is cognitive decline. Cognitive decline can result in confusion and difficulty making decisions. This can lead to the consumption of unhealthy foods or a lack of proper nutrition due to difficulty recognizing and preparing healthy foods.

The most apparent effect of unhealthy emotional relationships with food is physical. It can lead to weight gain and an increased risk of developing chronic diseases such as diabetes and heart disease. It can also lead to fatigue, weakness, and an overall decrease in physical fitness. Mentally and emotionally, unhealthy emotional relationships with food can cause depression and low self-esteem. It can also lead to isolation and feelings of guilt or shame. This can harm the older adult's overall well-being.

There are diverse impacts of unhealthy food on stress reactivity. For example, a diet high in processed foods and refined sugars can lead to a low mood and increased irritability and anxiety. A diet high in unhealthy fats and simple carbohydrates can also decrease concentration, memory, and mental clarity. This can further exacerbate the effects of stress as the individual struggles to cope with the psychological and physical health issues arising from unhealthy eating.

Unhealthy food can become a coping mechanism for stress as individuals may turn to unhealthy food to numb their anxiety, depression, and stress. This can lead to physical and psychological dependence on unhealthy food, further increasing stress levels and leading to an unhealthy and unbalanced lifestyle. McKay. et al. (2021) says that individuals who consume unhealthy food produce higher amounts of the hormones that regulate stress than those who take healthier diets.

Many approaches can assist humans in overcoming unhealthy relationships with food. For instance, learners must be cautious and work hard to maintain a healthy diet. The goal is achievable by avoiding junk food, eating a balanced diet, and regulating stress-eating. Students should look for nutritional approaches to managing their stress, like meditating, exercising, and sharing a talk with a trusted adult (Frayn. et al.,2018). All individuals should practice self-awareness by understanding how their thoughts, emotions, and behaviours affect their relationship with food. They need to take notice of every underlying feeling causing unhealthy eating behaviour, enabling them to devise health plans to deal with them.

Practising mindful eating is another way of preventing unhealthy emotional eating. Individuals should be aware of the sensations of hunger and fullness and eat to respond to these signals. Lattimore (2020) holds that mindful feeding assists people in reducing the urge to binge or overeat and helps them to uphold healthier relationships with food. Everyone should focus on nourishment for the body. This implies taking a balanced diet that comprises different whole-grain foods. It also means knowing the impacts of some foods on our bodies, like sugar and caffeine, and reducing them accordingly. In addition, the youths should undertake physical activities. Frequent exercise helps manage stress and anxiety, promoting a healthy relationship with food.

Also, educating the elderly about healthy eating habits and providing them with access to healthy foods can help promote proper nutrition. Older adults need to be provided with social and emotional support to enable them to reduce loneliness and encourage healthy behaviour. They also require access to mental health services to identify and address any underlying psychological issues among the aged individuals that may be contributing to the problem.

In conclusion, unhealthy relationships with food lead to issues like overeating, purging, binging, and emotional eating. Emotions affect different age groups, and everyone must know how to deal with them so they can easily manage their eating habits. Recognising and addressing specific behaviour patterns is necessary to prevent long-term health impacts. Individuals can develop healthier relationships with food by practising mindful eating, increasing self-awareness, emphasising nourishing the body, and undertaking frequent physical exercise.

References

Caso, D., Miriam, C., Rosa, F., & Mark, C. (2020). Unhealthy eating and academic stress: The moderating effect of eating style and BMI. *Health psychology open*, 7(2), 2055102920975274.

Frayn, M., Livshits, S., & Knäuper, B. (2018). Emotional eating and weight regulation: A qualitative study of compensatory behaviours and concerns. *Journal of eating disorders*, 6, 1-10.

Lattimore, P. (2020). Mindfulness-based emotional eating awareness training: taking the emotion out of eating. *Eating and Weight Disorders-Studies on Anorexia, Bulimia, and Obesity*, 25, 649-657.

Lopes Cortes, M., Andrade Louzado, J., Galvão Oliveira, M., Moraes Bezerra, V., Mistro, S., Souto Medeiros, D., ... & Serrate Mengue, S. (2021). Unhealthy food and psychological stress: The association between ultra-processed food consumption and perceived stress in working-class young adults. *International journal of environmental research and public* health, *18*(8), 3863.

McKay, N., Przybysz, J., Cavanaugh, A., Horvatits, E., Giorgianni, N., & Czajka, K. (2021). The effect of unhealthy food and liking on stress reactivity. *Physiology & Behavior, 229*, 113216.

Molnar, D. S., Jenkins, R., & Warshaw, D. (2015). Unhealthy eating behaviours and food insecurity among older adults. Journal of Nutrition in Gerontology and Geriatrics, 34(3), 248-262.

Scott, S., Muir, C., Stead, M., Fitzgerald, N., Kaner, E., Bradley, J., ... & Adamson, A. (2020). Exploring the links between unhealthy eating behaviour and heavy alcohol use in young adults' social, emotional, and cultural lives (aged 18–25): A qualitative research study*: appetite, 144*, 104449

Chapter   40

Author Qualifications and Honours

D.D, Doctor of Divinity

Certificate in Bible studies

Theology

Laws

(LLM)Master of Law.

Postgraduate Laws

legal research,

Business, CSR Corporate social responsibility

and human Right law."

Institutional development and management,

 International Law.

BA (Hons), Laws

Law: includes Criminal, Tort, damages, Contract,

Property, Equity and Trust, European Law,

Public, Constitutional, Judicial Review, and

Agency.

Advance Dip. Business Law, Level 4: include

Employment, Agency, Damages, Tort, Contract,

employment tribunal etc.

Dip. Criminology

Accounting

BA (Hons)op.

Financial Accountant

Management Accountant

Cert. Acct; (Certified accountant)

(PCA)Professional Certificate in Financial and

Management Accountant

Dip. Book-keeping, Level 3

Nursing

Nursing: RMN Registered Mental Nurse)

GN (General Trained Nurse)

Lecturer qualifications

DD Doctor of Divinity

LLM Master of Laws

BA (Hons)

BSc Hons o/g)psychology with counselling

Cert. in Education (Lecturer)

Business Certificate in Advanced Management

Cert. Business Enterprise

Advanced Food Hygiene

Intermediate Health and Safety

Dip. Safety Management

International Entrepreneur for over 25 years

(NVQ); Internal Verifier, (V1)

Trainer and Assessor A1 (NVQ)

Computers

Diploma; Cisco Level 2 Technician (build, repair, networking)

Microsoft Specialist

Dip. Claire Plus (in all software)

New Clait Dip. Level 2

ECDL Level 2

Scrip writer

Diploma in scrip writing.

TV, radio, stage, and film

Diploma in writing.

Autobiography

Biography

Family History

Certificate in Poetry

Psychology and Counselling

BSc(Hons o/g) psychology with counselling

Diploma in Counselling and Psychology

Cert. in Counselling and Psychology

Certificate in Social science

Photography

Cert. (PGFP).

Portrait, Glamour and Figure

Plumbing

Level 3 City and Guild

Hypnotherapy

Dip. Hypnotherapy

Chapter 41

Other Books by the Author James Safo

FAITH BOOKS- IN 5 DIFFERENT LANGUAGES

:

Arabic, Chinese, English, French & Spanish

ALL FAITHS

Theology

Love All Faiths

Faith Unity

Religion And Law; religion influence on National international laws.

CHRISTIANITY

BIBLE New Testament; 1,111 QUESTIONS AND ANSWERS : Plus, synopsis and Test yourself

Bible Old Testament 1,064 Questions and Answers And synopsis

Jesus Christ is Coming Soon

God Loves Christianity

God's/Allah's Messengers

Islam v. Christianity

Jesus Christ is Coming soon

Psychology of religion politics and marriage

Faith unity.

Faith unity simplified version.

Islamisme versus Christianism.

Love all faith.

ISLAM (In English)

QUR'AN; 1,044 Questions & Answers.

Allah Loves Islam

Islam v. Christianity

BUDDHISM (In English)

God Enlighten Buddhism

HINDUISM (In English)

Parama Nandra Loves Hindus

FREEMASON (In English)

In Search of Wisdom in Freemasonry

FRENCH BOOKS (Religious)

Allah Aimel'islam (Allah loves Islam)

Aimetouteslesfois (Love All Faiths)

Islamisme. V. christianisme (Islam v Christianity)

Dieu Aime Le Christianisme (God loves
Christianity)

Les Messagers De Dieu/ Allah (God/Allah
Messengers)

A LA Recherche De La Sagesse Dans La Franc -
Maconnerie (In Search of wisdom)

SPANISH BOOKS (Religious)

En Busca De Le Sabiduria Masoneri (In search
of wisdom in freemasonry)

Ametodas las creencias (Love All Faith)

Mensajeros de Dios (God Messengers)

4Dios Ama El Christianismo (God Loves
Christianity)

Islamities v Cristianismo (Islam V Christianity)

Allah am el Islam (Allah Loves Islam)

ARABIC (Religious)

الاسلام يحب الله. . (Allah loves Islam)

الأديان جميع حب . Love All Faith

CHINESS BOOKS (Religious)

Books in Chinese

伊斯蘭教訴基督教 (Islam v Christianity)

上帝爱伊斯兰教 (Allah Loves Islam) - Traditional

Chinese Edition

NON-FAITH BOOKS- IN ENGLISH
LANGUAGES

LAW:

Global Injustice

The Journey to Law Graduation

THE JOURNEY TO MASTER OF LAWS

International Laws plus 30 dissertation

Laws - United Kingdom +30 dissertation

The Law (Over 1,160 Questions and Answers)

Business Law volume 1; over 800 Q&A (
contract, employment, types of Human Right

Business Law Volume 2 over 600 Q&A (Tort,
CSR, Equity, Trust

Criminology: (Over 1,300 Questions and
Answers)

Religion And Law

POEMS

102 Poems on North America

70 Poems on South America countries and Cities

80 POEMS ON ARCTIC AND ANTARCTICA

102 POEMS ON AUSTRALIA, OCEANIA, NEW
ZEALAND

101 Poems on Asia countries and cities

118 USA POEMS : 50 States, Cities and Maps

114 Poems on 54 African countries

Over 200 Love Poems plus over 100 love
icebreakers

Over 100 Poems on Faith & Victory

107 Poems on Discrimination, Racism &
Suffering

Jesus Christ, Prophet, Arch Angels, Saint (Over
150 poems and Biography

The One - Over 130 Poems "DCF"

105 Poems on 54 European countries & Cities

BUSINESS

Developing and Managing Institutions and Organisations Volume 1

Developing and Managing Institutions and Organisations Volume 2

Set up and manage a business

How to set up a care home and care agency

How to manage a care Home and care agency

Care Home; Staff training

COMPUTER

Computing for beginners+310 questions and answers.

How to Build and Upgrade a Computer and Network

The Path of Information to the Computer Screen

Computer Programming, Coding & Science Dissertation

ACCOUNT

Financial Accounting (Over 1,241 Questions and Answers)

Management Accounting (1015 Questions &
Answers Plus 100 Self-Assessment Questions)

PSYCHOLOGY

Journey to Psychology Graduation Volume 1

Journey to Psychology Graduation Volume 2

Psychology of Religion, Politics & Marriage

COUNSELLING

Journey to Counselling Graduation Volume 1

Journey to Counselling Graduation Volume 2

Counselling; Journey to Graduation Volume 3

Mood Disorder & Therapy

HISTORY

History; Journey to Graduation: 38 Essays

ENEMIES Within the earth

Slavery And Suffering

Slavery to Mastership

GEOGRAPHY

Geography: The road to Graduation: 30 Essays

Medical/Nursing/ Health & Social

Drugs for Diseases : 1,007 Questions and Answers

Health and Social Care

Journey to Nursing Graduation: 51 Essays

Mental and Physical Diseases - Plus Nursing and 53 Dissertations

Health and Social Care - Plus 50 Dissertations

Social Science

Understanding Sociology Science - Plus 56 Dissertations

WOMEN

Women are superior to men

Sweet and Sour women (plus over 500 love letters from women)

Chapter   42

Glossary

A

Acquiescence response bias

A tendency to agree with statements
presented in scales regardless of content.

Alpha value (a)

The significance cut-off used to reject
the null hypothesis (usually 0.05).
 It is the probability of making a
Type 1 error (usually 5%).

B

Bar chart

A chart consisting of rectangular bars,
where the length of each bar is proportional
 to the value of what its represents.
So the bar will be longer for larger values,
and shorter for smaller values.
 Bar charts are often used to

represent the results of psychological experiments because bars of different length are a good way of representing graphically the differences in the mean scores obtained in the different conditions.

Battery of tests.

A series of tests aimed at measuring the same thing, such as intelligence.

Between-participants design.

Also referred to as an independent groups design.
This is a term used to describe the design
 of an experiment where participants take
 part in only one condition.

Bias
The introduction of systematic error into
a research design. This may affect your results

Case study

In neuropsychology a case study is the in-depth study of a single individual, which typically involves the collection of data from a variety of sources, using a range of different methods.

A way of describing observed behaviour using a set of predetermined categories.
A method of summarising the meaning of segments of qualitative data.

Cognitive Psychology

The study of the internal mental processes such as perception, attention, memory, thinking and learning.
Conditions
A variation in the experimental procedure.
By comparing different conditions researchers can make inferences about the effects of one variable on another.
Confidence intervals
The range of values between which
An accurate population statistic is likely to fall, with a specified certainty (often 95%).

Confirmatory bias

When a scientist's expectations unconsciously influence the outcome of their research. This occurs because of the tendency to pay the most attention to those features of a phenomenon that appear to confirm prior expectations.

Confounding variable

A variable that is not controlled by the researcher but that can affect the results.

Content analysis

It involves analysing the content of written material or audio-visual material, and coding this in terms of pre-selected features.

Contingency Table

A table showing the distribution of one variable i rows and another in column and used t study the correlation between the two variables.

Control condition

The 'baseline' condition, against which experimental conditions can be compared.

Control group
Participants who are a?located to the
 'baseline' or control condition.

Correlation
Involves measuring the relationship
between two (or more) variables.

Correlational designs
A type of research design that looks
at the relationship (or association)
between naturally-occurring variables,
without making statements about cause and
effect.
Correlation coefficient
This is a measure of the strength and
 direction of the relationship between two
variables.

Counterbalancing
An aspect of experimental design
that includes all possible orders
 in which participants complete

tasks or conditions, or in which experimenters
present stimuli – this is to control for order
effects.

Cycle of enquiry

How the questions that
research addresses are often derived
 from theories or explanations, and the
 findings of that
 research then generate new questions
 or refinements to theory or explanation.

D

Data mining

The computer-assisted identification
and retrieval of data from a vast database.

Debrief

A post-research interview designed to
 inform the participant of the true nature
of the study. It may also be used to gain
 useful feedback about the procedures in the
study.

Deductive Coding

Codes generated from existing literature.

Degrees of freedom

A feature of reporting inferential statistics which

indicates sample size and/or number of conditions.

Demand characteristics
The cues in an experiment that participants can use to work out how the experimenter expects them to behave.
Demand effects
The effects on behaviour when participants are aware of taking part in research and adapt their behaviour as a consequence.
Dependent variable
The outcome variable that is being measured in an experiment. In experiments, researchers are looking to see whether changes to an independent variable bring about significant changes in the dependent variable (the thing they are measuring).

Descriptive statistics
These are used to describe features of a data set; for example, the mean and the standard deviation.

Direction of effect

Describes which of two variables is the
initial cause and which is the resulting effect.

Distribution

The frequency with which unique data points,
values or scores are spread out for a given
 set of data (that are either real or hypothetical).

Double blind

A research design where neither the
participants nor the investigator know
which group the participants belong to,
 thus reducing the risk of bias in
measures and interpretations.

E

Ecological validity

The extent to which a study reflects
natural occurring or everyday situations.

Effect size

A quantitative measure of the
magnitude, or size, of an effect.

Ethics

Principles that determine right and wrong

conduct. In psychological research, ethics refers to the codes and principles that researchers should adhere to.

Ethnography

A research approach where the researcher carries out extensive observations of a group through being involved in their activities over a period of time.

Evaluating conditioning

Liking or disliking something because it has been associated with a negative or positive.

Experiment

A research method that looks at the effect of an independent variable on a dependent variable.

Experimental condition

A condition in an experiment where participants are exposed to a specific variation in the independent variable.

Experimental designs

A type of research design that systematically manipulates one or more variables to see whether this impacts another variable. This allows researchers to establish cause and effect.

Experimental hypothesis

The prediction made by researchers when they speculate about the likely outcome of their experiment.

Explicit measures

These are direct measures of what people think or say, such as the responses collected in survey questionnaires.

F

Factor analysis

A technique that generates a set of factors that summarises the relationships between variables in a correlation matrix.

Familiarisation

The process in which researchers become immersed in raw data.

fMRI

Functional magnetic resonance imaging is a technique that allows the blood flow in the brain to be monitored while the individual undertakes a particular task.

G

Galvanic skin response (GSR)

A measure of the change in electrical

 resistance of the skin, often used as

a measure of autonomic reaction and arousal.

Generalisability

The extent to which research findings

can be applied to people or settings

beyond those included in the original study.

Generalisation

Responding in the presence of a

 stimulus that is similar to the trained stimulus.

Generalise

To extend the findings of a single study to explain

behaviour in other situations or settings.

H

Holistic

Relating to the consideration of a person

 as a whole rather than focusing only on

 specific aspects.

Hypothesis

A hypothesis is a researcher's prediction about

what will happen when a quantitative study,

 such as an experiment, is conducted.

The researcher then tests this prediction.

Hypothesis testing

A process through which a researcher
tests a research hypothesis. Data is
collected and statistically analysed to either
reject or retain the null hypothesis.

I

Immersion

The process of becoming very
familiar with your data by scrutinising
it repeatedly over a period of time.

Independent t-test

This is used when your experiment is a
'between-participants' design, with two groups
of people assigned to different experimental
conditions (for example, when looking at the
pain perception of two different groups: one
who received a placebo and one who
received a new pain killer).

This is also known as the
between-participants t-test,
independent-samples t-test or unrelated t-test.

Independent variable

A variable which is manipulated by

the experimenter to see what effect this
has on another variable.

Individual differences
Any characteristics that are
susceptible to variation between individuals;
for example, personality or intelligence.
Inductive coding
Codes that are generated from the data.

Inferential statistics
Statistical tests that permit inferences
 to be made and conclusions to be
drawn from quantitative data generated by
research.

Informed consent
The principle in psychological research
whereby participants must be given
 comprehensive information concerning
the nature and purpose of the research
 and their role in it, in order that they can
 make an informed decision about whether
to participate.

Interaction

The combined effect of two or more
independent variables on a dependent variable.

Internal consistency

A measure of reliability, that looks at the extent
to which different items on a survey
(often Likert scales) agree.
It looks at how similar the scores are for
 the different items, which are all designed
to tap into the same underlying construct.

Internal validity

The extent to which a researcher can
be confident about the causal inferences
they are drawing from a study, and that the
results are not due to an alternative cause
(or confounding variable). Internal validity is
therefore only relevant to study designs trying
to establish cause and effect.

Interquartile range

The values between which the
middle fifty per cent of data fall
when the data set is numerically ordered.

Interval data

Data that has been measured
at the interval level.

Interval level
Measurement on a scale where
the differences, the intervals, between
the points on the scale are the same.

Interview
A 'conversation with a purpose',
 designed to gather in-depth
 information from research participants.
 Interviews may be structured, asking
the same questions of all participants,
 or semi-structured or unstructured
allowing interviewers to adapt
questions according to participants' responses.
L
Leading questions
Questions that suggest or imply an answer.
Levels
In the context of an independent variable,
the term 'levels' refers to the different
experimental conditions. ('Conditions'

refers to a variation in the experimental procedure.

By comparing different conditions researchers can make inferences about the effects of one variable on another.)

Likert scale

The sum of responses to several Likert items. Responses are usually provided on a questionnaire where items may be displayed with a choice of options on a continuum.

Likert-type scales

Likert-type scales are simple graduated rating scales from which respondents choose one option that best represents their view or experience. They tend to be 5 or 7 point scales (e.g. strongly agree, agree, neither agree nor disagree, disagree, strongly disagree), although this may vary.

Longitudinal studies

A research design where the same participants are followed over time with repeated monitoring allowing the researcher to track change at the individual level.

Studies that monitor and chart the development of psychological variables over long periods of time.

Love as a social construction

Definitions of love differ across and between societies, cultures and social groups. These different definitions act as a behavioural resource for people interacting within a particular collective.

M

Main effect

The specific effect of a single independent variable on a dependent variable.

Mean

An average that is calculated by adding together all the items to be averaged and then dividing the total by the number of items.

Measurement

To apply a numerical measure according to a fixed, defined rule.

Measures of central tendency

The mean, median and mode tell you what score sits at the 'middle' or 'centre' of a sample.

Measures of distribution

The standard deviation and the range tell you about the variability and spread of scores in a sample.

Median

The score in the middle of a set of scores placed in order of magnitude.

Meta-analysis

A technique for combining data from different studies on the same topic, and analysing them together, to derive an overall conclusion.

Mode

The score occurring with highest frequency in a data set.

N

Naturalistic observations

A study where researchers take advantage of naturally occurring events, rather than themselves manipulating variables.

Negative correlation
Changes in scores on one variable
are matched by changes in another
variable in the opposite direction;
 if one increases, the other decreases;
 if one decreases, the other increases.

Negative skew
An asymmetrical distribution,
where the most frequently obtained data
 points are gathered at the highest end of the
 distribution, with the tail pointing
 towards the lower, negative numbers.
Nominal level
Measurement involves naming an
 attribute of the participants or their responses.
Normal distribution
The assumption that characteristics which vary
between people will be distributed across the
population in such a way that values at or close
to the average will be more frequent than
extreme ones.
A common 'bell-curve' distribution of data
with specific mathematical properties.
 It underlies many important statistical concepts.

Null hypothesis

The opposite of your research hypothesis.

It predicts that there will be no significant

effect or relationship between your variables.

O

Objectivity

Judgement based on observable

 phenomena and without the influence of

 personal opinion, emotion or bias.

Object of thought

The object, event or activity that is being

evaluated.

This term would most commonly be used by

discursive psychologists as an alternative to

'attitude object'.

Observational learning

Learning that takes place by watching

 the action of others, and the consequences

of those actions.

One-tailed hypothesis

A one-tailed hypothesis predicts the

 direction of the relationship between

two variables or groups.

Ontology

The philosophical study of the nature of being, existence or reality.

Open-ended question

A question that does not suggest or imply an answer and usually invites the witness to provide as much detail as they can.

Operational definition

Describes exactly what your variables are and how they are measured in your study.

Operationalisation

The process of turning a psychological construct into something measurable.

Order effects

A term used to describe the influence that performing one task may have on performing another task, and therefore a consideration for any experiment with a within-participants design.

Ordinal data

Data that has been measured at the ordinal level.

Ordinal level

Measurement on a scale that allows
 data to be put in an order (or numerically ranked)
 but where the difference between adjacent
points
 on the scale are not necessarily equivalent.

P

Phenomenology
The way things appear or are
 experienced subjectively.
Placebo
A substance or procedure that has
 no physiological action or effect.
Often used as a control in testing
new drugs or therapeutic treatment programs.

Population
This refers to the overall set of people
that you are interested in and want to be
able to generalise your findings to.

Population distribution
The frequency with which data points or
 scores are spread out for your population of
interest.

Population validity

A type of external validity that indicates
how well a study's fidings can be applied to
 the wider population.

Positive correlation

Changes in scores on one variable
are matched by changes in another
variable in the same direction;
 if one increases,
so does the other, if one decreases,
so does the other.

Positive skew

An asymmetrical distribution, where
 the most frequently obtained data
points are gathered at the lowest
 end of the distribution, with the tail
pointing towards the higher, positive numbers.

Priming

Where exposure to a particular
behaviour renders more likely the
 display of that behaviour in subsequent
 similar situations.

Principle of localisation

The principle that the psychological functions can be associated with particular regions of the brain.

Pseudo-sciences

The appearance of scientific methods but lacking in proper application of those methods.

Psychoanalysis

A set of theories and therapeutic methods exploring the unconscious processes influencing human behaviour.

Psychological constructs

Psychological processes that are believed to occur, but cannot be directly observed or measured.

Psychometrics

A field of study in psychology concerned with psychological measurement of things like attitudes, personality traits, mood or intelligence.

Q

Qualitative data

Data which is not in numerical form.

There are different kinds of qualitative data for instance interview material, written text such as newspaper articles or diaries.

Qualitative methods

Methods which generate data that
are not in numerical form, for instance
 interviews, written text such as
newspaper articles or diaries,
 visual materials such as photographic records,
 or detailed observations of
 behaviour and practices.

Quantitative data

DE100

Data which can be measured, counted,
 or expressed in numerical terms,
for example scores, ratings and percentages.

DE200

Data that is collected using numerical
measurements and is expressed in
numerical form.

Quantitative methods

Methods which generate data that can
 be measured, counted or expressed in
numerical terms; for example, scores,
ratings or percentages.

Quartiles

The values at which a data set can be

split into four groups of equal size
(or quarters) once the data has been sorted
by numerical order.

Quasi-experimental design

A design where the experimenter
assigns people to a condition based
on naturally occurring characteristics,
such as sex, age, height, IQ or a personality trait.

R

Random allocation

A feature of between-participants design where
participants are randomly assigned to
different conditions. Random allocation is
another feature of a well-designed study.

Randomised interventions

Where individuals are allocated
 'at random' (by chance alone) to receive a
particular
intervention.

Random sample

A subset of individuals (or cases) that
 are randomly selected to represent a
larger population, where each member
of the population has an equal chance of
being selected to join the sample. It is

therefore an unbiased representation
of the population.

Range

A measure of dispersion representing the
difference between the smallest and the
largest score in a data set.

Reliability

Reliability refers to the consistency,
or stability, of a measure or study.
 In other words, it is the extent to which it
can produce the same results under similar
circumstances.

Repeated-measures t-test

This is used when you are comparing
the performance of the same group of
 people in two experimental conditions
(for example, when looking at the same
participants' anxiety scores before and
after a therapy intervention). This is also
 known as the within-participants t-test,
dependent-samples t-test,
 paired-samples t-test or related t-test.

Replication

DE100

When a result from a research study is found

again in a subsequent study. Replication is important to establishing the veracity of a finding.

DE200

To repeat a study in exactly the same way. Replications test reliability.

Report

A report is a written document describing information and/or findings to a certain audience, usually for a specific purpose.

Representative extracts

(or excerpts, or exemplars) from interviews can be included in the text to provide an example of what participants actually said.

Research hypothesis

The prediction made by researchers when they speculate about the probable outcome of their research.

Research question

A research question is a carefully worded question stating precisely what a researcher is trying to find out in a study.

Rigour

A careful and thorough approach to methods and argument.

S

Sample

Subset of the population of interest that
 is studied in a piece of research.

Sampling

The process of selecting participants for a study.

Sampling distribution

The hypothetical distribution you would get
 if you plotted all of the possible means from
 all of the possible combinations of samples
(of the same size) that you could potentially
draw from the population. In almost all cases,
 this will be a normal distribution.

Sampling error

This refers to the fact that any sample,
however chosen, is unlikely to represent exactly
 the population from which it was drawn.

Scale

A term which, in the context of intelligence
research, is often used instead of the
word 'test'. In psychology, the word
'scale' refers to any set of questionnaire
items or tasks which combine to measure

a bigger construct that cannot be measured directly, such as intelligence or personality.

Scattergraph/scatterplot

A graph that shows the relationship between two variables, where pairs of values concerning the two variables are plotted as a single point. One variable forms the horizontal axis and the other variable the vertical axis. The pattern of points suggests whether or not a positive or negative correlation exists between the two variables.

Scientific method

A systematic research method in which a problem or question is first identified and defined. Information relating to the question is then gathered to help form a hypothesis. Relevant data is then collected (often through experimentation) to empirically test the hypothesis, and a conclusion that either supports or refutes the hypothesis is made.

Self-report

Any method of collecting data that asks participants to supply information about themselves, such as their beliefs,

attitudes or feelings. Common examples
are questionnaires and interviews.
Semi-structured interviews
Questions are prepared in advance
 but the interviewer may ask additional
questions during the interview in
 response to the interviewee's comments.
Situational (or external) causes
Causes of an event or behaviour located
 in the environment.

Social constructionism
A theoretical approach that explores
how human knowledge and meaning
making is built through jointly constructed
 understandings of our world.
Social desirability bias
The tendency for people to respond
to questions in a way they
 believe would
meet the approval of others.
Social facilitation
How individual performance is
 impacted by the presence of others.

Standard deviation

A descriptive statistic that represents
the average amount by which individual
values in the data differ (or deviate)
from the mean.

Standard error

The standard deviation of the
sampling distribution. It gives an
estimate of the variability of in different
samples that can be drawn from the
same population.

Standardisation

The process of ensuring that all
participants undergo the same treatment
and that all data are recorded in the same way.
Standardised test

A test that is designed to capture a
specific psychological construct and
 is administered, scored and interpreted
 in a standard manner. Standardised
tests have usually been rigorously tested
 for reliability and validity
on a large number of individuals in an

array of different situations and contexts.
Structured coding scheme
This is a set of pre specified categories
that is used to code behaviour.

Structured interviews
These entail asking the same
 questions of all the participants,
 in the same order.
Subjectivity
Knowledge and understanding
 arising from personal involvement and
experience.
Subthemes
The individual components
of a theme.
Systematic variance
Systematic variance means the effect
of your experimental manipulation,
which if everything goes to plan should
be a result of your independent variable (IV).
 In other words, it refers to the amount of
variability in your data that can be accounted
 for by the differences between
the experimental conditions.

T

Test norms

Benchmarks used to assess an individual's
performance on intelligence tests.
They offer insight into how a person's test score
 compares with the scores of other test takers
 from the same population.

Test standardisation
The process of establishing test norms by
 administering the test to a large sample of
the population for which the test is intended.
We will return to the issue of standardisation and
 why it is important in Chapter 2 of Investigating
Intelligence.
Thematic analysis
A qualitative method used to identify,
analyse and report patterns (themes)
in qualitative data.

Theoretical generalisability
The relevance of Ideas and analytical
 concepts developed in a study should
extend beyond the immediate
 research context.

Theory

A set of propositions about a
psychological phenomenon (e.g.
intelligence) which forms the basis of
an explanation.

Transcription

The process of turning audio or
 spoken data into a written transcript.
Transcription conventions
a set of symbols denoting characteristics
 of speech and conversational action.

Transcription notation

(see also transcription conventions) – a set
of symbols
 denoting characteristics of speech and
conversational action.

Transformations

Changing how the data is organised
 or coded, e.g. changing raw qualitative data
into numerical data and/or subsuming data
 sets into overarching categories.

Troxler effect

A visual illusion where an
unchanging stimulus that is stable
 on the retina fades from perceptual
experience. The effect is largely
thought to be due to the fact the
most sensory neurons adapt to
an unchanging stimulus and cease
 sending a signal, known as sensory
adaptation.

t-test

The t-test is an inferential statistic that
 is used to test the difference between
group means.

Two-tailed hypothesis

A two-tailed hypothesis predicts a difference
between groups (or a relationship between
variables), but it makes no
reference to the direction of the effect.

Type 1 error

Accepting that there is a genuine effect
in the population, when in reality there isn't.
 A false positive.

Type 2 error

Incorrectly accepting the null hypothesis,

when in reality there is a genuine
effect in the population. A false negative.

U

Universalism
The assumption that phenomena
observed in a study can be generalised
 to other contexts.
Unstructured interviews
These are the most flexible interviews,
beginning with a provisional list of
questions which will be adapted to
suit the details that unfold in the interview.

Unsystematic variance
Unsystematic variance refers to the
 The unplanned variation that naturally
occurs within any set of data due to
individual differences
and error. As such, this is often referred
to as within-conditions or error variability.

V

Validity
Validity is the extent to which a

measure or study is measuring what it
 set out to measure.

Variables

In psychological research these are
anything that can vary and be measured,
 controlled or manipulated.

Variance

A measure of dispersion which
involves subtracting the mean
from each score and squaring the
result, and then arriving at an average
 of these values. By taking the square
 root of the variance, the standard deviation
can be calculated.

Vignette

A short story or description of events,
people or actions that is used in
research to elicit participant attitudes,
perspectives and beliefs.

W

Within-participants design

Also referred to as a repeated measures design.
 This is a term used to describe the design
of an experiment were participants
 complete all conditions.

Index

www.ingramcontent.com/pod-product-compliance
Lightning Source LLC
Chambersburg PA
CBHW051453030726
47592CB00006B/1899